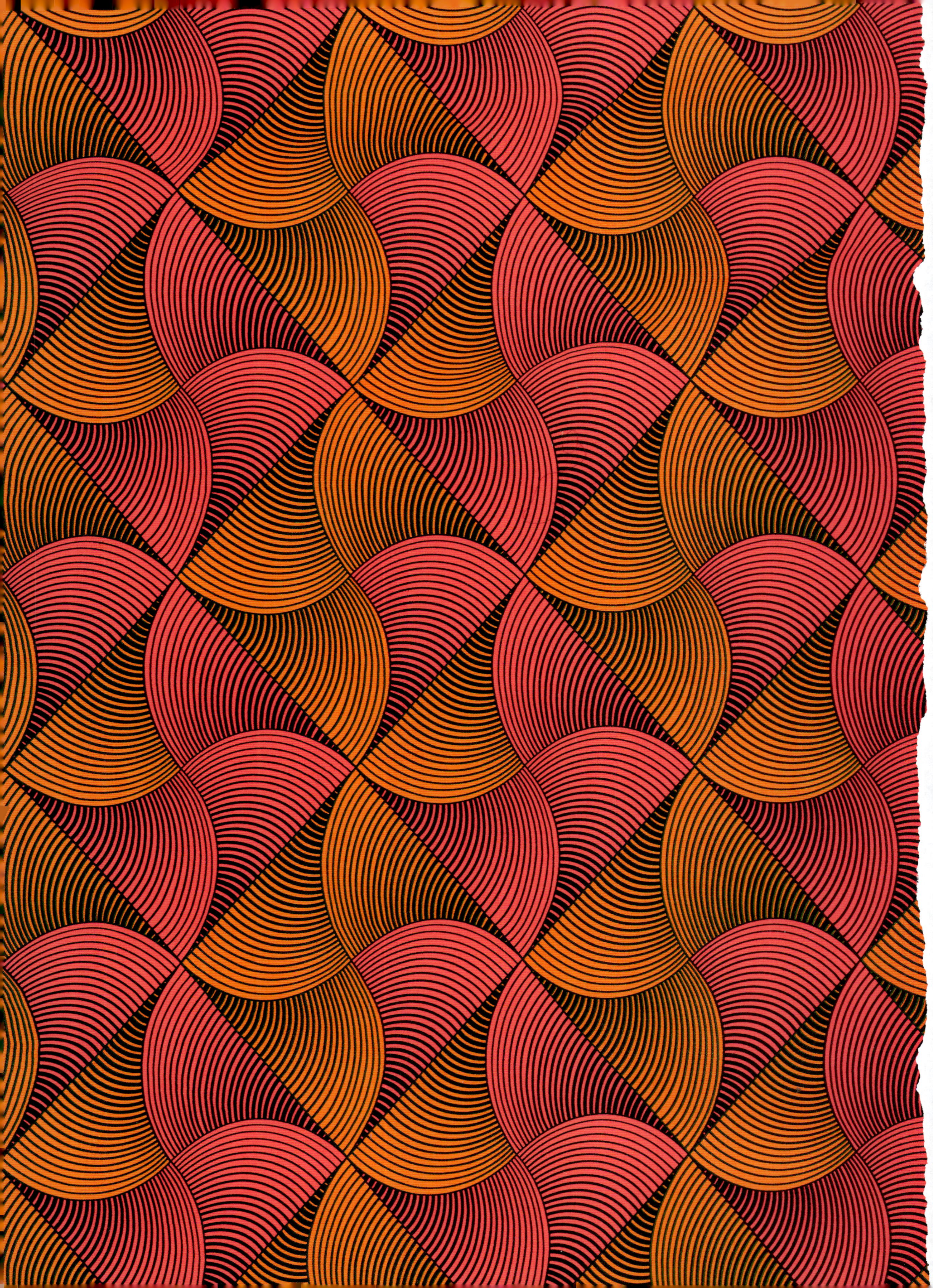

CAMO

Thandiwe Muriu

"With a little seed of imagination, you can grow a field of hope."
Proverb

Thandiwe Muriu

CHRONICLE CHROMA

Dad & Mum,

Thank you for empowering us to dream in Christ.

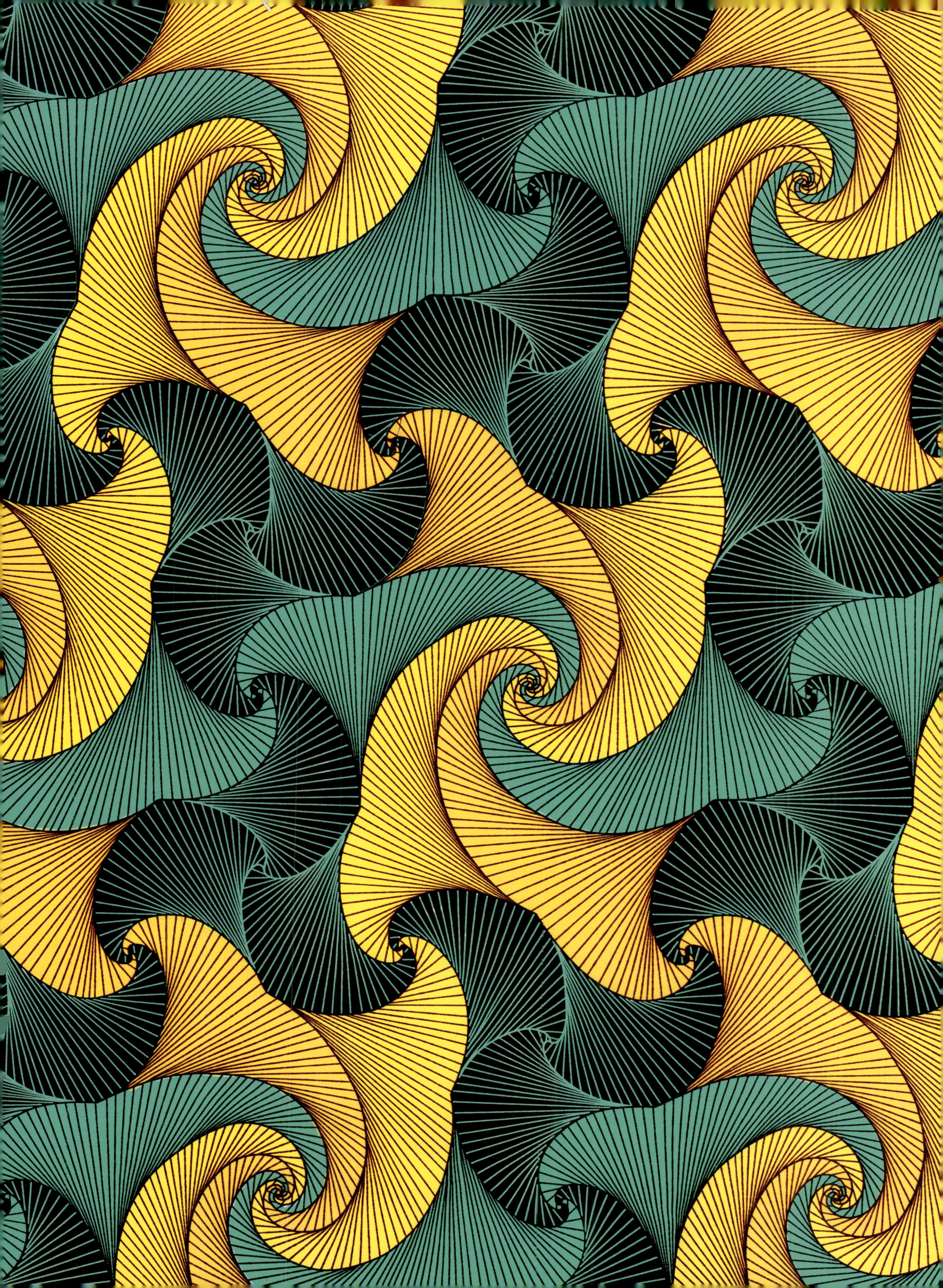

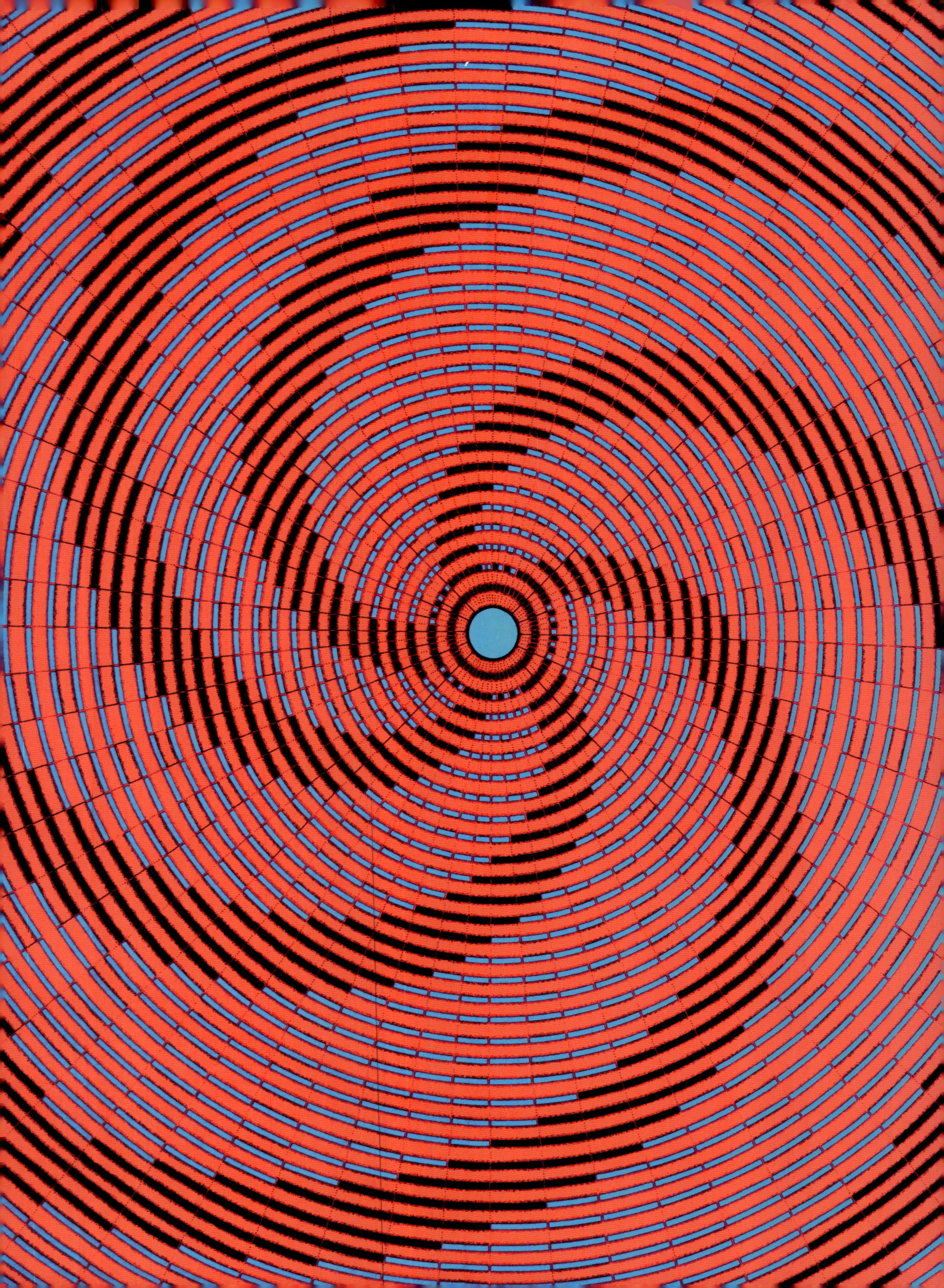

Foreword

by Oyindamola Fakeye

I am deeply honoured to be writing the foreword for this new publication from the artist Thandiwe Muriu, featuring more than seventy images that span eight years of her creative practice, from 2015 to 2023. In *Camo*, Thandiwe delves into the heart of African womanhood, weaving together threads of tradition, youthfulness, and the intricate tapestry of everyday life.

Thandiwe offers a profound celebration of womanhood and the role portrait photography plays in shaping societal perceptions of women, with a focus on women of African descent. In a world that often favours the familiar and mainstream, it is crucial to shed light on the overlooked and underrepresented narratives. Thandiwe's work exemplifies this necessity, as she gracefully captures the multifaceted perspectives of African women—stories that have long been confined to the periphery of mainstream publications.

Early adoption of photography in Africa had been tainted by a European colonial gaze, peddling exoticized and racist perspectives. As nationalism and independence movements arose, pioneering African photographers emerged, such as Seydou Keïta in Mali and Malick Sidibé in Burkina Faso, depicting the daily lives of the people in the communities, often in traditional attire, and showcasing the vibrancy of their cultures. Similarly, Thandiwe's work examines the intricate facets of identity representation, inviting us to question the influence of photography on our perceptions of self and others.

In 1955, at the age of eighteen, Felicia Abban, Ghana's first female photographer, established Mrs. Felicia Abban's Day and Night Quality Art Studio in Jamestown, Accra, close to J.K. Bruce Vanderpuije's Deo Gratias and James Barnor's Ever Young Studio. At fourteen, Abban had learnt photography from her father, Joseph Emmanuel Ansah, who ran a studio in Takoradi. Her practice, however, went relatively uncelebrated in comparison to her male counterparts. Her first exhibition was held in 2017 at ANO Gallery, Accra. Abban has since received international recognition as part of her inclusion in the Ghana Pavilion at the 58th Venice Biennale, both exhibitions curated by the art historian, writer, and curator Nana Oforiatta Ayim.

Like Abban, Thandiwe's relationship with photography also began at age fourteen, with her father teaching her photography on his Nikon camera. She would spend her time recreating shoots from *Vogue* magazine while experimenting with her siblings acting as her muses. Honing her photography skills within the male-dominated field of commercial photography, similarly to Abban, Thandiwe has also fought for her work to be recognised as equally as important as that of her male counterparts.

As someone connected to both the diaspora and Nigeria, having spent my formative years in the UK, I resonate with the space in which Thandiwe's images exist. Growing up just as enamoured by *Vogue* magazine, I also tried to recreate the extravagant images, which would lead me to visual merchandising and fashion styling in my early twenties and influence my love of fine art and fashion photography. Under the direction of the late Bisi Silva, I would further discover the symbiotic relationship between fashion and photography as part of my curatorial training at the Centre for Contemporary Art.

There is a playfulness with which I approach my own sense of style. This may be why I'm so drawn to "Our Collective Beauty," "I See You," and "Camo 42." Had I walked past these women in the street, I would have greeted them with a, "You look fabulous," before asking for all the details to recreate the looks. This is the testament to Thandiwe's eye for style, where eyewear, made out of thread, tissue rolls, and sink strainers are reminiscent of couture pieces. The styling of the hair, the pastel lipstick, and the cut of the garments reveal Thandiwe as not just a photographer but a true creative. They are a testament to the legacy she is creating—a legacy that finds beauty in the liminal spaces and captures the essence of care within her artistic approach.

In "Camo 01," Thandiwe celebrates the Jua Kali handymen who sit at the intersection of artist and innovator. I see Thandiwe the same way, each image revealing another layer of crafty creativity. From nylon brushes in "Camo 16" and "Camo 19" to the beaded eyewear in "Camo 39" and plastic spoons within "Camo 48," Thandiwe has brought an ability to take crafted and often disposable items to the level of high fashion. Each image, accompanied by African proverbs, creates a harmonious symphony that fosters a sense of interconnectedness, the perfect balance between the independence that contemporary society celebrates and the dependence associated with cultural norms. In many of the images, we find the subject's eyes obscured, yet their gaze remains penetrating and intense, a testament to the enduring strength that lies beneath the surface of many women.

Ankara emerges as the common thread throughout Thandiwe's work—a fabric that bridges socioeconomic divides and connects people across Africa, Europe, and Asia. Like my own experience donning ankara for the first time in a foreign land, her images evoke a sense of belonging and cultural interdependence. Through *Camo*, Thandiwe displays the shifting textile trends that mirror society's ebbs and flows. The fabrics speak volumes about the times we live in, whether it's the resilience found in the textiles during the COVID-19 pandemic or the evolution of fabrics post-pandemic. Her images capture the pulse of culture in each take.

I have several favourite images in the series, having struggled to settle on just one. Thandiwe's interpretation of the head wrap into what she would describe as a "fabric crown" in "Camo 39," as well as her reinterpretation of the duafe comb in "Camo 2.0 4322," a symbol of femininity and political struggle, both caught my attention. These images reflect the strength in womanhood, each ephemeral sculpture crafted perfectly for the subject's head. I am reminded of how I have felt taking off my gele, a head tie worn by Nigerian women during celebration, sometimes reluctantly because of how much I loved the way it sat so gloriously on my head throughout the day.

Thandiwe's personality shines through in these images. Her joy and playfulness resonate so strongly. It is clear to me that this is her labour of love, a passion that transcends the pages of this book and permeates through her ongoing practice. Thandiwe's own photographic journey is one of playful reflection, where her own childhood memories blend seamlessly with the experiences of young girls engaging in time-honoured games. Through her lens, we witness a narrative that transcends mere imagery—one that has been established amongst friends, in the hairdressers, at the market, and in the matatu on the way to church.

The publication flows like a kaleidoscope: each turn reveals a new pattern, a new perspective, a new narrative. We are invited to witness a sensory experience of colour, form, and light—a symphony that tells our stories, speaks to our struggles, and rejoices in our triumphs. From the hair braiders to the textile sellers, her images encapsulate the diverse roles that shape the tapestry of womanhood. Each photograph becomes a mirror for those seeking representation and a platform that celebrates their identity.

Many of the hair styles in this publication are reminiscent of those taken by the late Nigerian photographer J.D. 'Okhai Ojeikere, who photographed traditional hair and fashion trends in Nigeria between 1968 and 1999. Both Thandiwe and Pa Ojeikere, as he was fondly called, have been able to capture the possibility within our traditional hair styles, and in the case of Thandiwe, presented an expanded view through a contemporary and Afro-futuristic lens.

Camo captures the beauty, the complexity, and the essence of womanhood through Thandiwe's context as a Kenyan woman based in Nairobi, empowering representations of African women that transcend cultural boundaries. As a British-born Nigerian woman, I celebrate our differences but have come to the greater awareness of our similar experiences. I celebrate Thandiwe's legacy as a visionary artist and storyteller, telling African stories from our own perspective, and I have no doubt that you will enjoy discovering the layers within each page as I have.

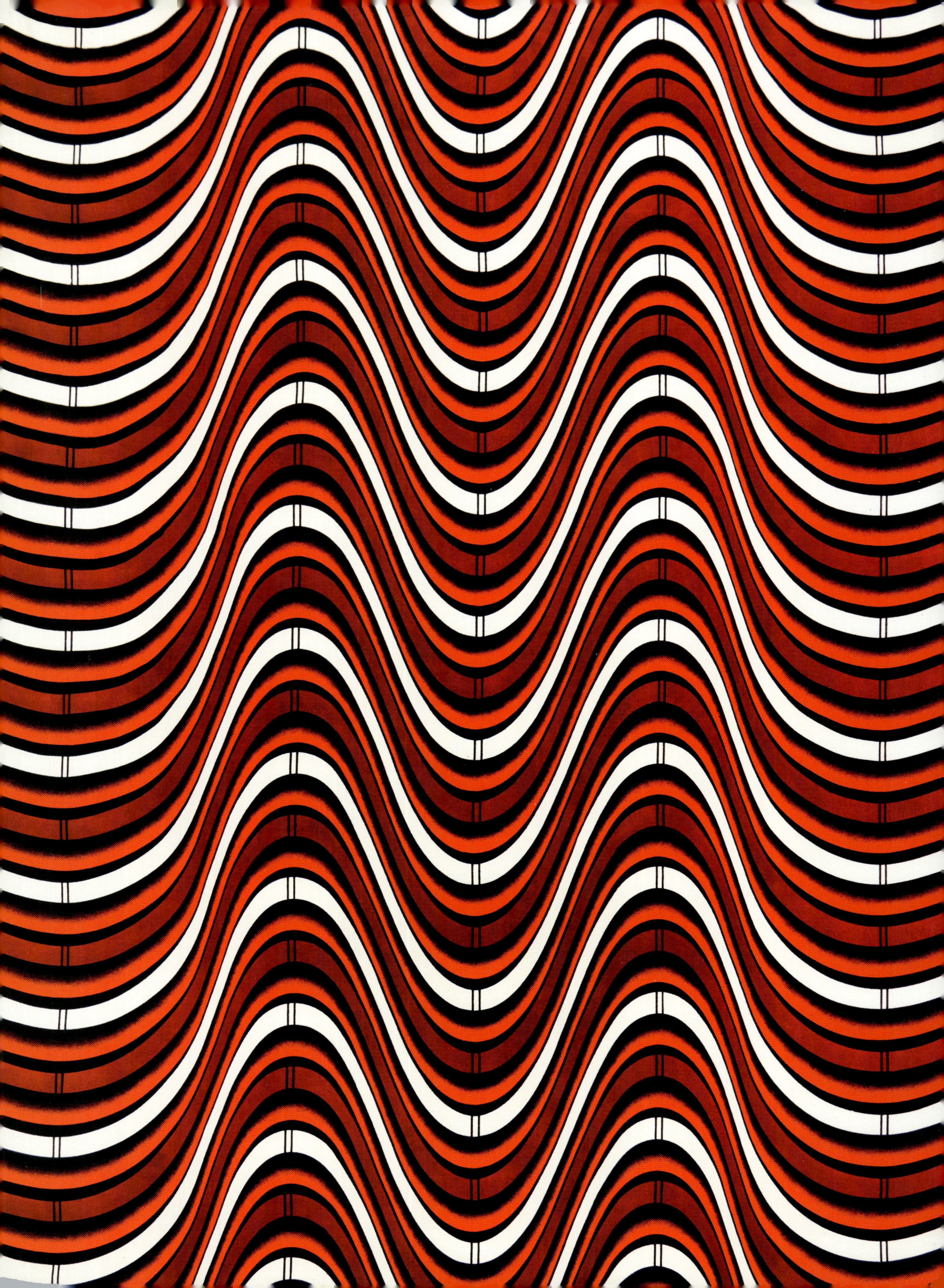

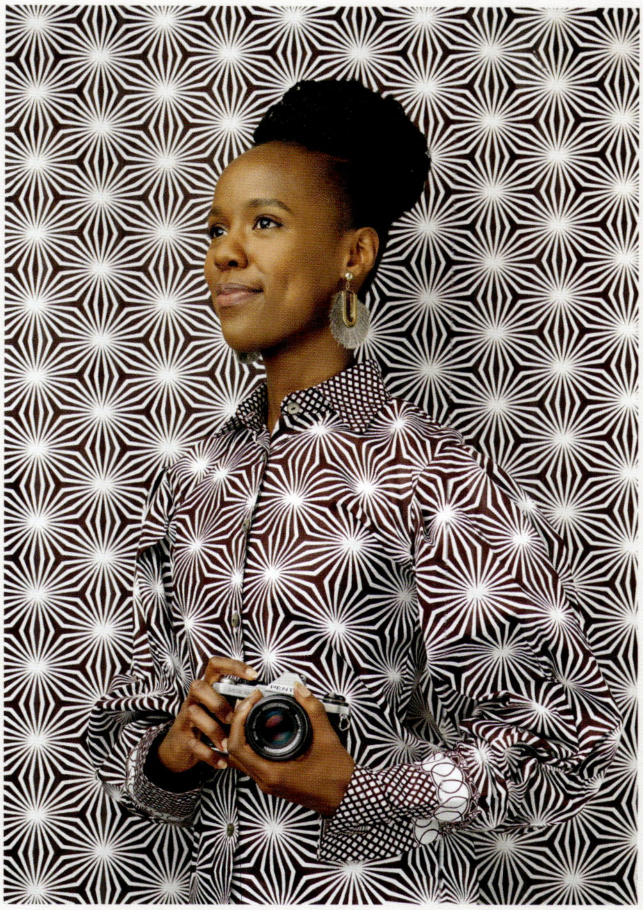

Introduction

By Thandiwe Muriu

PAINTING WITH LIGHT

I was fourteen years old when I first discovered that light could be my paintbrush. Born and raised in Nairobi, Kenya, in a family of all girls, it was a unique privilege that my parents affirmed our dreams. My father was my first teacher and cheerleader, encouraging me as I experimented with his old Nikon camera after school. Recognizing my growing love for photography and aware of the absence of formal training opportunities, my father taught me everything he knew. He diligently brought home secondhand magazines purchased on the roadside so I could immerse myself in learning.

The African proverb, "Do not let what you cannot do tear from your hands what you can," became the driving force of my artistic exploration. The lessons flowed from all quarters. My mother taught me to problem solve. She lovingly helped me cobble together a home studio using her bed sheets as backdrops. We MacGyvered a DIY photography reflector from aluminium foil. She opened my eyes to see creative possibilities everywhere. I still view the world this way.

Realising a growing delight for vibrant colour and portraiture, I turned my lens towards my sisters. Without realising it, my lifelong curiosity and observations around beauty had begun. With school and mountains of homework done, we would dash to the garden and dive into chaotic, elaborate *Vogue*-inspired photoshoots before the sun set. My elder sister collected the iconic magazine, and we were enthralled by the glamorous high fashion on display. The limitless boundaries of our own imagination took us from the rooftop of our house to dressing up the family dog and precariously balancing in a pond, all to explore the joy of photography. A brazen desire to share my newfound passion drove me to post every single image online.

As my skill grew through the years, photography became a large part of my identity. It was a fusion of all the things I loved: an artistic blend of both technology and physics. Right from the start, I had a natural inclination for it. Within four years, I had saved enough to buy my first camera, a Nikon D7000. My parents encouraged my passion, which was certainly countercultural. In Kenya, we are taught to aspire towards an academic career and white-collar jobs. To be a doctor, lawyer, or engineer holds more social value and prestige than being an artist. Perhaps it is a parent's desire for a better future for their children. As an A-student, this is simply what was expected of me. Even though I didn't feel this pressure at home, I struggled. There's an African proverb: "Man's greatest battles are the ones he fights within himself." As the transition into higher education drew closer, I agonised about which path to take.

UNCONVENTIONAL PATH

Then came Mutua Matheka, a Kenyan architect-turned-photographer, with a revolutionary way of storytelling through a lens. He discovered my online treasure trove and understood how determined I was to craft a distinct style and visual voice. Mutua was already renowned for his excellent photography, and

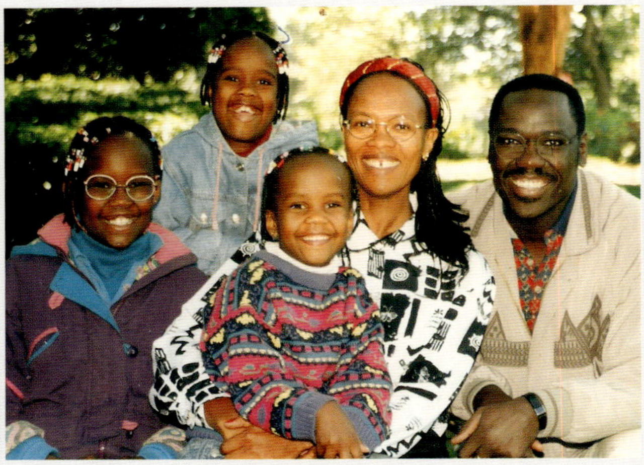

by reaching out, I felt an instant kinship. I'll never forget one distinct statement that he calmly shared that rocked my world and challenged my perspective entirely: "Thandiwe, shoot the work everybody else is too lazy or too busy to shoot."

In my first year of university, he extended an invitation to join a pioneering group of photographers under an agency called ProKraft. It was here that I met Osborne Macharia. Under his tutelage I learnt how to hone my voice, preparing me to tell the stories on my heart. It cemented my passion for creating, rather than simply recording stories, and showed me that fashion photography wasn't my only creative outlet. My career in commercial advertising kicked off and grew by leaps and bounds.

The rise of Osborne and Mutua challenged the perception of the advertising industry at a time when most creative work automatically went to foreign photographers. These international imports were talented for sure, but they had also monopolised the space for years. It was difficult for local artists to make headway. "Until the lion has his own storyteller, the hunter will always have the best stories" (African proverb).

ProKraft rewrote history and their revolutionary approach had a ripple effect. All our hard work was beginning to pay off. I made a swift, upward climb that allowed me—a complete anomaly, being both young and a woman—to shoot my first commercial campaign for Swedish multinational company Oriflame. I was twenty-three and still a varsity student.

That year, I won the Portraiture Photographer of the Year and Most Promising Young Photographer of the Year awards. I started teaching workshops and sharing what I knew widely, and in less than ten years since I had bought my first camera, I began shooting major campaigns across greater East Africa.

I thought I would be happy photographing commercials. It was a long way from using bed sheets as backdrops, my sisters as models, and foil paper as a reflector. However, I felt creatively empty. Despite all my growth, the fire and passion I had carried at the start had settled into embers. I had gotten into the routine of creation but had lost the heart for it. Sharing my frustration with Osborne, he challenged me to begin photographing personal work. It was this conversation that began the journey of Camo.

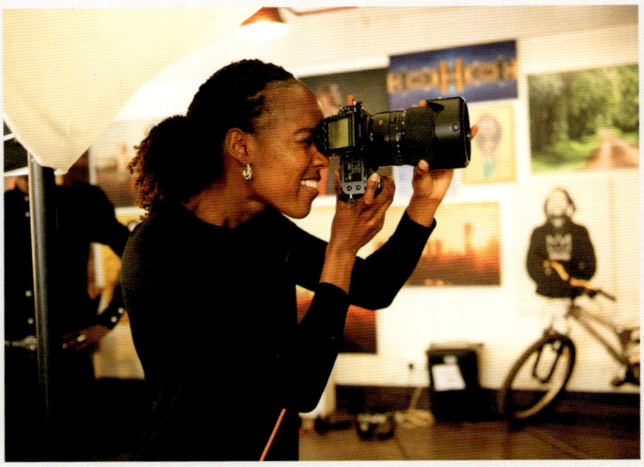

My passion for sharing my work online, thankfully much tamed now, never ceased. Instagram became my stomping ground, and it was there that I slowly built a community of supporters who enthusiastically followed each new project, experiment, and triumph. Camo combined all the elements I loved: colour, women, and African identity. Instagram served as the perfect visual diary with a window into this return to my roots. I posted *Camo 01* on July 15, 2015, with the caption, *Hello #afrobeauty!* I was excited to share this new direction in my artistic journey, back in the groove of things, creating art for art's sake.

By 2020, I had photographed fourteen Camo images, and my life was about to change yet again. The pandemic had brought everything to a stop. I was trapped in my small apartment in Nairobi watching what felt like the world coming to an end. Like everyone else, my days were filled with hand sanitizers, masks, and laughing at tissue roll memes. Little did I know that my couch would become the stage for my big breakthrough. It was there that I received a message from Paris-based 193 Gallery requesting my participation in a group exhibition titled *Colors of Africa*. It would feature the work of Hassan Hajjaj and several other African artists. I was sceptical but intrigued. The only arts education I had received in school involved drawing, shading, making papier-mâché, and the like. We all saw our art classes as a welcome reprieve from endless notetaking rather than an opportunity to develop a career. 193 Gallery's invitation opened up a doorway of artistic growth and self-discovery.

I couldn't quite fathom the magnitude of what was happening. My work was showing abroad for the first time . . . in France! The respect with which the gallery handled the images and how the audience responded to the work surprised me. I had been trained to believe that my work had a set value. Over the next few months, even after signing on with 193 Gallery, I watched a new world unfold in front of me within the walls of my home. Camo was exhibited at the 2020 Photo London Fair and nominated for the Emerging Photographer of the Year Award. It felt surreal.

The art world was a fascinating new realm for me, one full of opportunity to release myself fully to the joy of creating personal work. My new art education came hard and fast.

The first time I travelled, when I saw my work hanging in a gallery, I immediately rushed towards it in pure delight, touching the vibrant print much to the horror of everyone watching. Back then, I had never interacted with more than historical artefacts in gloomy museums. I had no idea that it was forbidden to touch any artwork. Dirt and body oils could corrode the work. Who knew handling art was a skill to be learned?

THE QUESTION OF IDENTITY

Globally the 1980s were a time of synth-pop, bold colours, and exaggerated silhouettes.

On the continent, the distinctive kaunda suits had become all the rage. Popularised by Zambia's first president, Kenneth Kaunda, this double-breasted safari suit was a mark of class and sophistication for those who were fashion-forward. Bursting with energy, the world was striding down the same path when suddenly, Ethiopia was hit by a devastating famine. Millions were affected, triggering a large-scale humanitarian crisis that rightly required the world's attention to help resolve. The result of this dramatic pivot though, the image of the starving African with a begging bowl, became front and centre within the public imagination.

A 1984 BBC news report on the drought-stricken region was transmitted to more than four hundred television stations worldwide[1]. A few years later, Kevin Carter's haunting Pulitzer-winning image, "The Vulture and the Little Girl,"[2] from Sudan's 1993 famine would further reinforce this portrait of Africans as hungry, fly-ridden figures. Undoubtedly, there is a great deal to unpack regarding poverty indices and quality of life across the continent. However, these images shaped narrow and enduring ideas about Africans.

Multiple truths can exist at the same time.

Switching on my television as a child, I saw these projected images of Africa, but it confused me because that was not the Kenya I knew. Yes, things were difficult, but we went to our public parks on Sundays to enjoy the lush greenery. Together we walked to work in droves and lived in close-knit communities, sharing unbridled joy in the spirit of *harambee*—a Swahili word meaning "pulling together for a good cause." We were much more nuanced than those images implied.

In many ways I feel my work is a response to those images of starving Africans—a passionate, contrarian argument against entrenched ideas regarding who and what we are. My work considers beauty and possibility, and I define myself as part of the *New Africa*. More than just a look, it is a heartfelt philosophy lived out in vivid African reality. This is a hybrid culture merging the reality of westernization without losing our beloved, innate African values. My grandparents had come out of a fight for independence and saw westernization as a threat. It was a destroyer of their precious culture in a post-colonial world.

But the truth is that my generation are the children of globalisation and we have lived our lives with digital exposure; and now? Now we have taken parts of Western modernism and fashion and made it our own. Like the joining of hands, African youth have grasped both worlds and created a new blended culture that is a unique middle ground—a way that bridges the generations and successfully brings together two seemingly opposing worlds. It is what Burna Boy, Sho Madjozi, Sauti Sol, and Just a Band have done. It is at the core of every photograph I shoot.

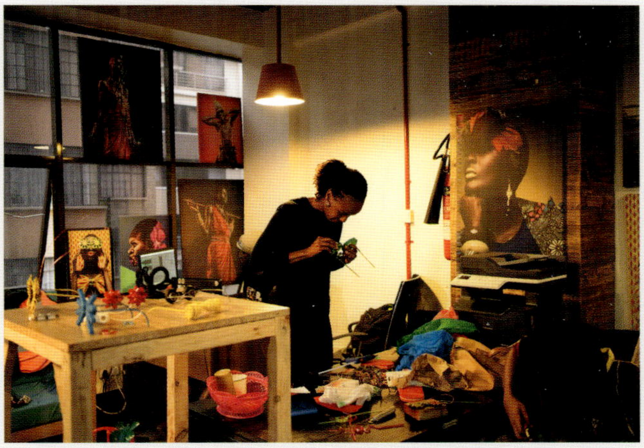

But this exciting, untravelled territory invariably raised new questions regarding identity; for how can you fuse the new and the known without them? I repeatedly confronted my own thoughts around the role of women in society, the place of tradition, and my own self-perception. Who was I if I defined myself outside the boundaries that my culture dictated for me? Did artistic contribution hold value when weighed against an academic career?

Camo was the catalyst into new boundaries in my photography, leading me on a deeply personal artistic journey. I was twenty-five when I developed the first images in the series. They were vibrant and provocative, an amalgamation of beauty and strength and an emblem of my *New Africa*. "Birds sing not because they have answers but because they have songs" (African proverb).

THE FABRIC OF OUR LIVES

There is a fine thread linking all of us. Perhaps it is the tea, bread, and Blueband (margarine) breakfasts that connect us. The memories of chilly mornings heading out to school. The playground games we revelled in. The camaraderie of knowing the lyrics to the same songs. The "me I" that Kenyans use in conversation for emphasis, saying things like: "Me I love my mum."

[1] Suzanne Franks, "Ethiopian famine: how landmark BBC report influenced modern coverage," The Guardian (October 22, 2014), https://www.theguardian.com/global-development/poverty-matters/2014/oct/22/ethiopian-famine-report-influence-modern-coverage.
[2] The Pulitzer Prizes, "The 1994 Pulitzer Prize Winner in Feature Photography," https://www.pulitzer.org/winners/kevin-carter-free-lance-photographer.

This love for Nairobi, for Kenya and our singular charm, always shows up in my work. I constantly ask myself if there is a new dimension yet to be explored. We are creative and resourceful, refusing to be defeated and finding practical ways to deal with the harsh realities of life. We laugh to keep despair at bay and always show up in our 'Sunday best'—quite literally a tailored shirt, jacket, or dress made from West African ankara fabric. I parallel this joyful exuberance in my work. I use the same fabric (also referred to locally as *kitenge*) and amplify its wondrous qualities tenfold.

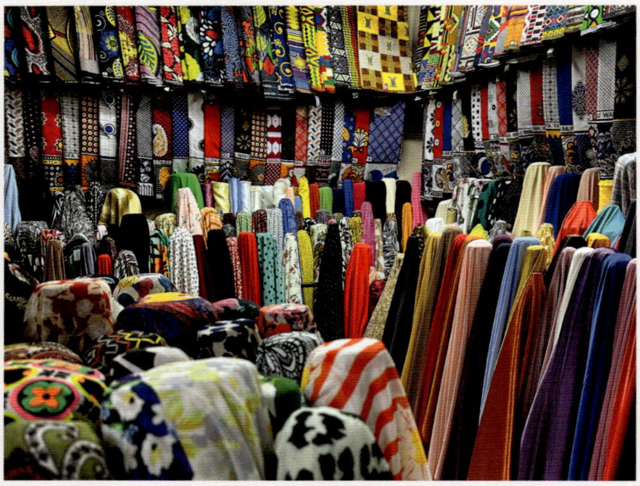

I grew up around ankara. My mother, like many mothers, was my first reference for beauty, and she loved to wear head wraps. Watching her deft motions, tucking here, pulling there, is a map that remains drawn inside my head. It seemed to me like she was crowning herself each morning. That's the magic of the ankara. Despite not being an indigenous African fabric, its bold patterns and saturated colours easily lend themselves to the type of flamboyance we delight in.

Ankara finds its roots in a traditional Indonesian printing process called batik, where designs are made on a fabric using wax and then immersed in dye. In the 1800s, the Dutch colonised the Asian nation and later developed a method to mass produce this cloth. Indonesians maintained a fidelity to their indigenous batik. The Dutch version had cracks in the wax used to create patterns on the fabric, therefore the resulting prints were seen as poor craftsmanship. The only market available to the Dutch for this particular cloth was in Africa. We looked beyond it as a rejected fabric and embraced its beauty[3].

For me, ankara is so much more than a piece of cloth; it is a record of history. Dutch fabric company Vlisco began producing ankara textiles as early as 1846[4]. Designs such as the speedbird pattern, which features a bird nestled in an air bubble, have long been interpreted as a symbol of change or transition. Ghanaians embrace it as a marker of the transience of riches, while the people of Togo called it "Air Afrique" because the fabric was used in the uniform of a local airline company. This marriage of symbol and story has continued on across the many centuries of the textile's evolution. It is common for certain patterns to cycle in and out of popularity. One year it was all about tribal markings within the pattern. The next year, pink and brown were in. Another year was all about the colour blue and angular lines. In its own special way, Camo serves as a dynamic, living archive of these patterns and trends.

Ankara embodies my *New Africa* ethos. It is the heart of my work. I honour it as a traditional cloth but select geometric shapes that my generation can identify with, rather than the symbolic prints my mother would choose. Obsessed with the idea of creating movement within a static image, I select textiles with patterns that seem to flow, dizzy, throb, or pulse. After considering the scale of a print and whether it possesses a kaleidoscopic quality, I am not afraid to change a fabric's colour as part of my creative process to enhance its 3D effect. My goal? To create an optical illusion.

When I look at a piece of fabric, I'm not just seeing colour, I see movement. I will scour the catalogues of online retailers and hop out of a car to get a better look at pieces sold on the side of the road. Finding the right fabric is a conscious and meticulous process that I enjoy engaging in especially because fabric shops possess such an otherworldly charm. The air smells faintly of cotton, dye, and newness. Hundreds of textiles nestle in open shelves that run from floor to ceiling. They sit in thick horizontal and vertical stacks, are splayed across tabletops, or stand in waist-height piles by the door. Folded into the smallest square possible, the fabrics spark curiosity and invite exploration, only offering subtle hints of their full colour and motif. Hopeful hands unfurl a chosen fabric, customers from all walks of life eager to gauge a material's suitability for their special event. It peels apart with ease, cracking a little at the spine from the wax that gives the fabric a glossy sheen.

There is a hue and sequence for every mood and every circumstance. No one leaves empty-handed: not the woman with a wedding to attend, the couple making new outfits for their family portrait, or the tailor updating his personal stock. This textile is as dynamic as the people who continue to print it and wear it. "However far the stream flows, it never forgets its source" (African proverb).

QUIRKY AND AVANT-GARDE

It is a well-known truth that a woman's secret weapon is her tailor. She knows them by name and keeps their number on speed dial when an important social event beckons.

Tailors are often found in busy, open-air marketplaces, small wooden or corrugated stalls in urban centres, or tucked away in the corner room of an office building. They slide material under obedient needles powered by paddling feet or the electric zing of a motor. The Kenyan tailor is often surrounded by heaps of dazzling

[3] Anne Grosfilley, African Wax Print Textiles, (Germany: Prestel, 2018).
[4] Vlisco, "About Vlisco," https://www.vlisco.com/about-vlisco.
[5] Vlisco, "Speedbird," https://www.vlisco.com/fabric-stories/speedbird.

fabric, tape measures, and threads in haphazard assemblage. Elaborate garments waiting for collection hang on their walls, marketing their maker's prowess. They hunch over their machines, eyes glued to the work. They must complete the task before them before a new customer shows up with an urgent need and the temptation of ready cash. The Kenyan tailor is notorious for missing deadlines and being caught flat-footed when an item is due. The key is to stay at the top of their list of tasks for the day; otherwise they will never deliver on time.

It is within this dynamic space that the Camo garments emerge. Beyond these little quirks, the Kenyan tailor's skill is undeniable. There is a communal collaboration to the Camo garment's creation. This is my culturally embedded process where we refine the design ideas until a garment seamlessly blends into its paired background. One time when I laid out a new fabric, the tailors laughed and told me the pattern was favoured by church choirs that year. They are just as delighted when my selected fabric pleases them. Through our combined efforts, the resulting outfits are quirky, stylish, and modern cuts. Colourful and avant-garde, they play up the electrifying nature of the prints. Everything is exaggerated: billowing sleeves, gigantic collars, and skirts by the yard. They are complete originals.

THE *JUA KALI* WAY

Nostalgia associated with domestic Kenyan life permeates throughout the Camo series.

I have a tactile relationship with objects from my youth and those found in the cupboards and drawers of millions of other households. They are items we all grew up with. Plastic pegs which held up our clothes on the hanging lines and never discoloured, strings of safety pins every woman kept handy. The sieves we use to transfer hot, milky tea from a saucepan to a thermal flask. The metal afro combs that accurately and somewhat ruthlessly part our natural hair into small, neat portions. The rotary phones that took a place of pride in our sitting rooms with strict instructions not to play with.

When in need, we develop the ability to give everyday objects a second life out of practical necessity. I once spotted a cyclist weaving through traffic with two small beauty mirrors mounted at each end of his handlebars to give him increased visibility. In rural Kenya, newspapers are often transformed into bedroom wallpaper. Plastic soda tops and thin steel wires become race cars. Flattened bottle tops convert into makeshift playing cards and, if fed through a curved wire, can turn into tambourines.

This habit of combining and remodelling materials is very much the Kenyan way. It is commonplace for a population often lacking in means but not in ingenuity. It goes a step further than achieving a do-it-yourself objective. We call it *jua kali*: a Swahili phrase to mean "hot or fierce sun." The term is used to refer to our informal, blue-collar economy and the ways in which these workers labour—often outside in the blazing sun—to handcraft items through methods such as welding or carpentry.

I follow the *jua kali* philosophy in the creation of the whimsical spectacles or accoutrements that my subjects don. Laying the items out on a table, I play with different placements and combinations, and once satisfied I set about glueing, wiring, and painting them to perfection. I have cultivated the ability to see the potential in all things. It is what my mother taught me in my formative years. Now, through my hands, an item of single utilitarian function is elevated into fashion.

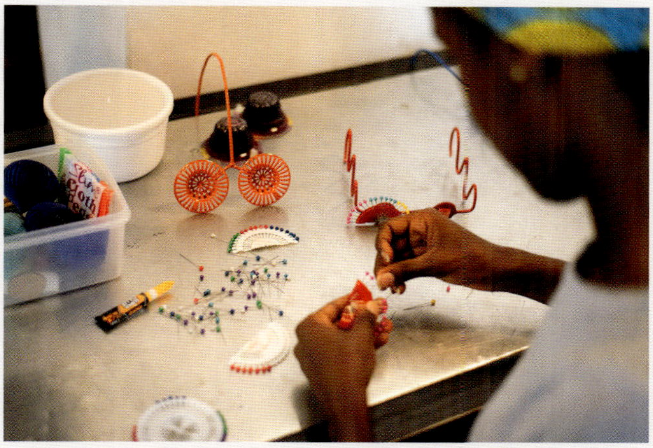

Over the years, I have accumulated various objects in a small chest christened my "box of limitless opportunities." They are odds and ends waiting for me to discover what kind of eye pieces they want to be. For the image *Tempest*, I converted a security torch popular with Nairobi watchmen into hot pink spectacles. In *Camo 31*, stainless-steel spiral scourers used by women to scrub their pots to gleaming perfection became green and yellow stunners. In *Camo 30*, mosquito coils, a smelly but practical bug repellant, took on a radiant pink hue as they perched on my subject's face.

Creative recycling is peppered across the Camo series with pieces made from shoe polish, tissue rolls, stick-on nail extensions, sink drains, plastic cutlery, and hair rollers. Perhaps this offers an African-led model for sustainability that is necessary in these times. We should all see the true, unappreciated beauty of every object and its potential to be upscaled and reused more than once.

THE WISDOM OF PROVERBS

The great Nigerian author Chinua Achebe once wrote: "Proverbs are the palm oil with which words are eaten."[6] Nearly every African community developed short, pithy sayings that conveyed their society's morals and values. With more than three thousand tribes and two thousand languages and dialects on the continent[7], proverbs number in their thousands. They were passed down through oral traditions from one generation to the next. The texts employ abstract ideas and metaphors to relay powerful messages about the human condition. Proverbs motivate, chastise, warn, affirm, and offer good counsel.

Written records historically legitimised a culture. Where there is an archive of written work, the world perceives proof of existence. As part of colonization, historical records were often overwritten, and spoken word did not hold the same permanency against this Western documentation. However, this does not devalue the significance of oral history and wisdom. Our words held weight in their capture of civilisations, cultures, and way of life. Our heritage gives us the ground on which to stand in self-reflection, rather than encumbering us.

Sadly, proverbs have fallen out of daily use. They are a dying art form relegated to books on dusty library shelves. Even as I examine and interrogate the place of culture and tradition in my generation, there is an importance in paying homage to these statements of wisdom that continue to resonate truth today. I am building on the foundation of other cultural observers before me. Heritage informs and shapes our contemporary African identity, even as the continent rapidly changes under the influence of the forces of globalisation.

As a result of my growing fascination with proverbs as the spoken poetry to my visual poetry, *Camo 2.0 4415* became the first image where I experimented with marrying African proverbs to my images: "Beauty and greatness do not belong to the gods alone". These powerful words resonated deeply within my soul. Going forward, Camo adopted this fusion of image and proverb.

A LOVE LETTER TO WOMEN

It is easy to feel invisible as a woman. The teachings of the patriarchy infiltrate every aspect of our lives. We are taught to be small and quiet at home. To shrink even further at work. To never occupy space in public. To only cater to others. Being the sole female photographer in Kenya's advertising industry, I was constantly overlooked. Over the course of my career, I have witnessed clients make a beeline for my male assistants, assuming they were the hired talent, not me. Only men were expected to be operating at that professional level.

The circumferences of disregard extend into beauty standards. There is a preferred archetype everywhere. In Kenya it is curvy with a fair complexion and long, soft hair. This view is exclusionary by design and fosters feelings of inadequacy in the women who do not present in the prescribed fashion. These women are, in actual fact, the vast majority within their cultures. They possess a valid beauty that such ideologies work to diminish.

[6] Chinua Achebe, *Things Fall Apart* (London: William Heinemann Ltd, 1959).
[7] Ruth Finnegan, "14. Proverbs," Oral Literature in Africa (Cambridge: Open Book Publishers, 2012), 379-411.

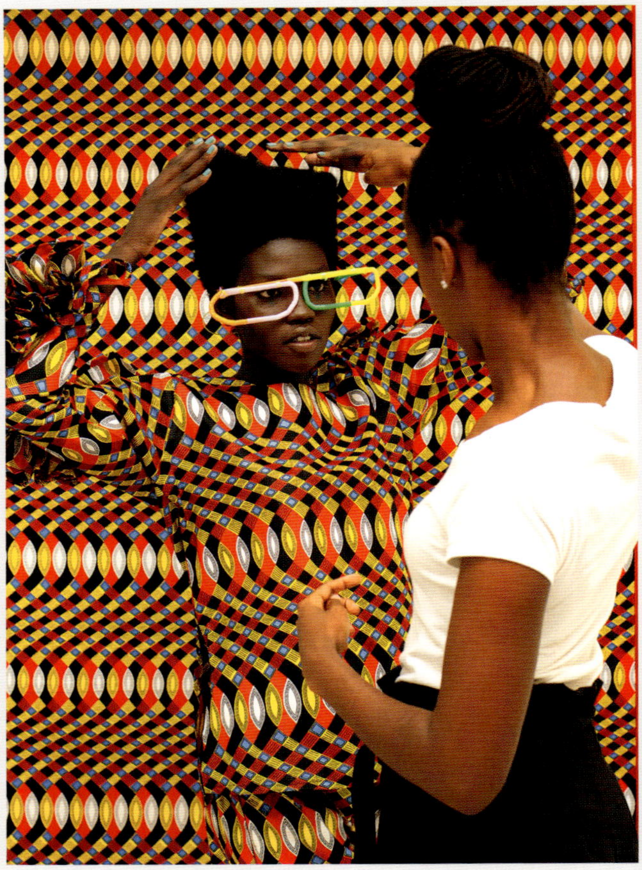

I am lucky that my parents built an unconventional home for their children. It was an oasis of liberal thinking in a world holding onto narrow perceptions regarding what a woman could do and be. Home empowered us, but we still had to confront the world beyond our doorstep, a place that continued to uphold prejudiced views against women. Camo pushes back against these narratives. It is my way of resituating the place of women in society, the position of tradition, and my own self-perceptions as I struggle against limiting beauty standards.

I believe beauty can be anything we decide it is.

Featuring subjects that have natural hair and dark complexions, Camo is purposefully designed as a love letter to myself and other women. I want us to see ourselves in our true fullness, to be unapologetic and harness our power of self-assurance. This extends to overturning our negative perceptions about natural hair. Straight hair and flowing weaves still reign supreme in a post-colonial world. For a long time, society has enforced the idea that natural hair is undesirable. We spend our time hiding our tightly wound, sometimes unruly curls, yet our hair has always possessed the power to unlock our true selves. Part of the *New Africa* narrative in my work is to reclaim our hair heritage. Our ancestors were wildly imaginative and sculptural in their inventions. Their designs had an incredible, almost architectural quality. In my images, I modernise these hairdos and make them slightly more outrageous. I turn them into art pieces.

Once fabric, garment, accessory, and subject are all assembled, the final image is composed in-camera. It is not postproduction that produces the surreal effect but rather a studious juxtaposition of subject against background. The goal is to have them blend

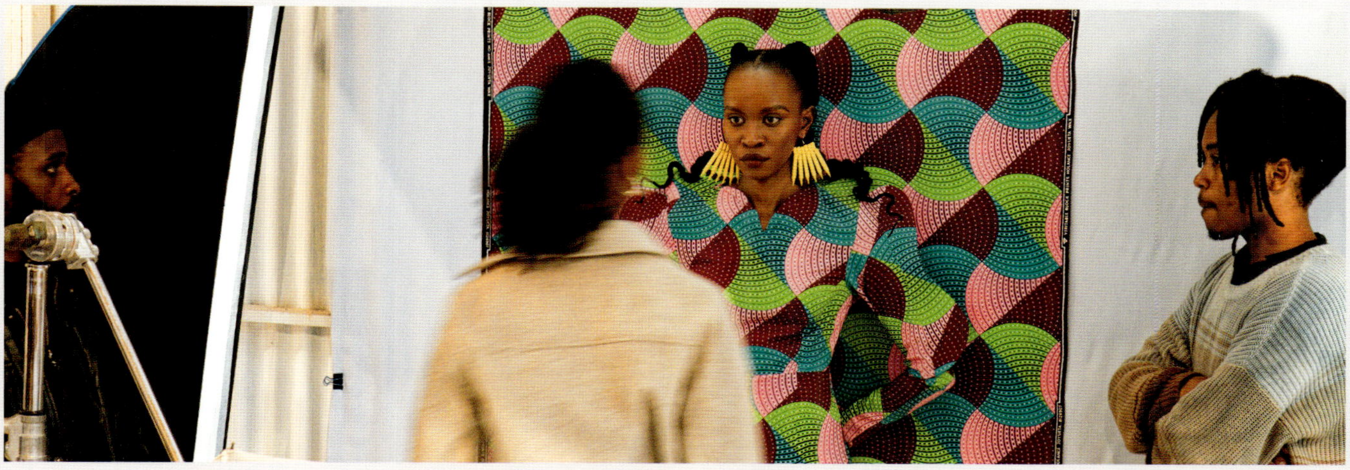

together so beautifully that they create a type of steganography where the viewer cannot easily detect the exact boundaries of the subject or the items they are wearing. It becomes a true camouflage, where the subject disappears both literally and metaphorically, in one sense magically vanishing and in another mirroring the way society can make a woman feel invisible.

As the Camo series has travelled around the world, from New York to London to China, I have come to recognize that this is a struggle for all women. It is not just a fight for the Kenyan or African woman. Every culture measures beauty in ways that don't necessarily reflect the true spectrum of all its people. An opportunity is lost to affirm the diversity beauty holds. Hopefully, I get to make the journey of life a little more comforting for women and leave them seeing themselves with renewed respect, confidence, and awe.

TOUCHING THE WORLD

"Hope is a good thing, and good things never die" (African proverb). At a time when I felt creatively spent, Camo was a way to fall in love with photography again. I have spent the last eight years developing more than seventy reflective images and learning things about myself that I didn't know. Camo has sweetened my journey of self-discovery. Even though I don't have all the answers, engaging in this work has enhanced a feeling of being at home within myself. I have learnt that the power is in sharing my struggles. Through Camo I revealed myself to the world openly and honestly.

The series compelled me to take a deep dive into my community's beliefs and practices. I have been delighted to find hidden gems within a deeply patriarchal culture, for instance, the issue of dowry: an amount of money or monetary equivalent that a groom gives to his bride's parents upon their marriage. The goal of dowry negotiations was to put prospective in-laws in a high-stress situation to allow for their real personalities to emerge. This was a way to gauge whether their child was going to join with a good family. And, instead of seeing dowry as the purchase of a woman, I learnt that it was an opportunity for the two families to come together. The full amount was never paid to the girl's parents. Instead, small amounts were given across their years of marriage. It gave their son-in-law a justifiable excuse to constantly visit his new parents.

I have come to realise that the reasons behind some aspects of my community's traditional beliefs were powerful and wise. They vindicated their incorporation into the *New Africa* narrative within my work. I see how important it is to speak back to spaces that suppressed women. It has been a joy, and sometimes a moment of shared pain and struggle, to commune with other women in this fight against invisibility. The Camo series has been received as a work that emphasises how women everywhere are capable, fully autonomous individuals who deserve the care and support of their communities.

Travelling for my first fair in New York, it was amazing to see how art was truly a universal language. There were people from all walks of life in attendance. There are no words to describe the wonder in my heart watching collectors so deeply connect with Camo that they wanted to give it a permanent place in their homes. This was the first time a museum acquired one of my pieces. Equally exciting, pieces were purchased by an elderly couple and a schoolteacher. Newlyweds purchased my art as a wedding gift to themselves, and Camo was also added to the Joy Simmons Collection. In the middle of this beautiful environment, it was an emotional experience to see my work sold out. Shortly after that, I had the opportunity to view the Contemporary African Art Collection by Pigozzi, of which, much to my joy, Camo is a part.

Witnessing the gravitational force of the work firsthand affirmed that the vulnerability with which I approached the questions of beauty, identity, and culture was worth it. Camo has resonated well beyond Kenya's borders. I am so glad to be a part of those who are sending a harmonious positive message about our *New Africa*. Camo serves as a mirror that lets others see themselves and another side of Africans with greater clarity. "With a little seed of imagination, you can grow a field of hope" (African proverb).

Tears have been shed, kindred spirits found, dialogue amplified. That is the power of art

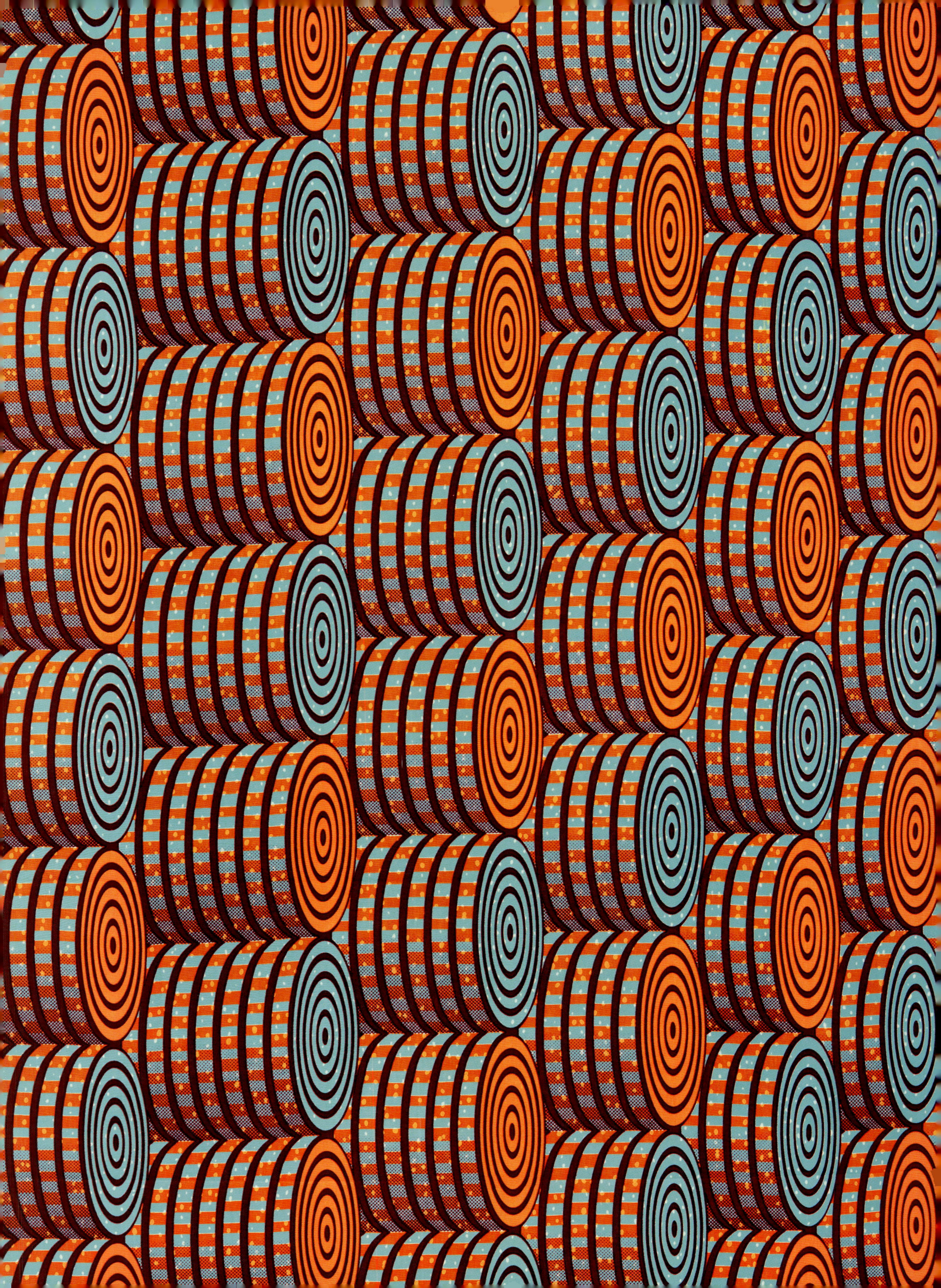

CAMO

Under the scorching equatorial sun, remarkable individuals embody the spirit of innovation, problem-solving, and artistic brilliance as they craft furniture, and metal fabrications that become cherished fixtures in Kenyan homes. These informal artists are known as Jua Kali craftsmen. Translated from Kiswahili, the term means 'fierce sun' and refers to the fact that very few own a physical shop so must work under the sweltering sun.

Sweat glistening on their brows, they innovate and create with unwavering determination and skilled hands, offering practical solutions for any customer needs that arise. Be it repairing a broken table, mending a burst pipe, or conjuring objects from your wildest imagination, these artisans are always ready for a challenge, eager to forge objects of both functionality and artistry. They are the living embodiment of the Kenyan spirit of hard work, moonlighting as innovator, artist and problem solver.

Camo 01, the first of Thandiwe's powerful series, all started with an observation of her daily life.

Eyewear constructed from metal sheets.

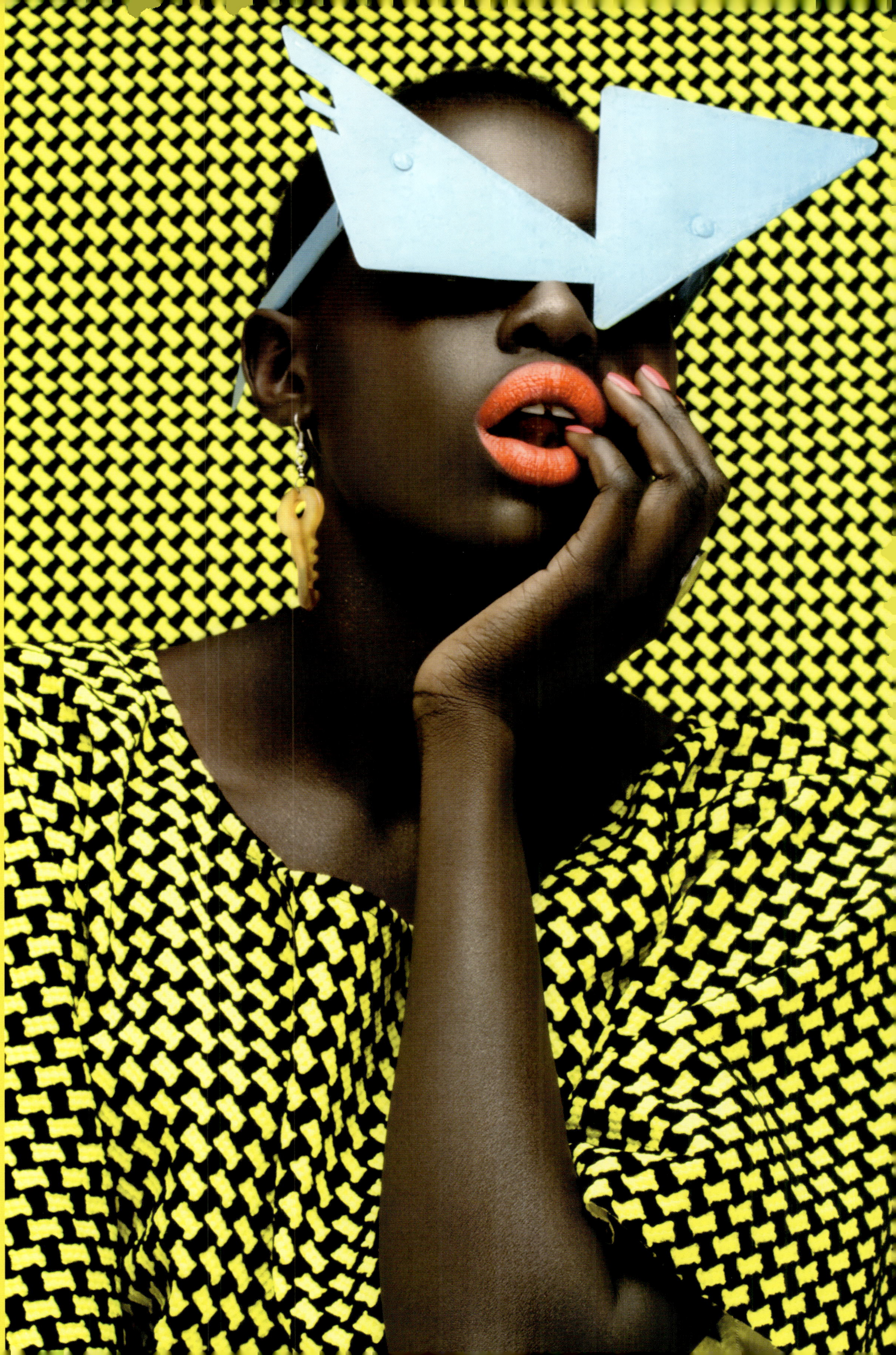

“Being happy is better than being King.”

“Kuwa na furaha ni bora kuliko kuwa mfalme.”

A timeless tradition is cherished in Africa - the joy of coming together with loved ones under the power of connection and celebration, which thrives in Camo 02. In Kenya, no meal is meant to be savored alone. Instead, it is a communal experience that nurtures the spirit and warms the heart. The smoky aroma of goat meat barbecue known as Nyama Choma is paired with soft drinks like Coca Cola, Fanta Orange, and Sprite which effervescently add to the festivities. Laughter and merriment fill the air, creating a symphony of happiness.

Camo 02 encapsulates the camaraderie, the bubbling joy, and the sense of unity shared by friends and loved ones around the world. We drink soda around gatherings and good times.

Eyewear constructed from Coke cans.

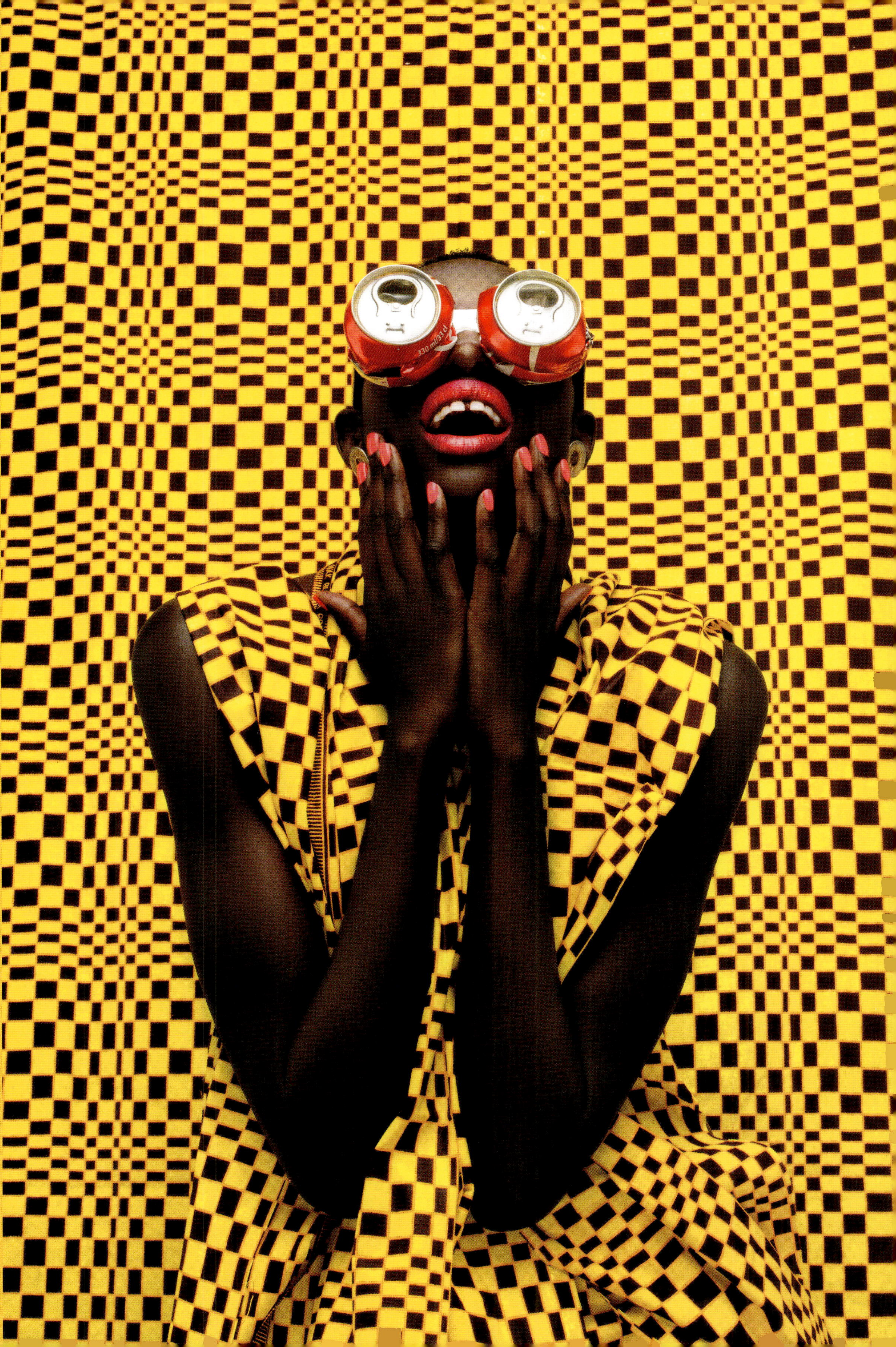

Thandiwe remembers her school days where computers, like ancient relics, would grumble with a distinctive whirr as if protesting against the hot and dusty conditions of Nairobi. With their bulky presence and outdated design they stood as testaments to a time when the world wide web was still a novelty and technology a laborious trek of zeros and ones. Patience was required to journey through the digital realm.

Camo 03 captures the very spirit of those schoolroom computers, their frowning attitude, clunky keyboards and pixelated screens of limited color palette reminding Thandiwe of an era gone by under sweltering Thursday afternoon lessons.

Eyewear constructed from computer fans.

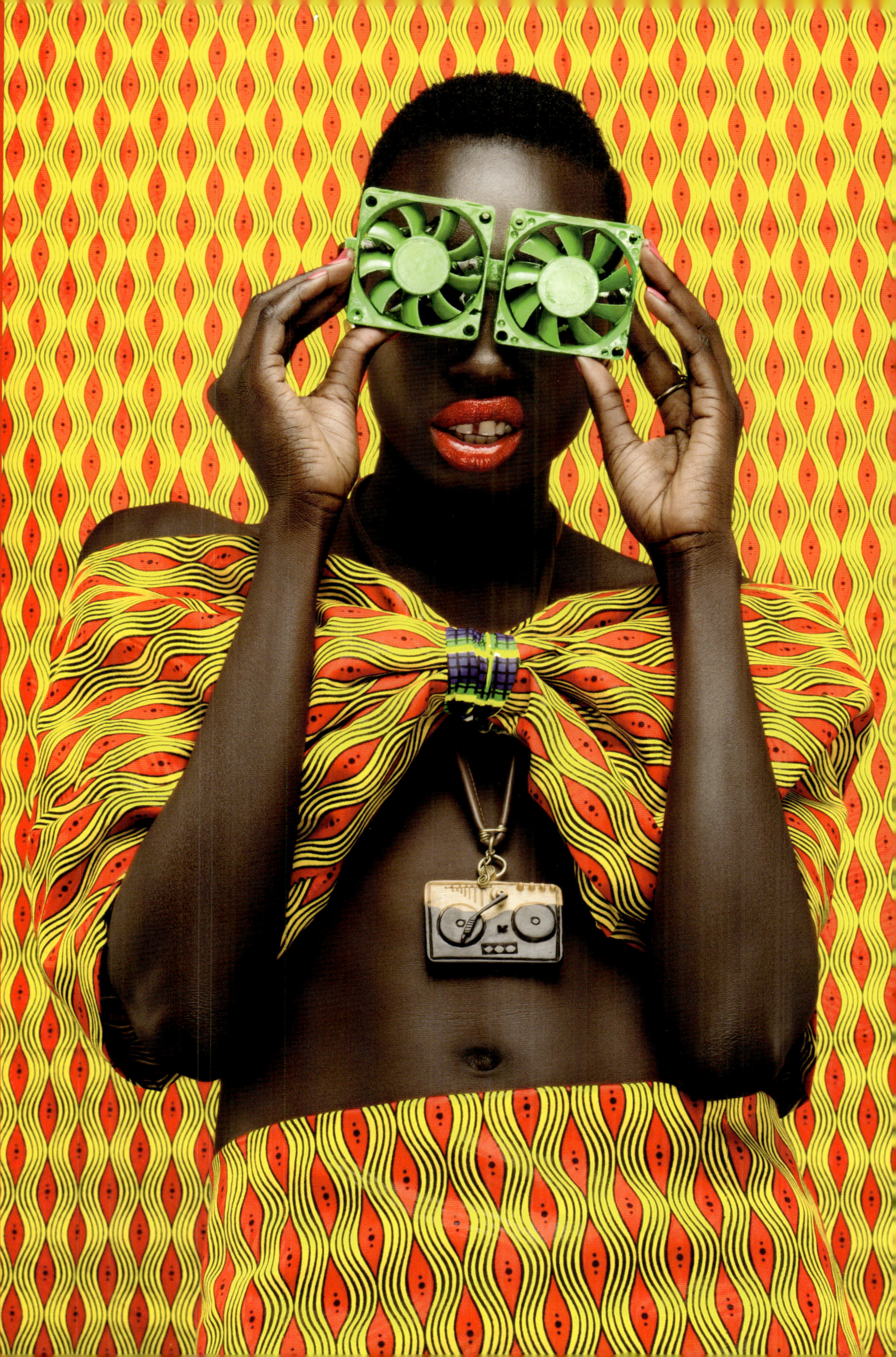

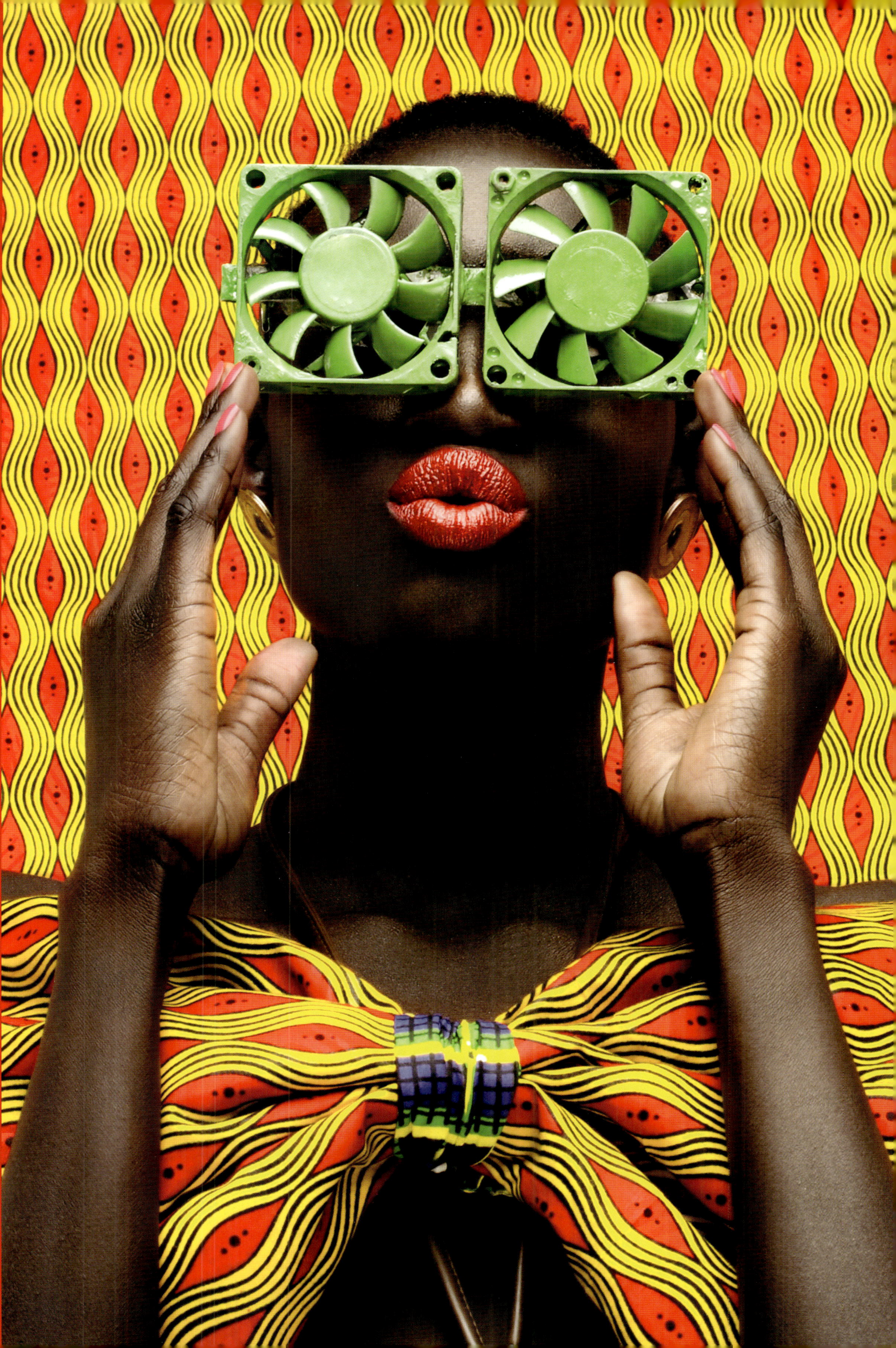

“Seeing is different than being told.”

“Kuona ni tofauti kuliko kuambiwa.”

There is a delectable charm to Camo 05, where the eyewear reimagined cupcake holders, a sweet delight from Thandiwe’s childhood. The air would fill with the ambrosial aroma of freshly baked cakes lovingly prepared by her mother or aunties for special occasions. Wafting scents would dance throughout the house, enchanting Thandiwe and her excited friends, their youthful anticipation bubbling over as they were eagerly drawn to the delightful treats.

A playful reminder of those scrumptious moments, Camo 05 is a flavourful artwork on what love, community and celebration tastes like, the sweetness of life.

Eyewear constructed from baking tins.

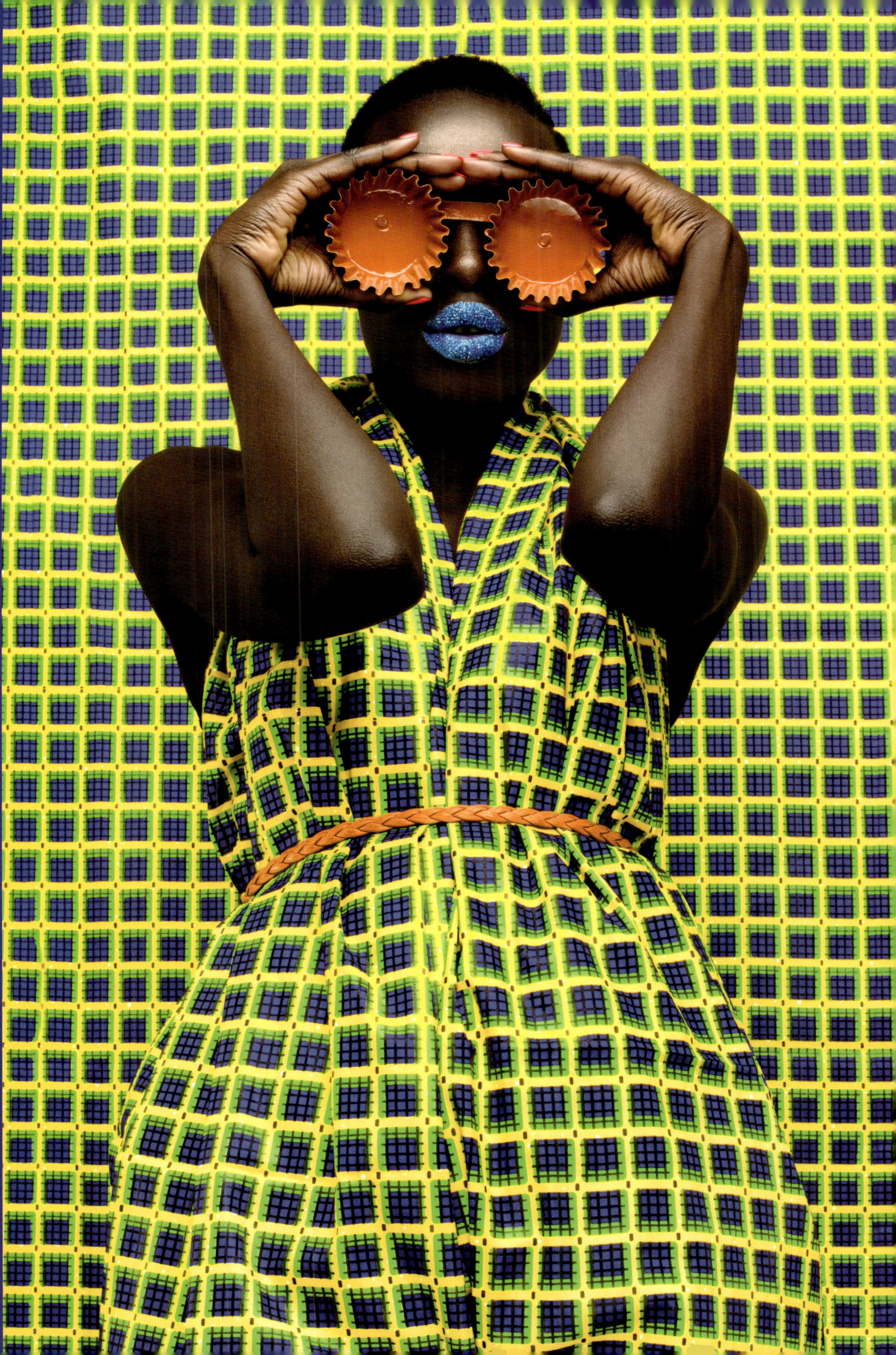

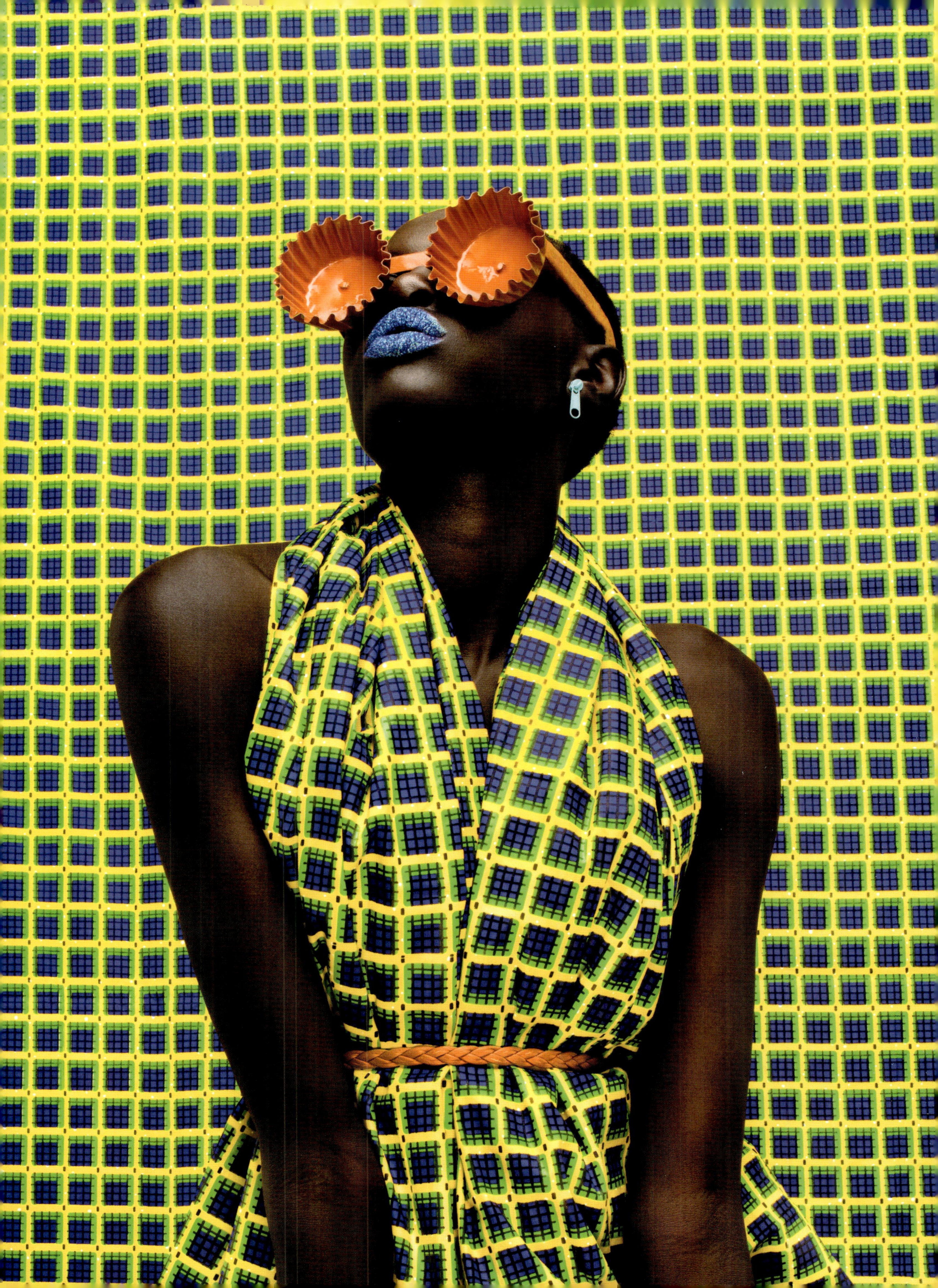

A whimsical celebration on spectacles, Camo 06 captures the Kiswahili word "Macho nne" which directly translates to "person with four eyes". A figurative phrase for a person who wears glasses, it caught Thandiwe's imagination, igniting an enchanting play on perspective.

The subject's glasses, crafted from carefully sliced pieces of vibrant glass, effortlessly channel her pop art perspective. Each fragment shines with captivating colors, transforming the functionality of eyewear into a mesmerizing kaleidoscope of individuality and creativity. With each glance through these enchanting lenses, a new world is revealed; celebrating a unique vision and the beauty that lies within their gaze.

Eyewear constructed from glass.

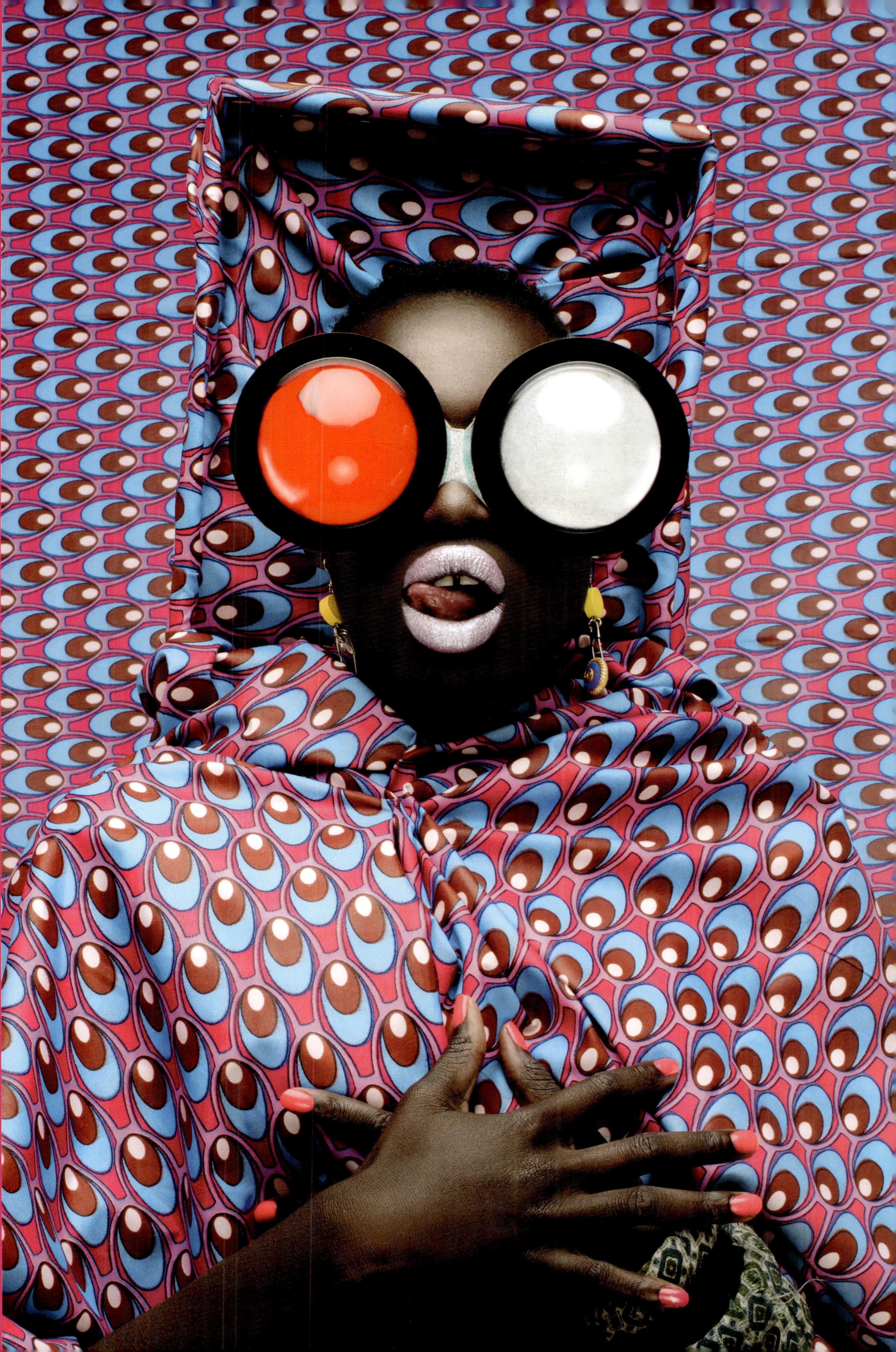

African stunners languidly perch on the subject's face in a unique Camo nod to the huge early 2000's trend of shutter shades. These stunners sport horizontal lines instead of tinted lenses. The vibrant pink slats intricately intertwined, resembling the modern interpretation of the Afro comb—an emblem of both style and status that holds ancient roots dating back to Egyptian hieroglyphics. Thandiwe reminisces about the confidence and fashionable aura she felt as a child when wearing sunglasses. An emotion she seamlessly translates into this Camo piece through the subject's nonchalant pose and effortlessly protruding handles that evoke the essence of the comb.

The stunners represent not only a fashion statement but also a tribute to the rich heritage and cultural significance inherent in the Afro comb. Its presence is a reminder that beauty is not confined to external perceptions but is a reflection of history, identity, and the enduring spirit of the African people.

Eyewear constructed from plastic combs.

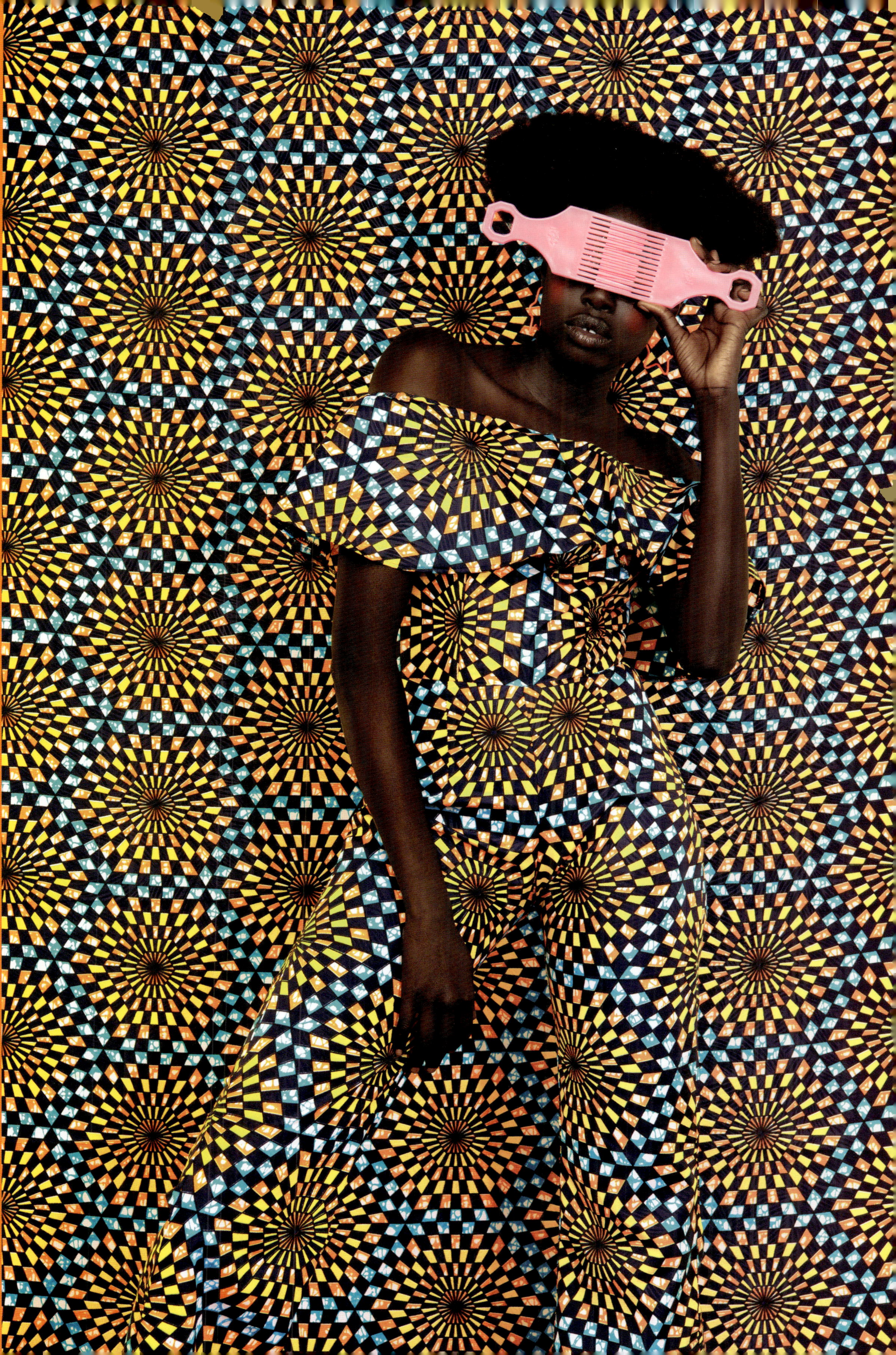

Against a backdrop of vibrant African prints, the subject seems to symbolically disappear into her background, mirroring the way in which the expectations of culture can cause any individual to lose their identity to cultural uniformity. But the camouflage is halted by her beauty; an exquisite imprint Thandiwe allegorically affirms the individual's contribution towards communal success. Her bold and confident step is a powerful reminder that we can still remain true to ourselves, even if our gifts are unconventional or different from the norm. Authenticity can be the catalyst to connection. And the most beautiful communities are completed, in part, from the contribution of the unique individual.

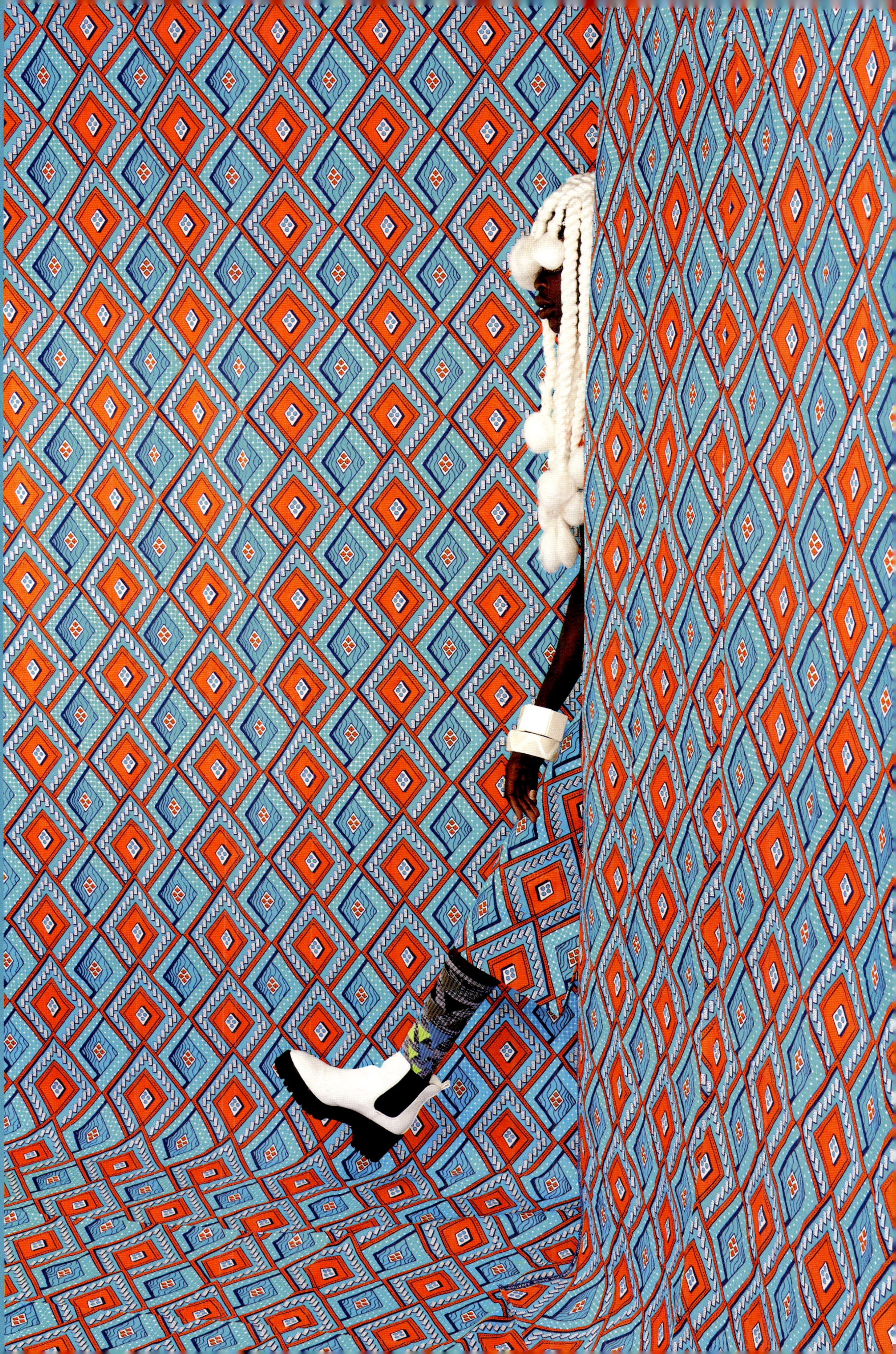

"Where a woman rules, streams run uphill."

"Penye mwanamke hutawala, mkondo wa mito hupanda mlima."

Nestled gracefully within the subject's luscious locks, a row of vibrant orange combs transforms the humble everyday tool into a royal symbol of strength. These plastic styling tools hold a special place in the morning routine of many women as they determine the impact and beauty of their coiffure.

To every woman her hair is her crowning glory, the combs of this image a symbolic celebration of the strength, shine and swirl of curly hair. Within this regal frame of Camo 2.0 4322 lies a radiant reminder to cherish the beauty that stems from our heritage. It honors the untamed beauty, resilience, and the unyielding spirit of women who proudly take ownership of their unique hair journeys.

Crown constructed from plastic combs.

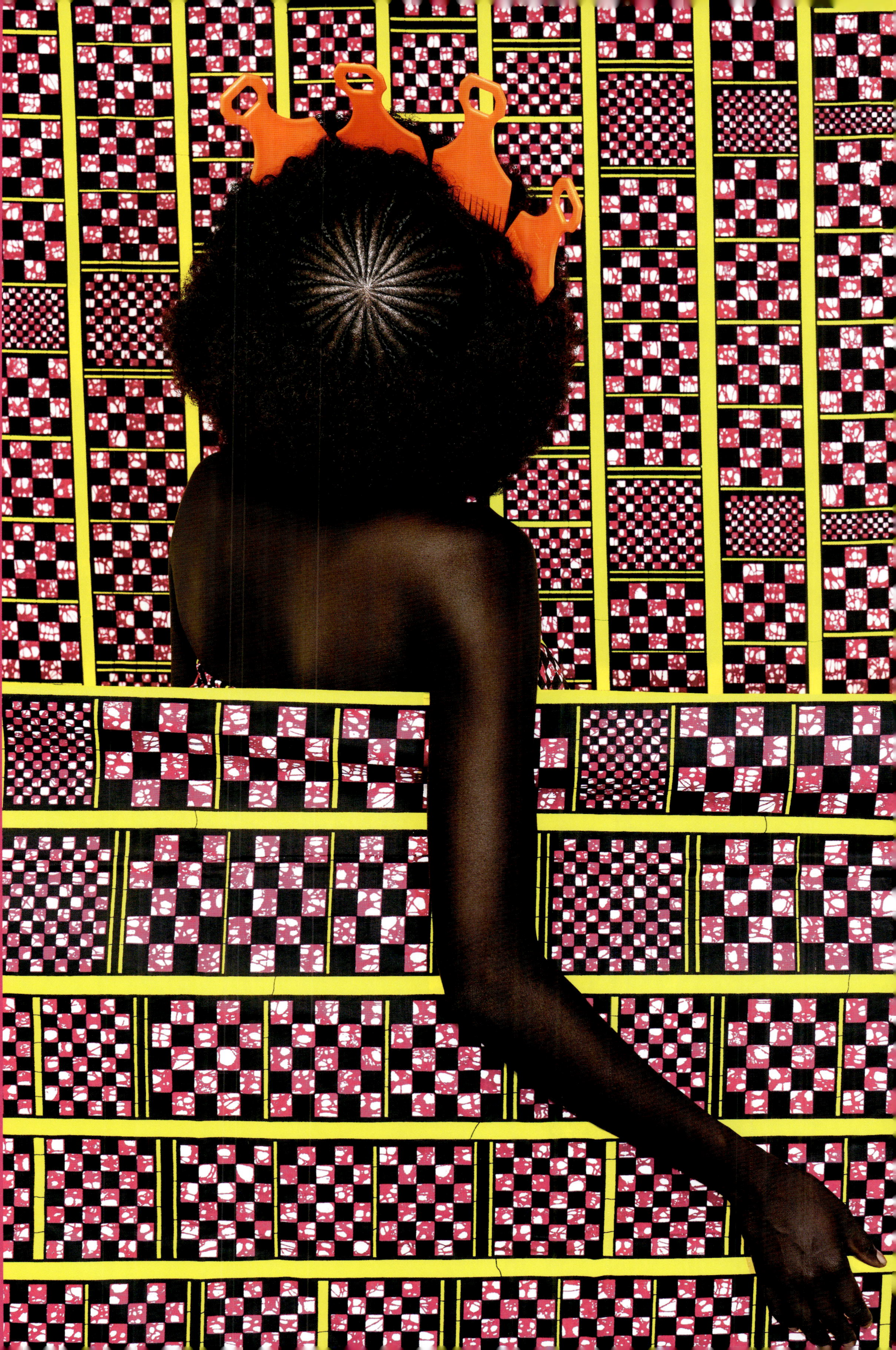

"Beauty and greatness do not belong to the gods alone."

"Urembo na ukuu sio wa miungu pekee."

Beads have a rich history of being worn for both beauty and to symbolize messages of status, age group and more to the larger community in one glance—without speaking a word. At the heart of adornment in Africa, whether for children or adults, was the threading of delicate cowrie shells, large etched wooden tubes, shimmering cutout metallic strands and everything in between. In a less nuanced context, for special occasions, Thandiwe's mother would string plastic neon beads into the lengths of Thandiwe's childhood hairstyle. Any little Nairobi girl's coiffure became extra special, extra good looking with beads in her hair, and Thandiwe was no different.

Beads have surged back into fashion as the younger generations rediscover them from their traditional roots. Within the trendy circles of African cities, many women and men are incorporating them into their chic hairstyles. Camo 2.0 4415 celebrates this with the vibrant nonchalance and strings of dotted delight from the subject's face. Thandiwe's' homage to the beauty of beadwork won the British Journal of Photography's Female in Focus Single Image Award of 2021.

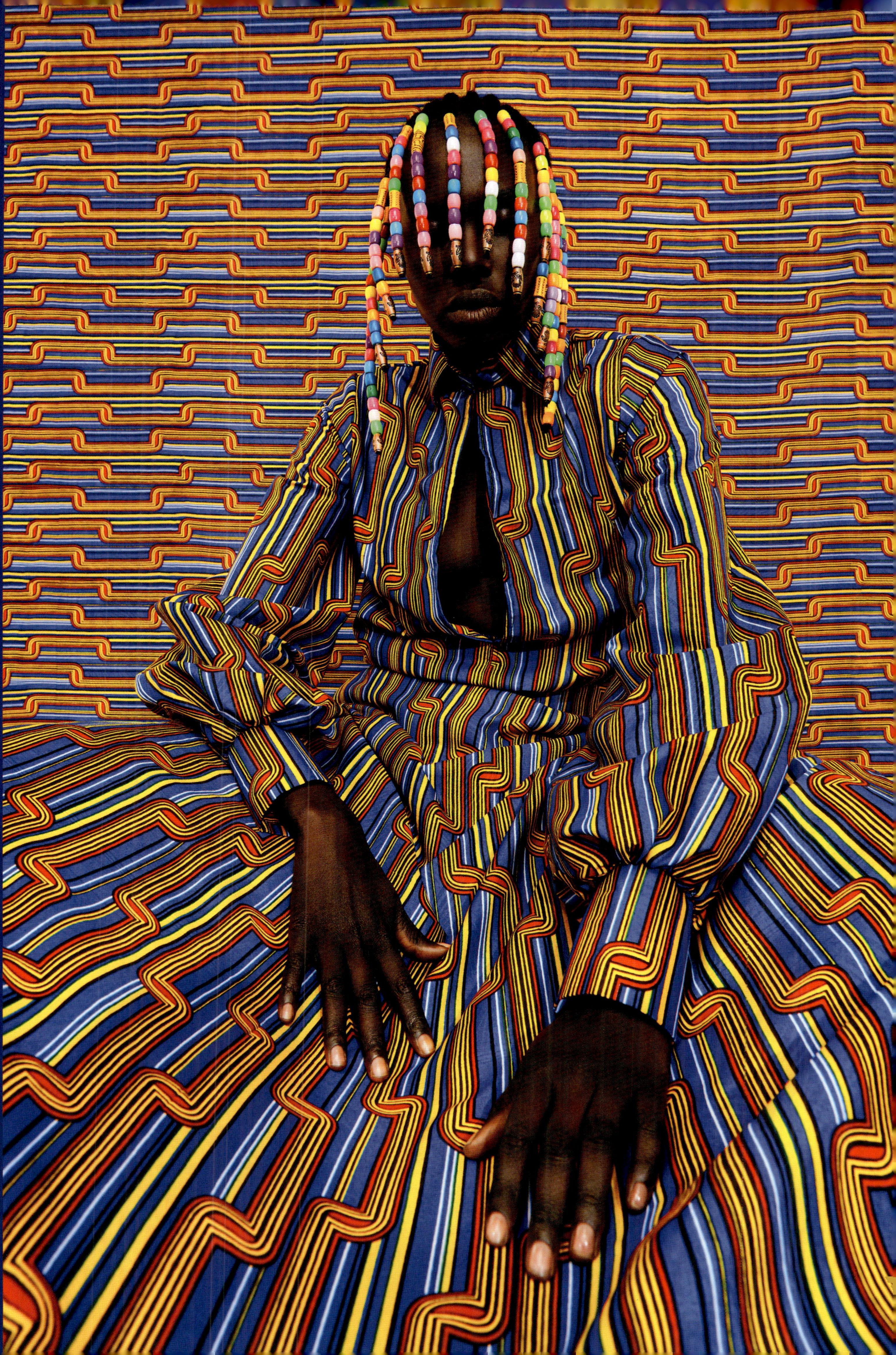

With an almost childlike distortion of its shimmering plaits, the dynamic perspective within Camo 2.0 4452 pulls the viewer upwards along the length of the subject's dark coils.

This visual reminds Thandiwe of her desire for long, and longer, and longer braids as a little girl. Caught in motion, the glistening plaits extend to such extraordinary lengths that they could easily be mistaken for jump ropes instead of mere braids. Beckoning you to explore the realm of dreams and endless possibilities, this is a bold and audacious homage to the imaginary elongated braids that Thandiwe always wanted to have as a girl (but never did!).

This piece serves as a testament to the limitless possibilities of creativity. It invites us to appreciate and to be inspired by the remarkable ability of art to capture our imagination.

Eyewear constructed from comb covers.

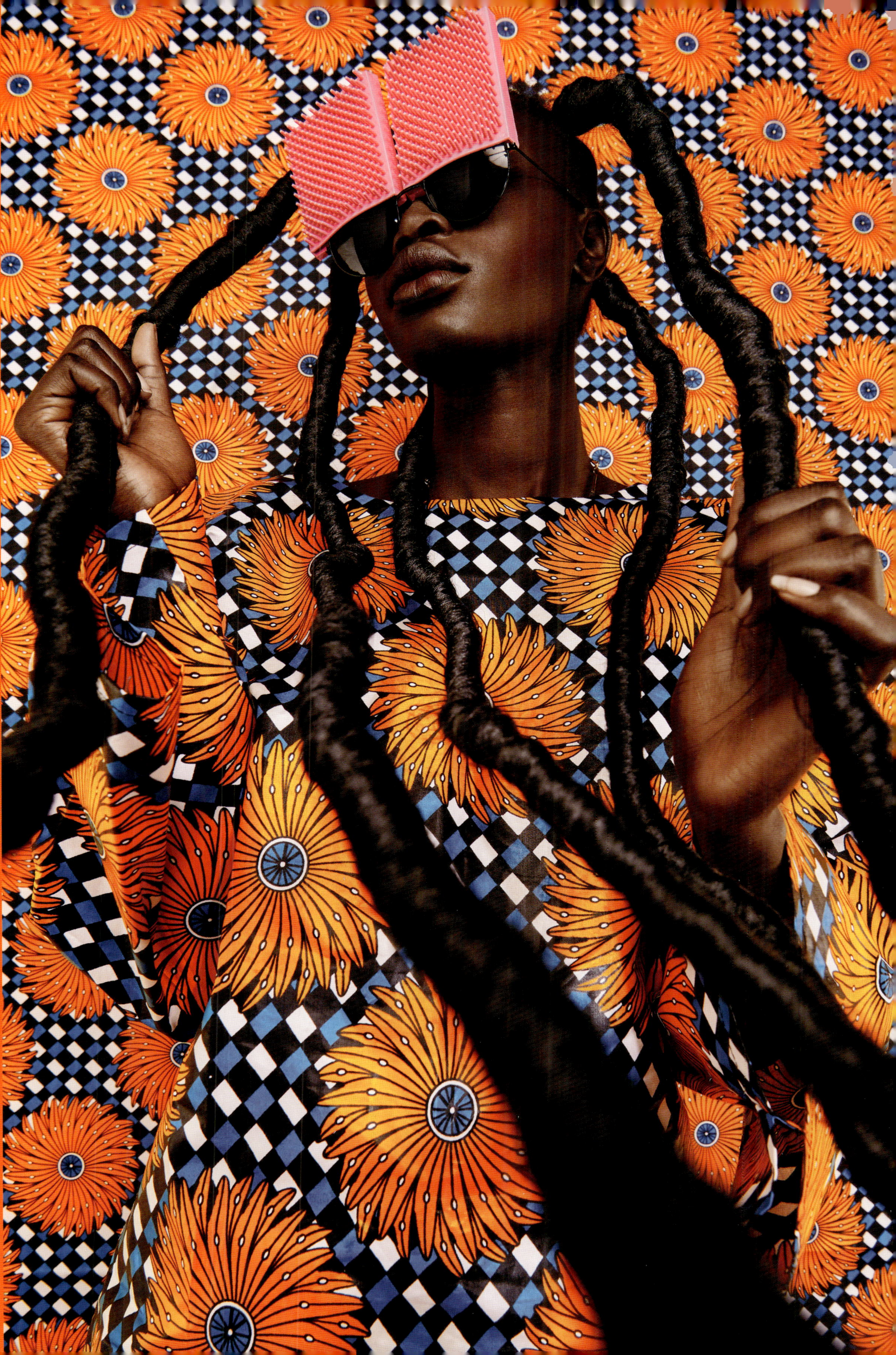

The unique yellow brim seen in Child's Play can trace its roots back to the cover of a humble plastic laundry basket, one produced by a Kenyan factory known for its distinctive finish. These baskets have a special place in the local community - found in any supermarket across Kenya.

As a child, Thandiwe would play hide-and-seek and sometimes curl up inside the large sized laundry basket to avoid being 'found.' More grown up now, Thandiwe elevated a hamper lid, repurposing it as a Vogue-worthy statement hat within a small, enclosed space for Child's Play.

And the name? Well, it couldn't be more fitting. The image is part of a series in which Thandiwe takes us on a nostalgic trip, exploring the toys and games that filled her childhood.

Hat constructed from laundry basket lid.

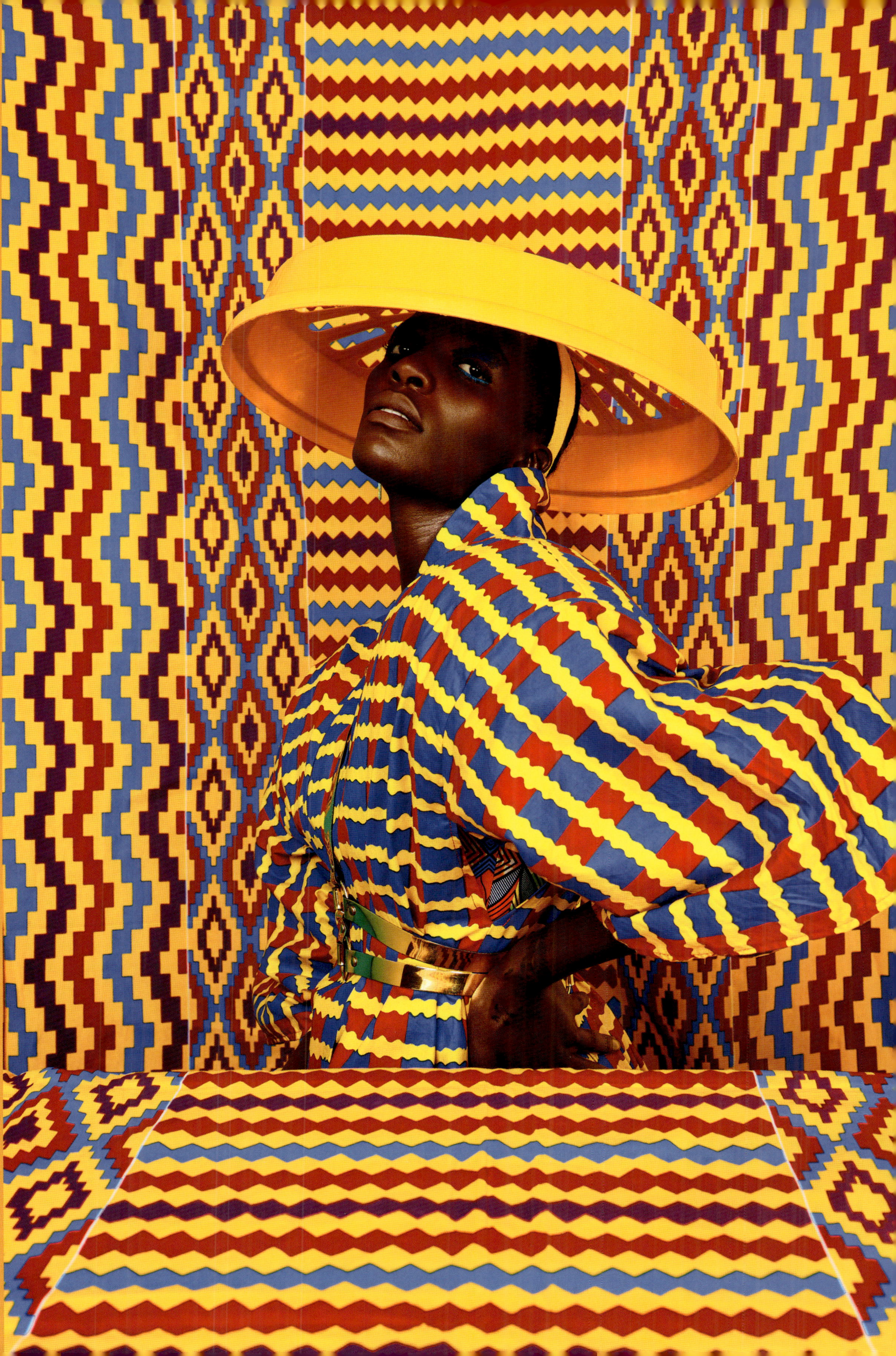

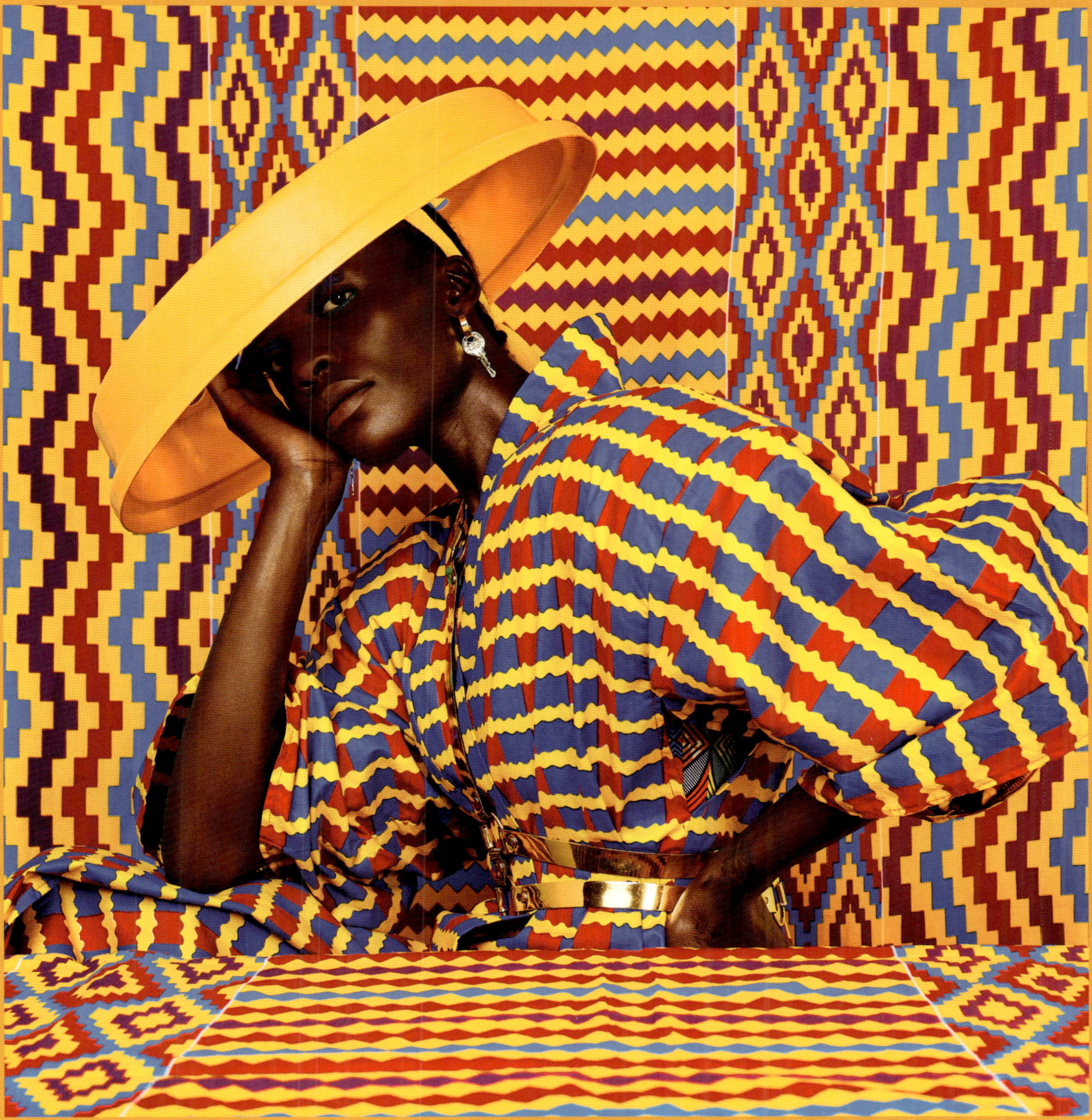

"We desire to bequeath two things to our children; the first one is roots, the other one is wings."

"Twatamani kuwarithisha watoto wetu vitu viwili: cha kwanza ni mizizi, cha pili ni mabawa."

In an artistic emphasis of the hair pin eyewear of Camo 08, the subject's zig zag braids are based on a common Kenyan hairstyle technique. Braiding is usually done at local Kenyan hair stalls, clustered together in open air markets. The most noteworthy within Nairobi is Kenyatta Market—renown for the diversity of skill and speed that its hair stylists offer. The local hairdressers aggressively shout their wares or sit perched on plastic chairs with combs in their hands ready to braid, weave, straighten or cut any Kenyan woman's hair if she only steps into their booth. Once complete, the trendy, pristine braids are pinned in place with the black hair pins used as she steps away from the grid-like market that bursts with energy.

As tribute to the timelessness of African culture, the subject's eyewear is made from long black hair pins in distinct red and yellow fan-shaped holders. The long black bobby pins have never changed—used by Thandiwe, her mother and grandmother for generations—and remain as pragmatic as they were in the past. This is a nod to African consistency—even though there is always change and development in the continent, the important things remain the same.

Eyewear constructed from bobby pin sets.

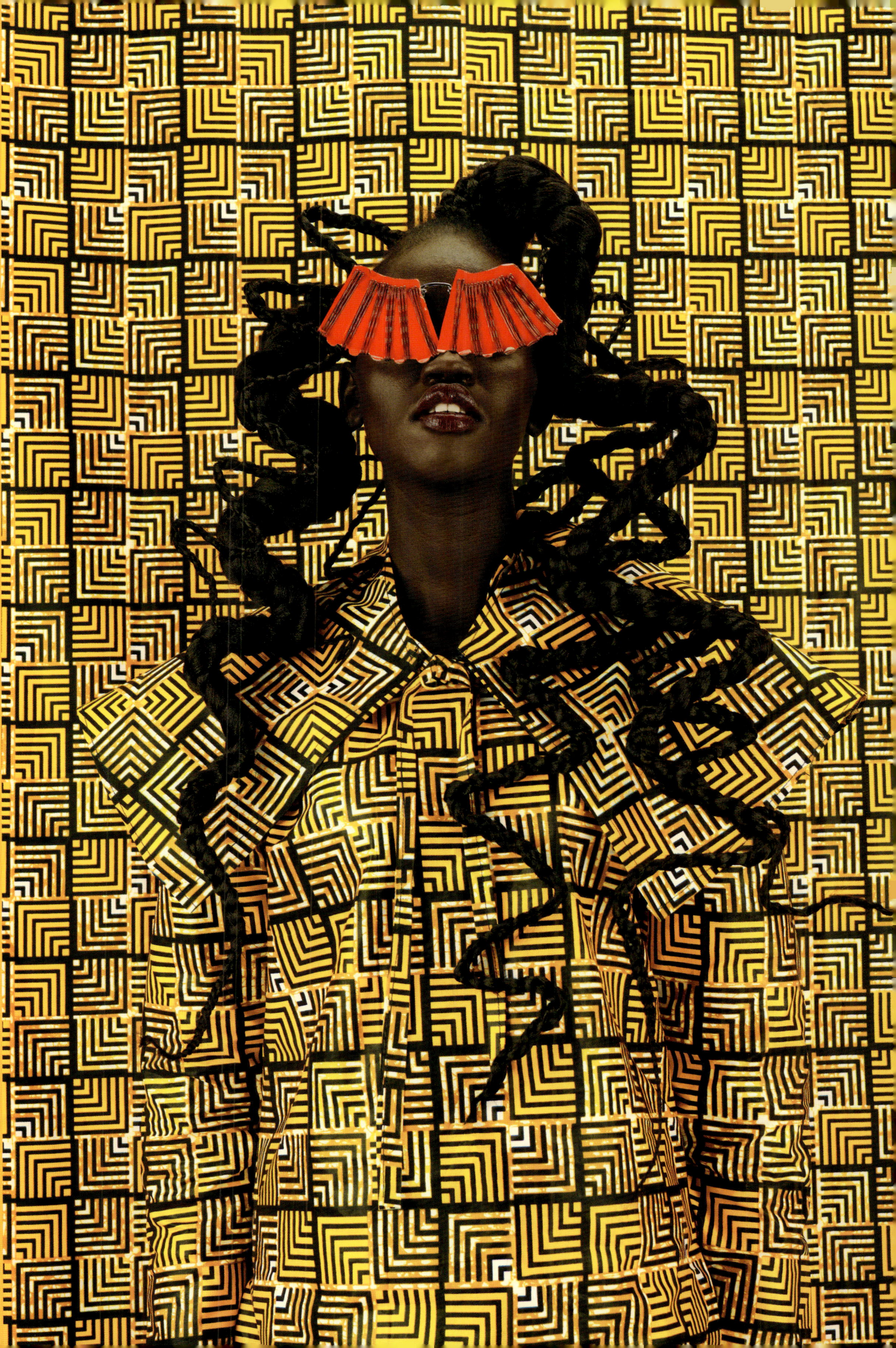

“Rising early makes the road short.”

“Kurauka mapema hufupisha njia.”

The evocative essence of Camo 11 lies within the bottle caps adorning the subject’s hair. The colorful metallic lids are popped from drinks found throughout Kenya, most notably Tusker, a beloved local beer brand that has earned global recognition. These bottle caps, imbued with Kenyan traditional significance, hold subtle cultural cues that present a striking departure from Western engagement rituals. Instead of traditional porridge, these sugary drinks now carry the weight of acceptance or rejection to a marriage proposal. A girl’s decision to pour a soft drink for her suitor symbolizes she has agreed to marry him, while a refusal becomes a profound “no” to his intentions. Within this rich heritage, soft drinks symbolically speak to everyone involved, without a single word being spoken.

Hair accessorised with bottle caps.

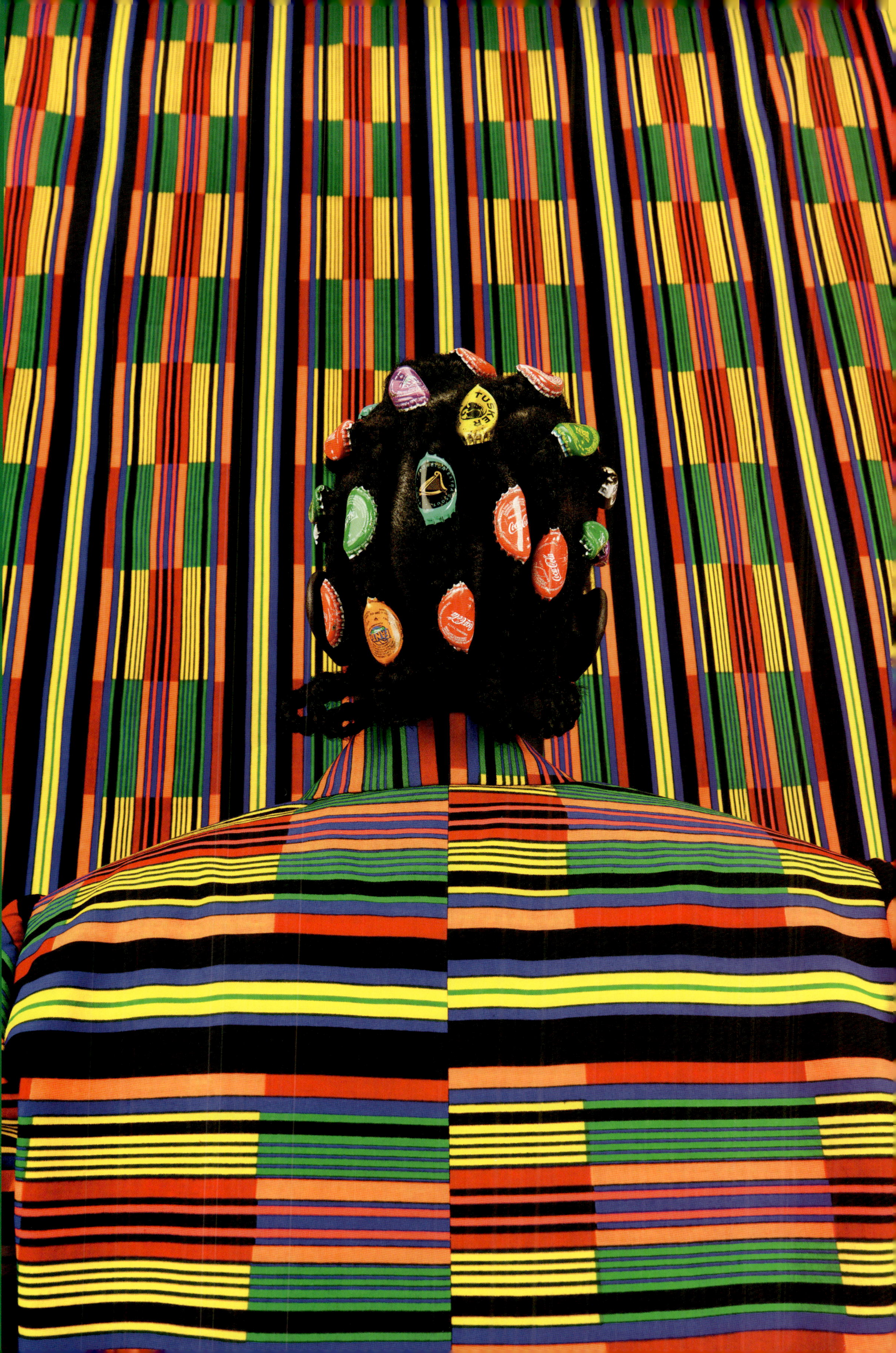
TUSKER
Coca-Cola

“Life is lived forwards, but understood backwards.”

“Maisha yatazamwa mbele, lakini yafahamika nyuma.”

Circles of intricate braids rhythmically radiate, like auditory waves in the ether, within Camo 13. These delicate, woven strands make a striking contrast against a musically rich backdrop of turquoise and orange drum prints.

Through her lens, Thandiwe sees more than just patterns in Camo 13. She sees echoes of her Kenyan heritage manifested in the slender, elongated Mbeere tribal drum. Traditionally, these drums were pounded by the unmarried men of the tribe, their beats piercing the village air in a vibrant call for love and marriage.

Indeed, Camo 13 seems to hum with that same vitality, the aura of Mbeere men’s determination permeating the canvas. Hidden within its captivating aesthetics lie whispers of courtship and unity, resonating secret messages of affection and commitment. “Can you hear the rhythm?” it seems to ask.

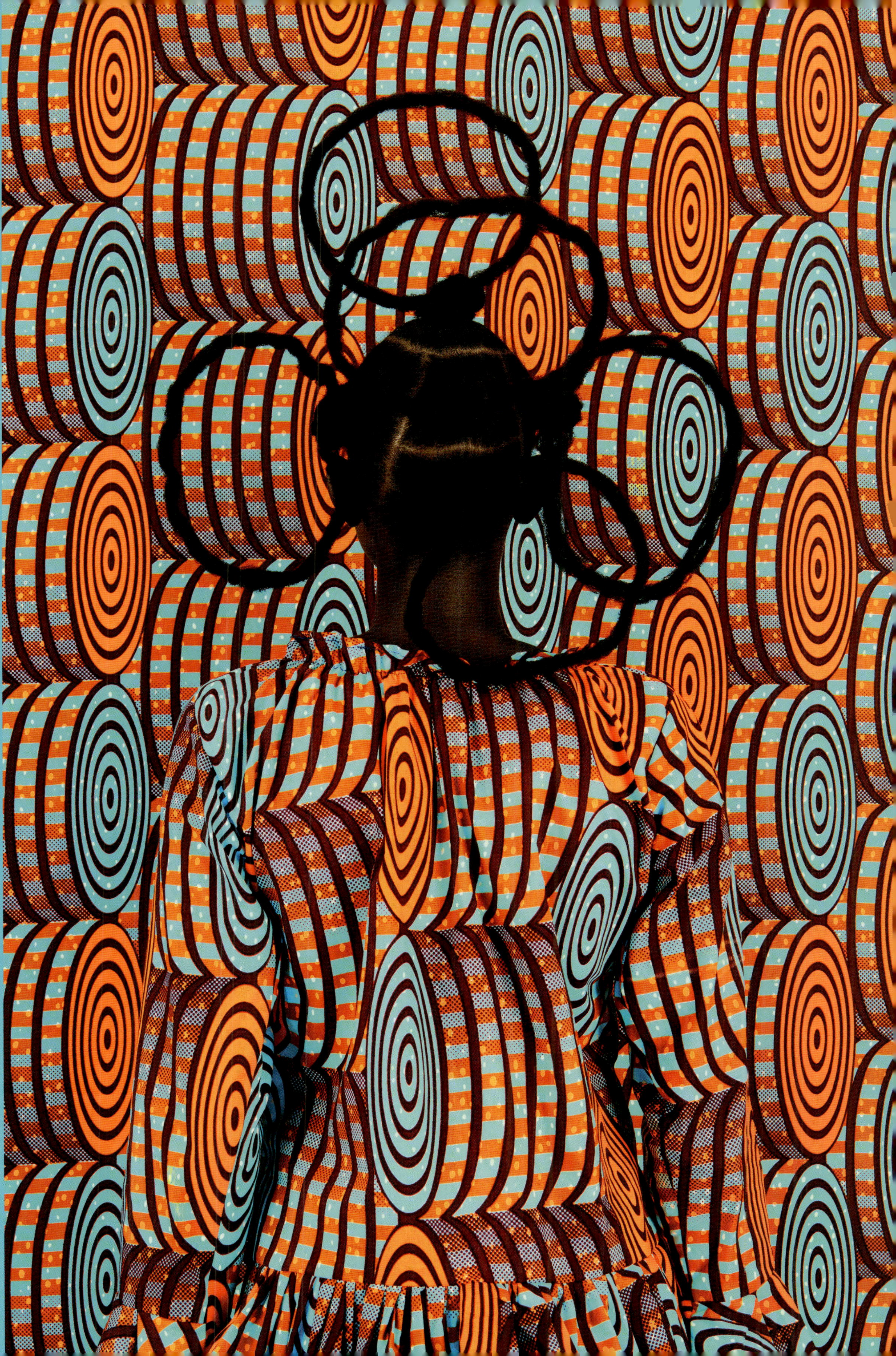

For children, drinking straws were the source of countless hours of fun. For Thandiwe, the simple act of receiving a soda came with the added excitement of playing with the bright tube after slurping up her drink!

In Kenyan culture, sodas hold significance, but to Thandiwe, the drinking straws held even greater importance. They weren't just tools for drinking; they were versatile objects that could transform into sculptures, snorkeling tubes, or even fashionable bracelets. All it took was a child's boundless imagination to unlock their potential.

Eyewear constructed from drinking straws.

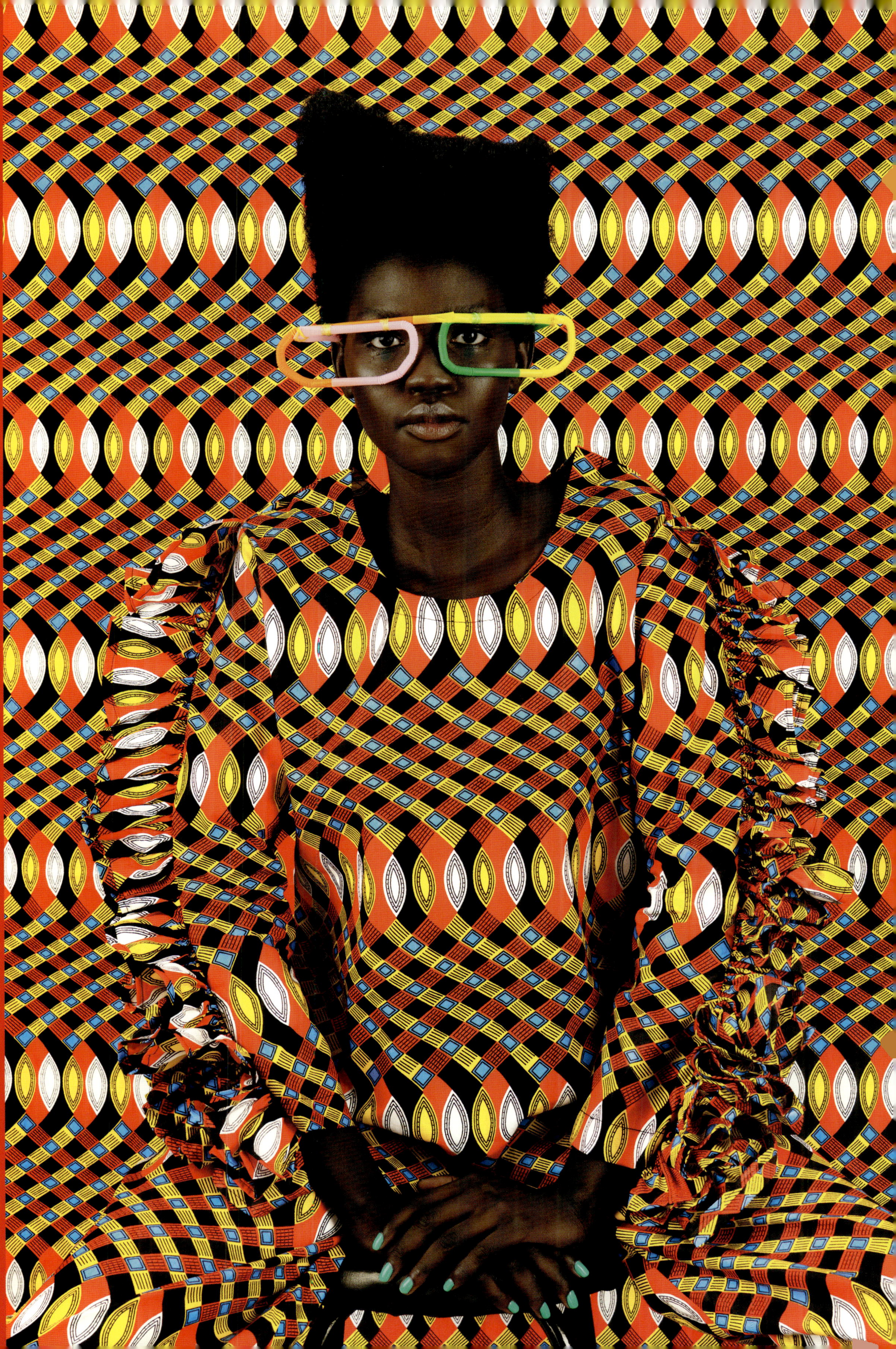

"The pillar of the world is hope."

"Nguzo ya dunia ni tumaini."

Nuanced and layered, Camo 15 carries an eccentric print that is a nod to the former logo of an established state-owned TV station. Thandiwe would lose herself to the Saturday morning cartoons sprawled across its broadcasts. The station, founded in Kenya in 1928, was instrumental in supporting the nation during the COVID-19 pandemic and remains a popular choice in lifting the hearts and hopes of it's viewers.

Thandiwe gives her own tribute to the impact of the global crisis, presenting her subject in a spiky, virus-like hairdo, bright and playful. Made from Kichungi, a common Kiswahili term for sieves, alluring yellow and green goggles add a whimsical dash to the look. They are iconic plastic strainers used to brew a good, hot cup of tea—the universal comfort in the face of trying times.

Eyewear constructed from plastic seives.

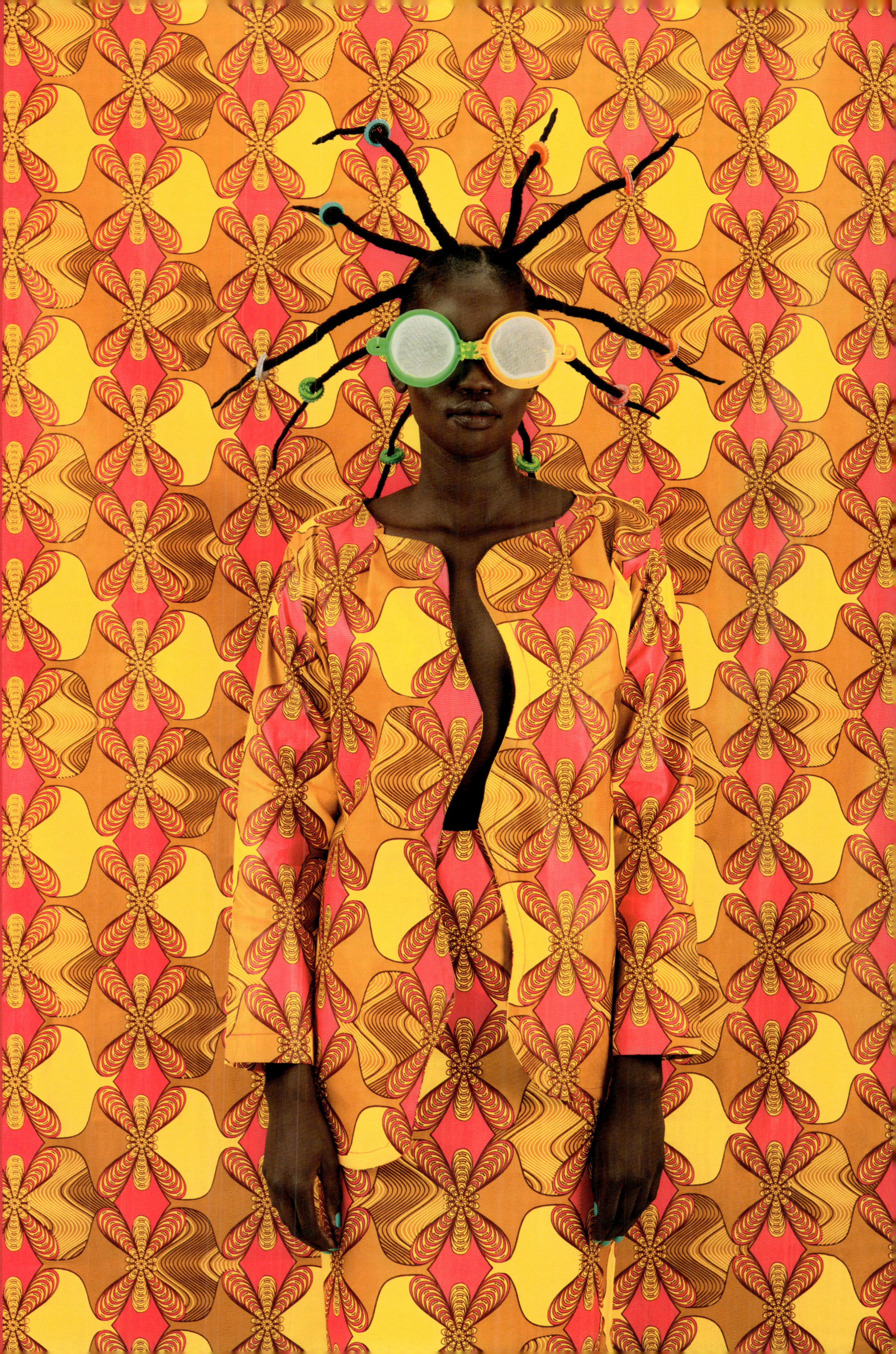

"A beautiful thing is never perfect."

"Linalopendeza sio timilifu."

Looped into textured eyewear, long-bristle nylon brushes sit perched on the subjects face suddenly becoming significant within the mesmerising blue and yellow print. She gazes into the distance as if she can see the future, her eyes filled with foresight and anticipation.

Thandiwe utilizes these simple bottle-cleaning brushes, often associated with routine cleaning tasks, to signify the prevalent plastic culture within African kitchens and households.

Eyewear constructed from bottle bristle brushes.

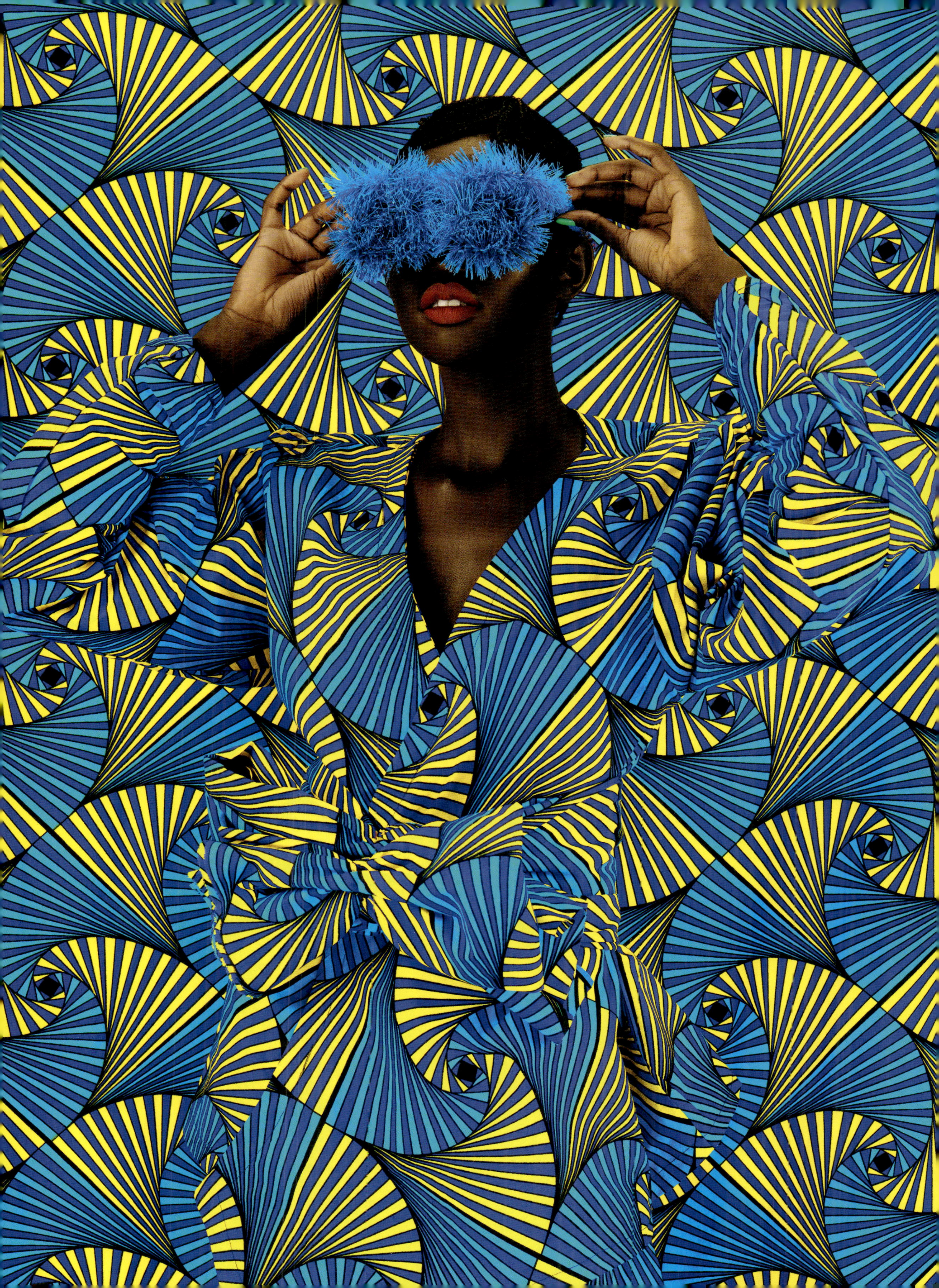

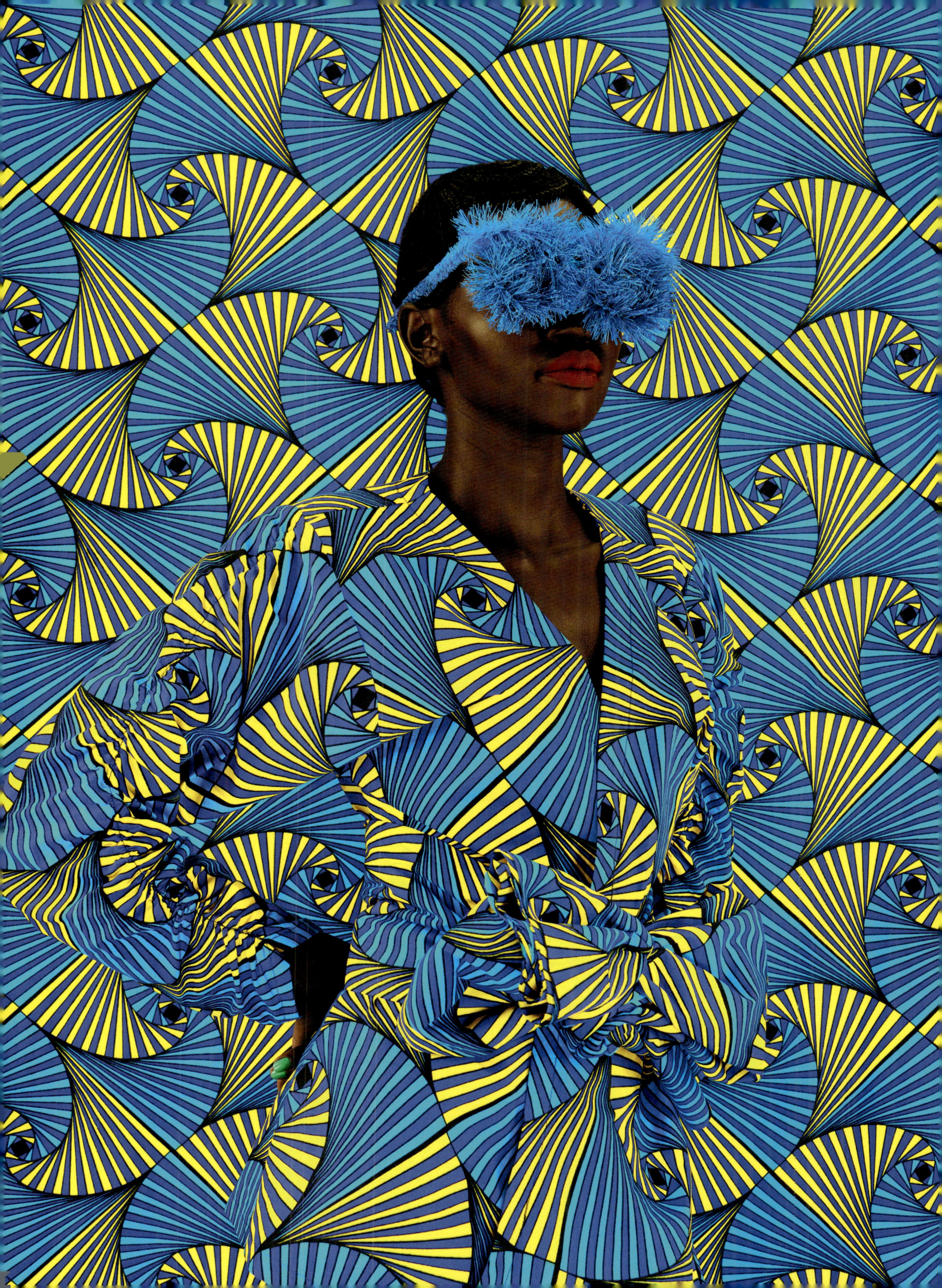

Every Camo image is inspired by everyday objects found in the average Kenyan home. Commonplace objects which are often unappreciated but beautiful in their own way, are transformed into a mesmerizing avant-garde tableau. A garish red lemon squeezer and an upside-down wavy bowl in muted pink become a juxtaposition of fun.

These objects dance harmoniously, weaving a tapestry of playfulness and creativity, a heartfelt tribute to the countless women who embrace these tools each day, engaging in the timeless art of homemaking. Camo 17 is a celebration of the wonders concealed in the unassuming corners of our household.

Eyewear constructed from lemon squeezer.

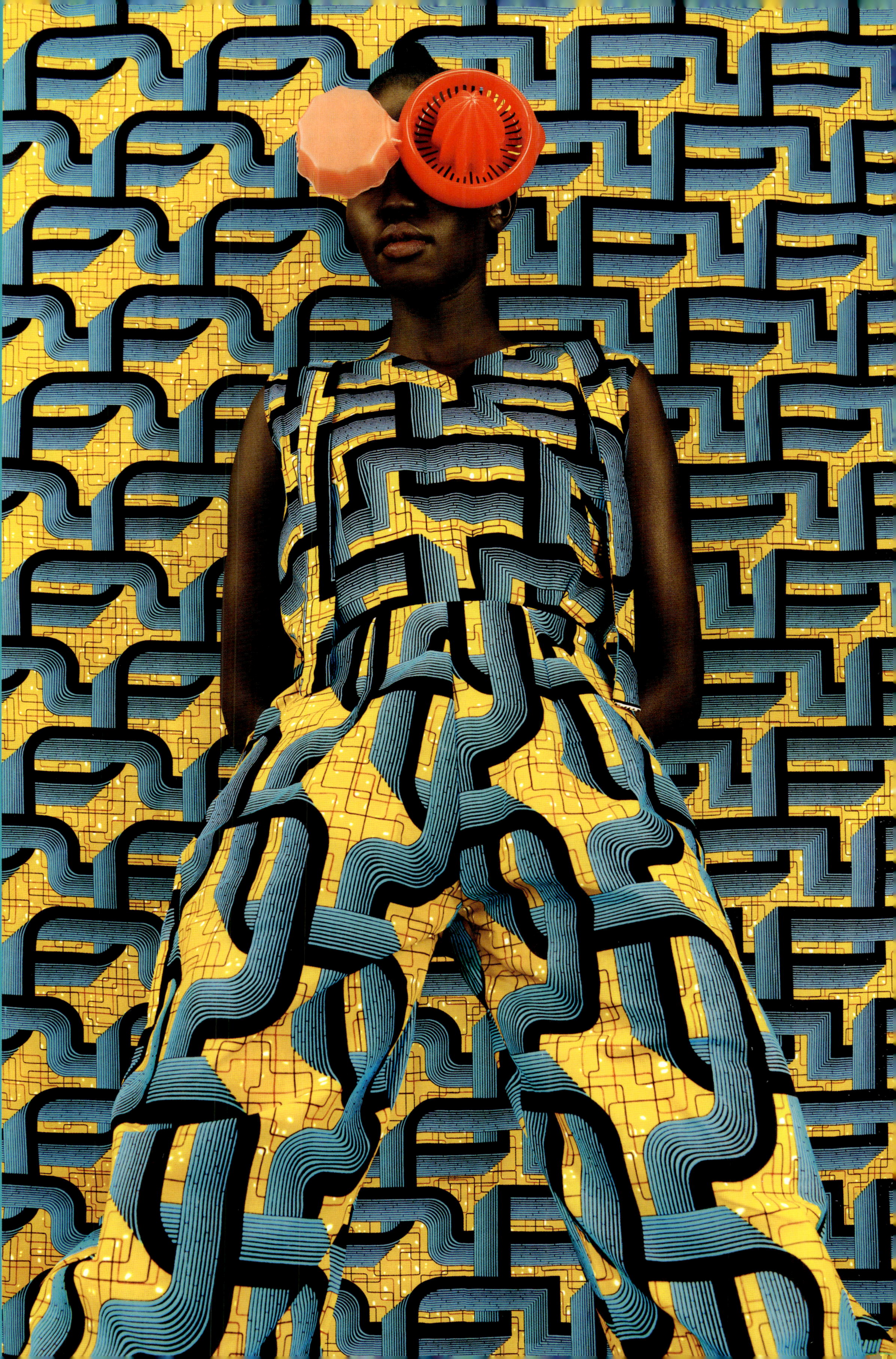

Set against the backdrop of daily rituals, Camo 18 pays homage to the art of handwashing clothes and the vibrant colors that adorn the drying process. As the garments are meticulously hung out under cloudless blue skies, a symphony of color emerges with garish pops of bright hues. Plastic pegs gleefully clash against the fabrics they hold in place elevating the simple act of drying clothes into a vivid spectacle. Camo 18 beautifully reflects the spirit of the Kenyan woman—resilient, creative, and unapologetically radiant—even in the midst of her daily rituals and tasks.

Eyewear constructed from pegs.

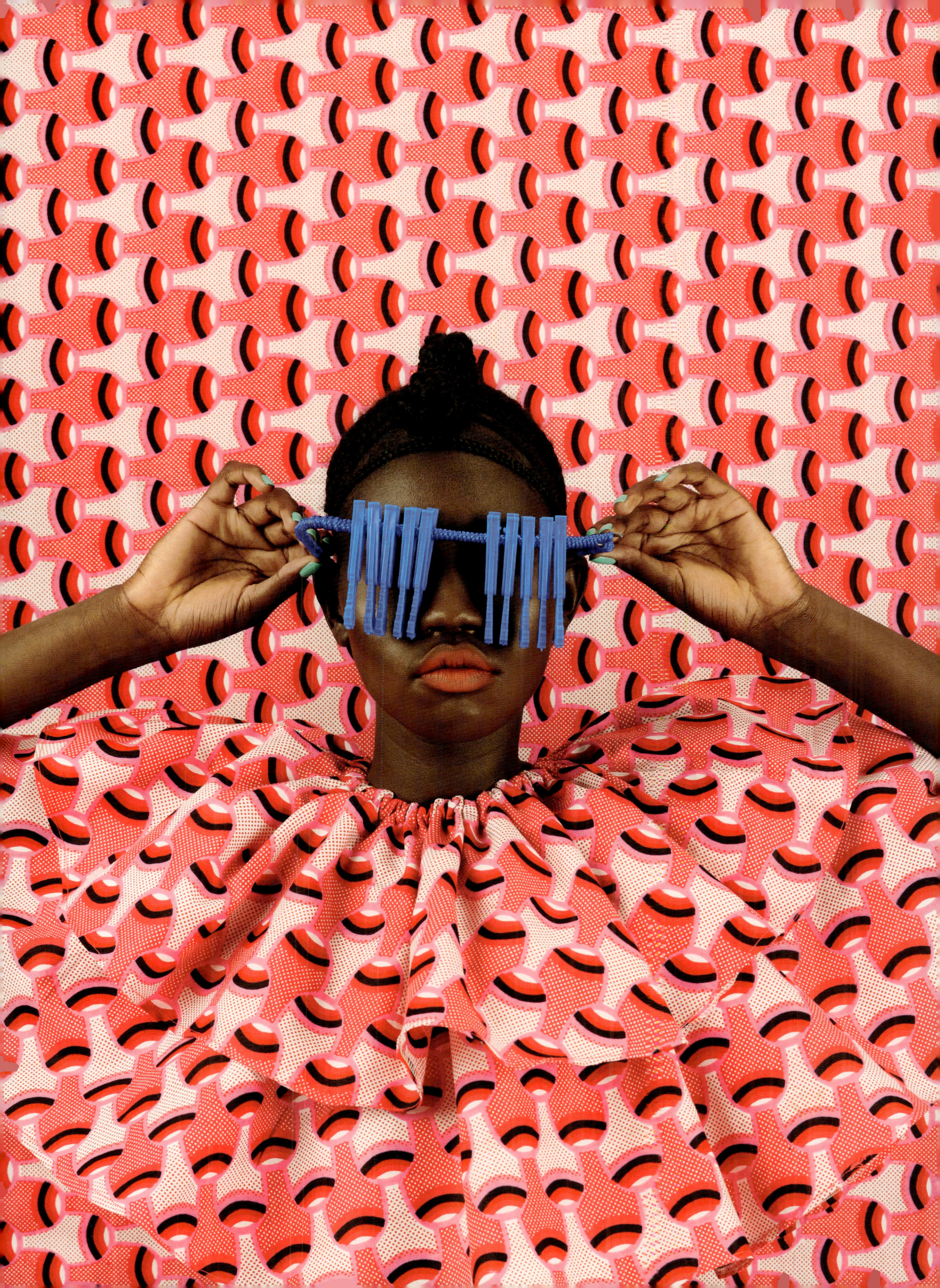

"The eyes that have seen an ocean cannot be satisfied with a mere lagoon."

"Macho yaliyotazama bahari hayatosheki na wangwa."

At first glance, this dapper monocle seems to be a bespoke accent to a swirling pink story, but in fact, it is ingeniously crafted from a simple and unglamorous clothing hanger. Ubiquitous in the wardrobe of the hard working Kenyan, these unappealing hangers find new life as props, hooks, impromptu TV antennas, and even latches to stubborn doors.

In Camo 20, the multi-use metal strip is reinterpreted into a new, eye catching focal point that demands attention and intrigue. The work explores the potential hidden within the mundane, providing a unique and thought-provoking twist that leaves you hung on its captivating charm.

Monocle constructed from wire hanger.

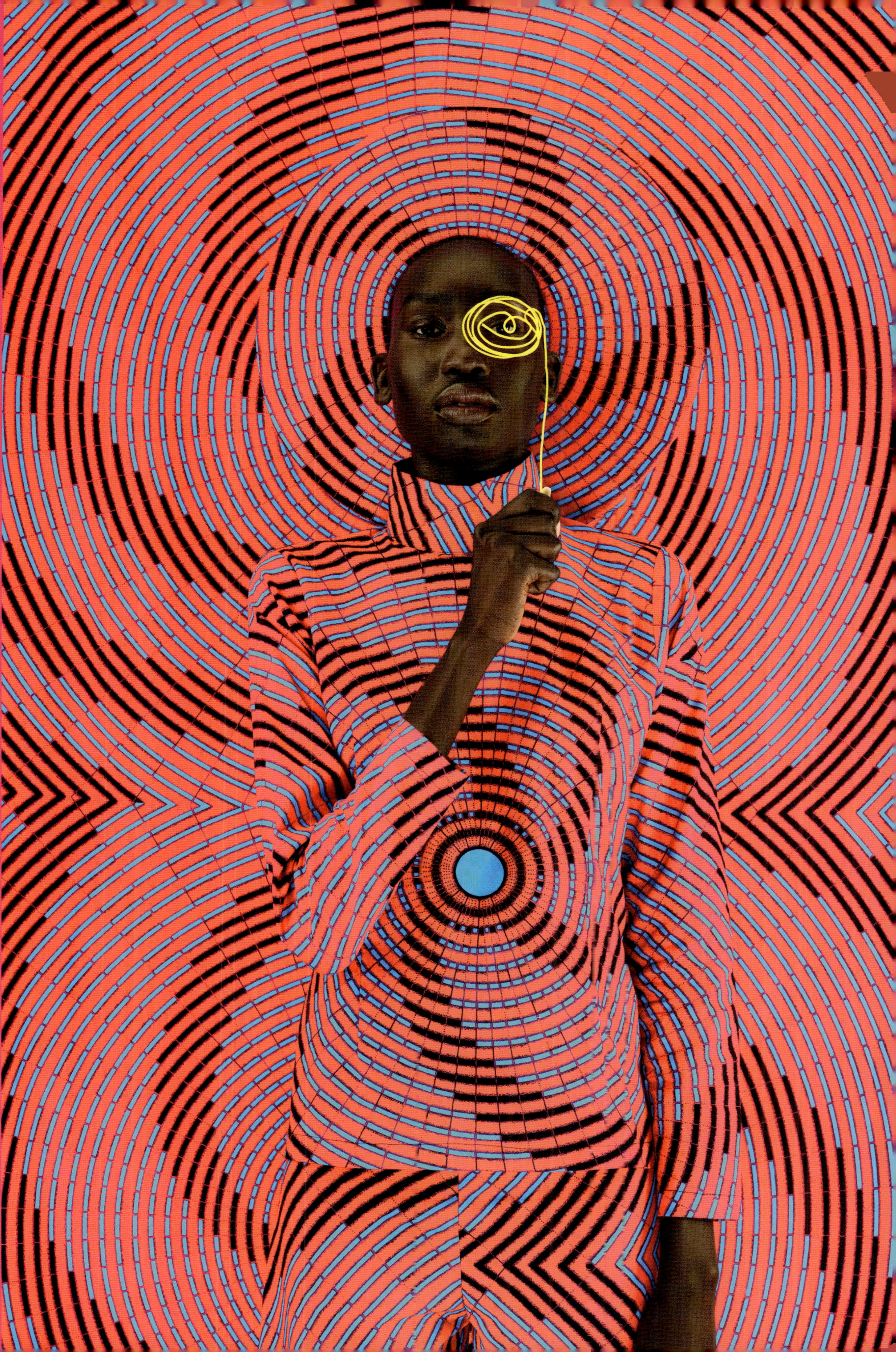

"Patience puts a crown on the head."

"Subira huvika taji kichwani."

Within Camo 21 lies a fusion of cultural artistry and nostalgic symbolism. The glasses, meticulously hand beaded by talented local Maasai artisans, embody the captivating allure of their traditional jewelry. Despite not being Maasai themselves, all Kenyan women are drawn to the beauty of this distinctive tribal adornment. They appreciate the intricate craftsmanship that goes into creating each piece and Thandiwe is no different.

Standing guard, padlock and key protect and unveil our most treasured possessions. Thandiwe is transported back to her student days where small locks kept her precious books and knowledge safely nestled within her desk. Camo 21's uniquely celebrates this personal history and appreciated treasure trove.

Eyewear constructed from Maasai bracelet and padlocks.

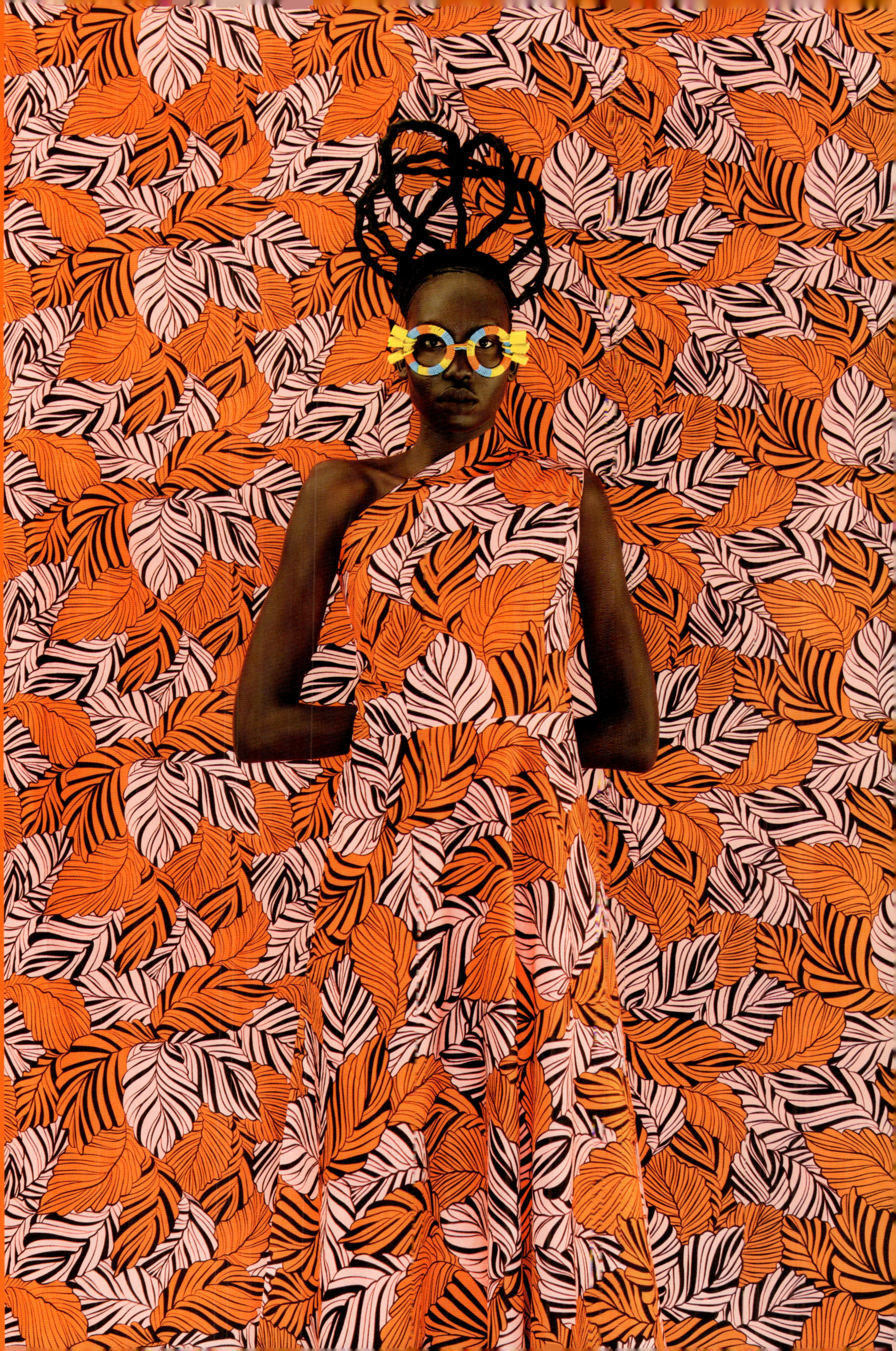

"He who is destined for power does not have to fight for it."

"Aliyenuiwa kumiliki nguvu hastahili kuipigania."

It is a very strong, confident woman who gazes into the lens of Camo 23, her face exuding a calm defiance that is truly formidable. She balances five fisted hands within her strong armed hair, the bright dashes of color made from iconic afro combs. Light but fierce, the piece visualizes the gentle power of a woman who is confident in herself. In her powerful silence, she radiates a quiet strength that commands attention.

Hair accessories made from power combs.

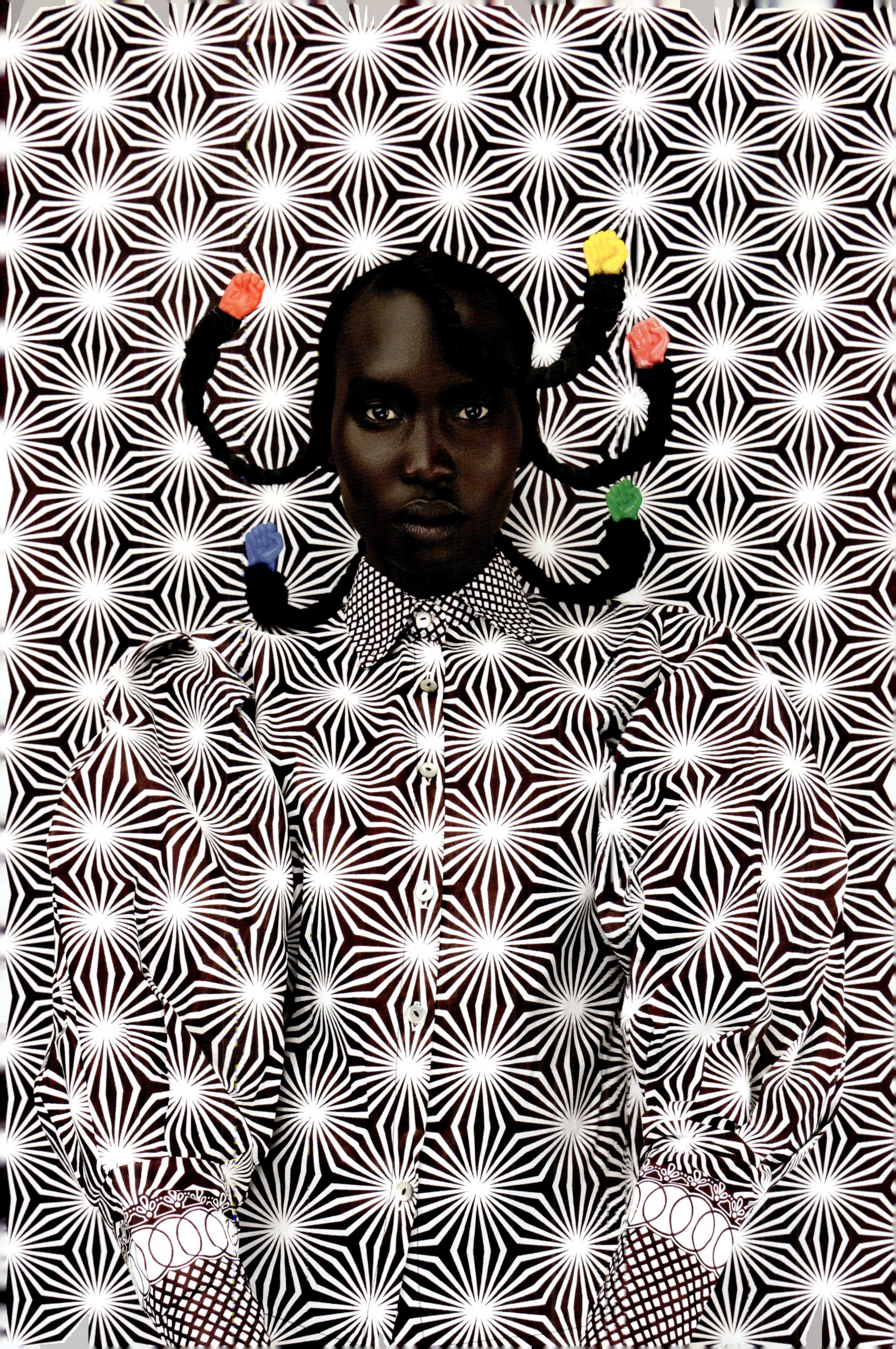

To speak of shells is to speak of Mombasa, part of the coastal region of Kenya where pristine white beaches meet the mesmerizing turquoise waves. Known locally as "the white and blue city", Mombasa's coral reefs, seafaring traditions and rich, shimmering customs add to the majestic, cresting waves and swaying palm trees. Stumbling upon an empty shell becomes an enchanting moment, filled with a sense of wonder and delight. Camo 24 captures the aquatic essence of shell collecting, exploring their structures, colors, patterns, pressing them to your ear once miles away from the ocean just to hear the echo of waves, allowing the listener to carry the magic of Mombasa with them wherever they go.

Eyewear constructed from soda cans.

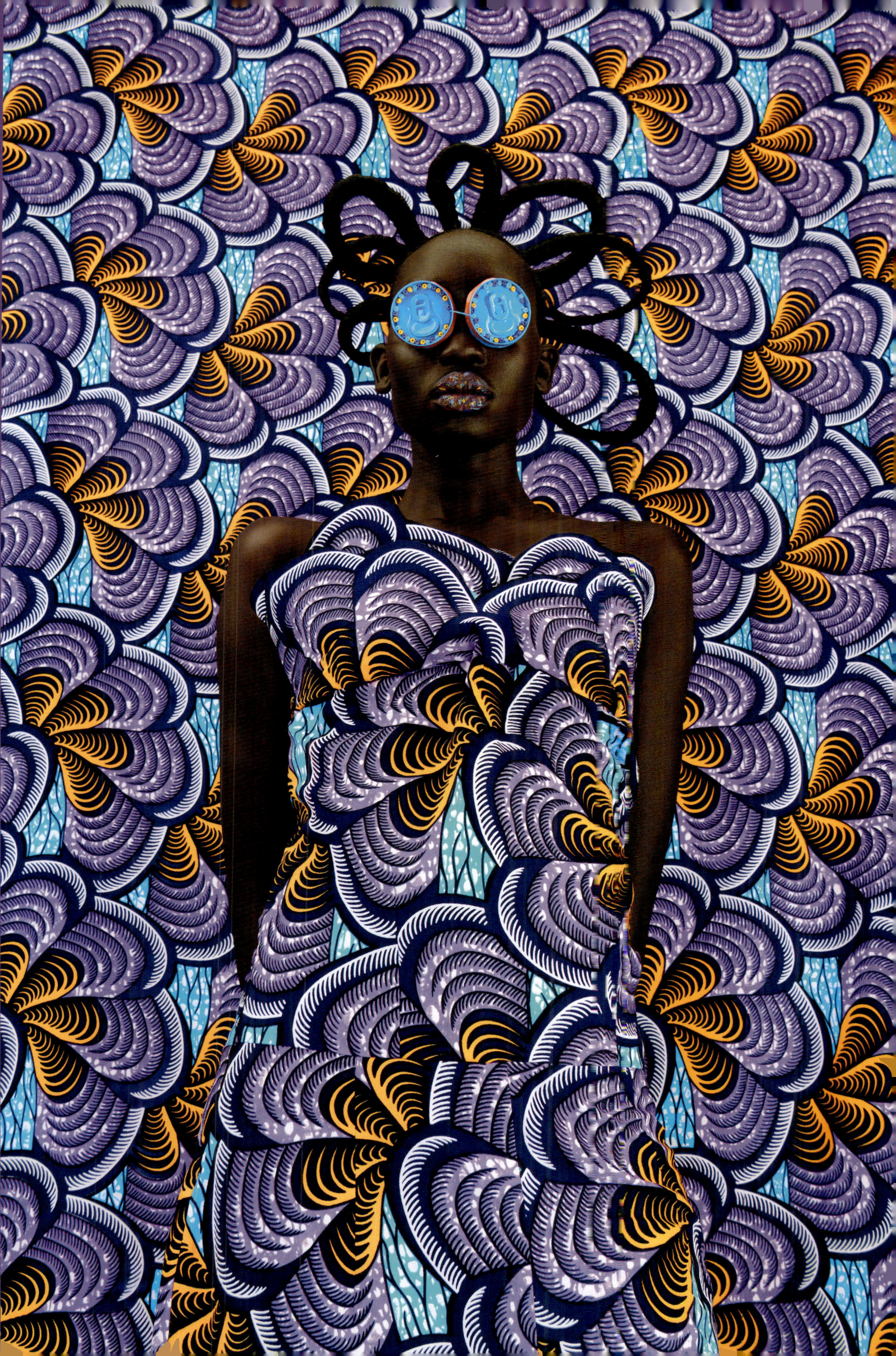

"Even if you close your eyes while looking in the mirror the image remains yours."

"Hata kama ukifumba macho mbele ya kioo, picha itasalia yako."

Like a mesmerizing plaything, the pattern on Camo 27's frames is a vibrant kaleidoscope of ever-changing colors, reminiscent of the engrossing toys Thandiwe enjoyed as a child. The psychedelic print reflects fond memories of playful imagination, basking in the naive innocence of youth.

This playful ingenuity is the distinctive style of the Jua Kali-Kiswahili for fierce sun-metalwork artisans in Kenya. Thandiwe drew inspiration from their signature looping sculpture, transforming metal earrings into avant-garde frames, infusing them with a burst of artistic flair.

Eyewear constructed from earrings.

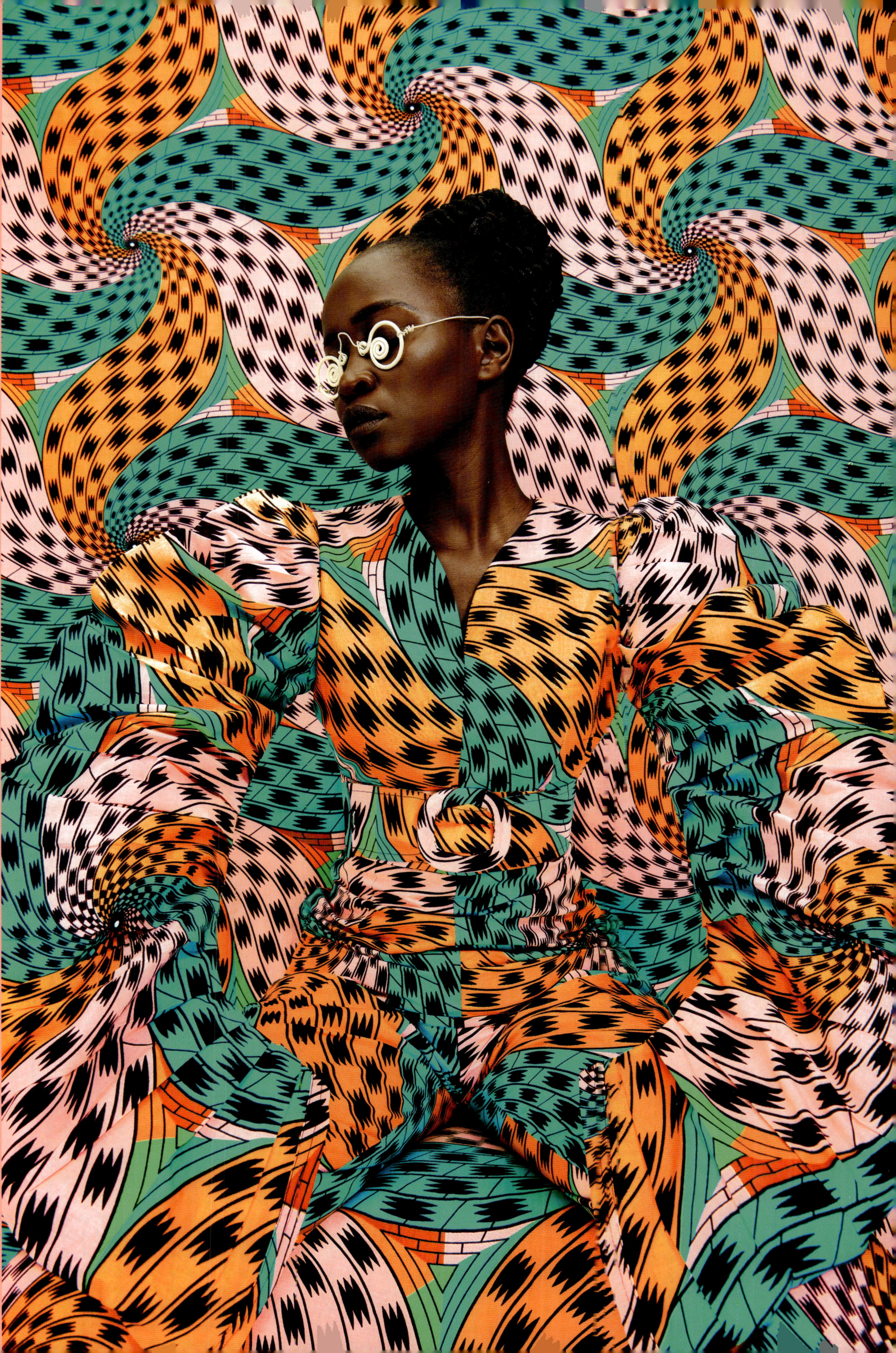

"With a little seed of imagination you can grow a field of hope."

"Ukiwa na mbegu ndogo ya dhana unaweza kukuza shamba la tumaini."

In Kenya, tinsel is a key part of any heartfelt celebration, moving beyond decoration on a christmas tree into everyday festivities. Whether it's draped proudly over a successful graduate at their degree ceremony or gleefully thrown around the neck of a family member returning from overseas study, the frizzled, garish boa loudly adds to the joy and warmth of any good party. The dazzling and shining eyewear of Camo 28 is a Happy New Year party mixed with an explosive coiffure and complemented by riotous swirls of yellow. It's Thandiwe's crackling, bursting visual masterpiece that embodies the excitement and exuberance of celebrations in Kenya.

Eyewear constructed from tinsel.

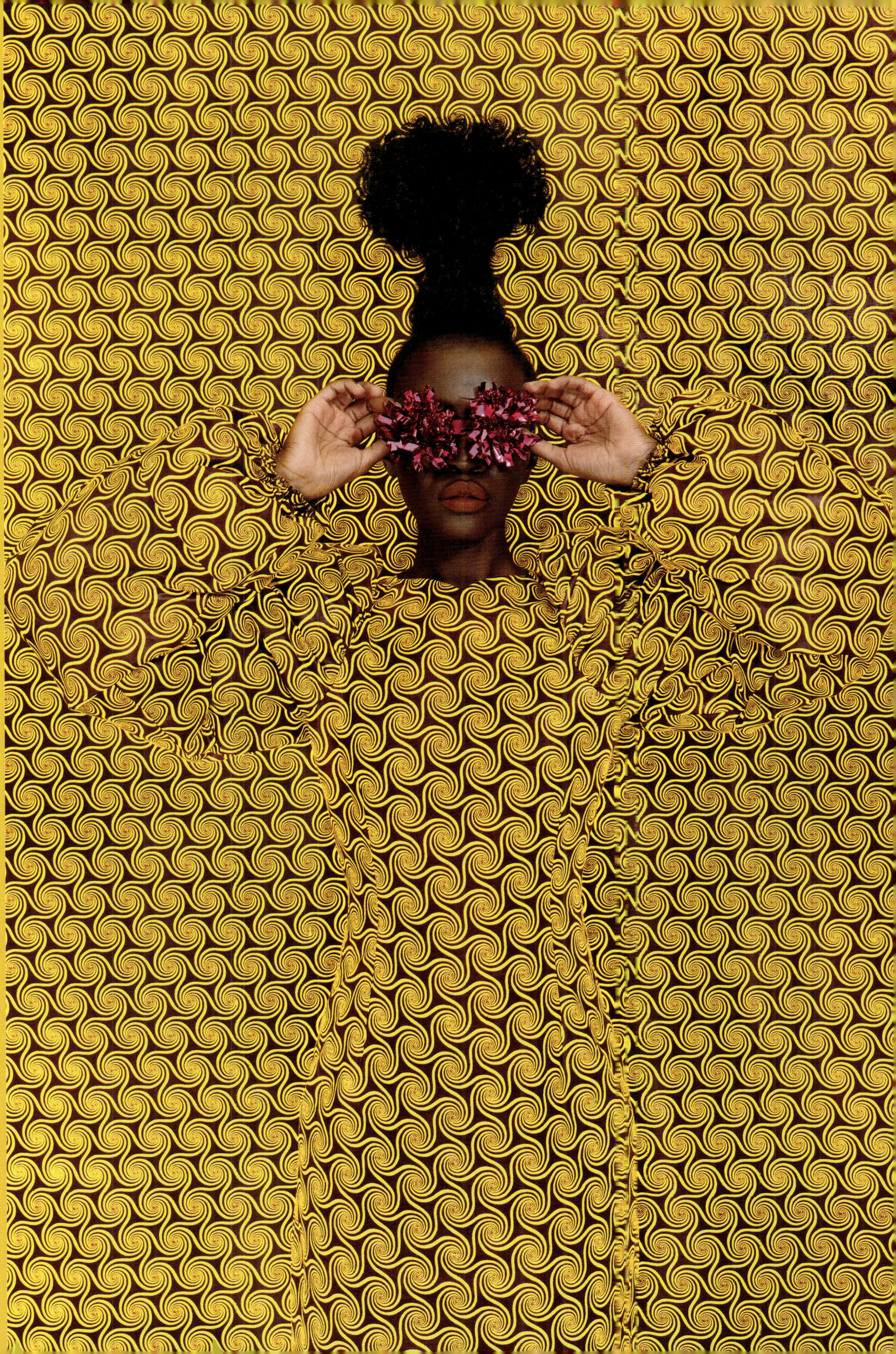

“If you think you’re too small to make a difference, try spending the night with a mosquito.”

“Ukihofia kuwa udogo wako hauwezi kufanya mabadiliko, jaribu kulala usiku na mbu.”

There’s nothing more annoying than the high-pitched whine of a mosquito weaving around your ears as you sleep. Jolted awake one time too many, Thandiwe ingeniously repurposed a local mosquito repelling solution into mesmerizing eyewear.

In homes across Kenya, mosquito coils are used to ward off these nap-interrupting-annoyance, particularly in areas without electricity, ensuring serene, bite-free rest. In this way Camo 29 offers a hypnotic twist on an everyday tool.

Eyewear constructed from mosquito coils.

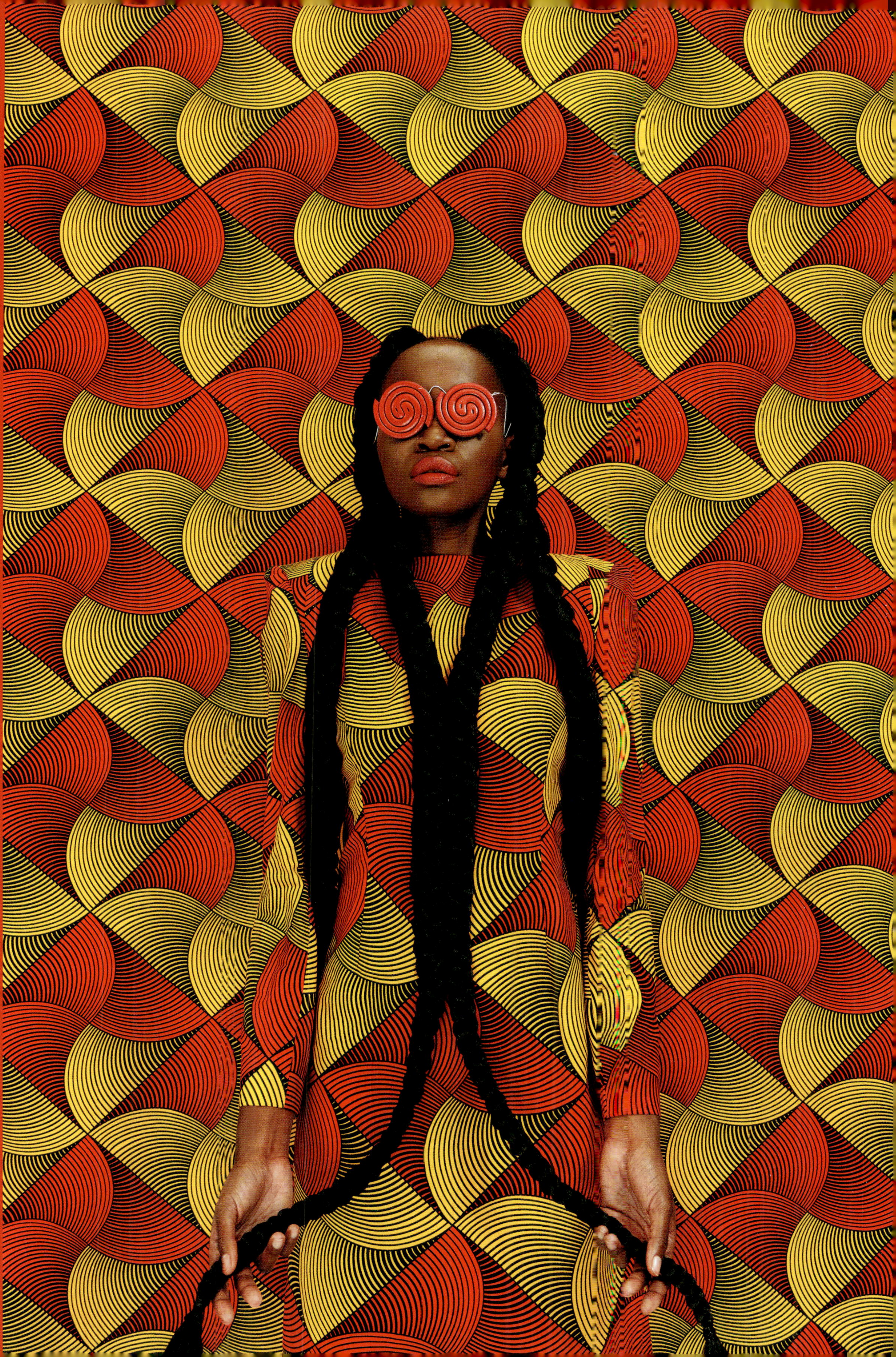

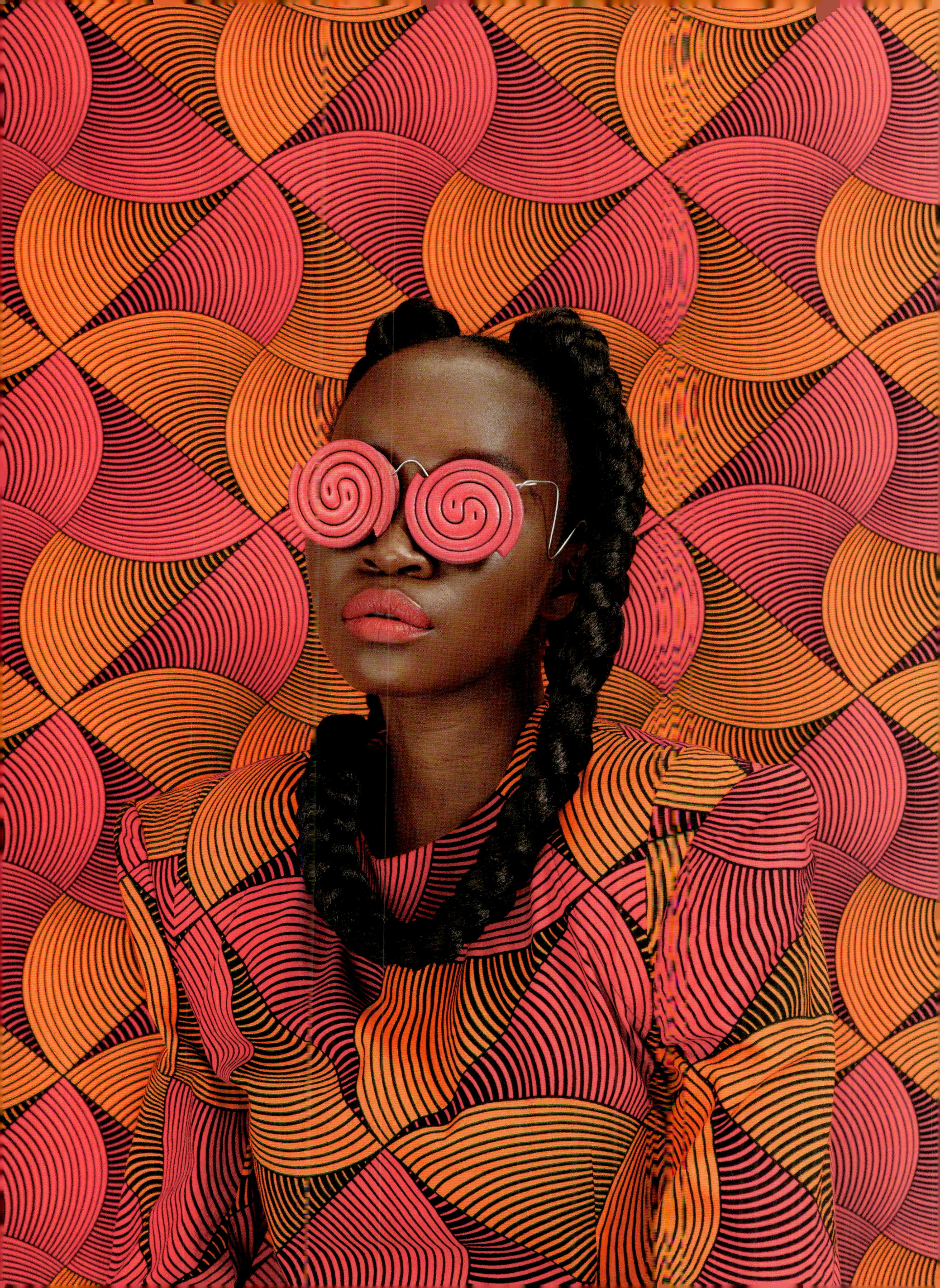

"You are not born a leader, you become one."

"Huzaliwi kiongozi, wajitahidi kuwa kiongozi."

An everyday item becomes a power woman's enhancement. Green aviators, a statement piece for the high necked domina, are crafted from steel wool scouring pads. Steel wool is found in every homestead in Kenya because it efficiently scrubs the commonly used Sufuria—Kiswahili for 'aluminium cooking pot'—to shining perfection. It is a mark of pride for every good Kenyan housewife to have her collection of sufurias glistening in silver brilliance. Thandiwe has many fond memories of dishwashing in her childhood, using steel wool to quickly scour the sufurias used to cook that day's family meal, then stacking them like a Russian babushka doll before dashing off to grab her camera for a photo session with her sisters.

Eyewear constructed from stainless steel spiral scourers.

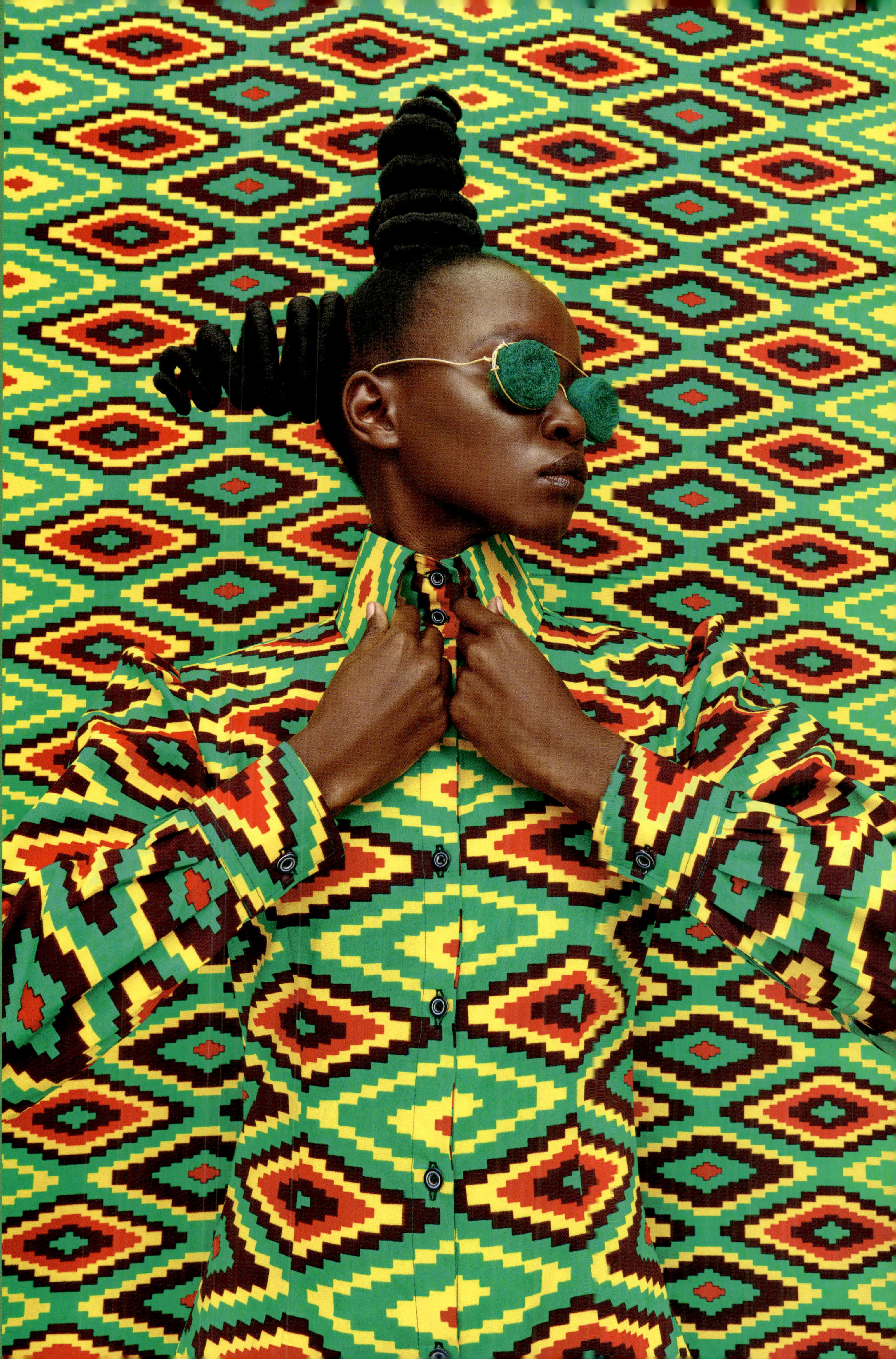

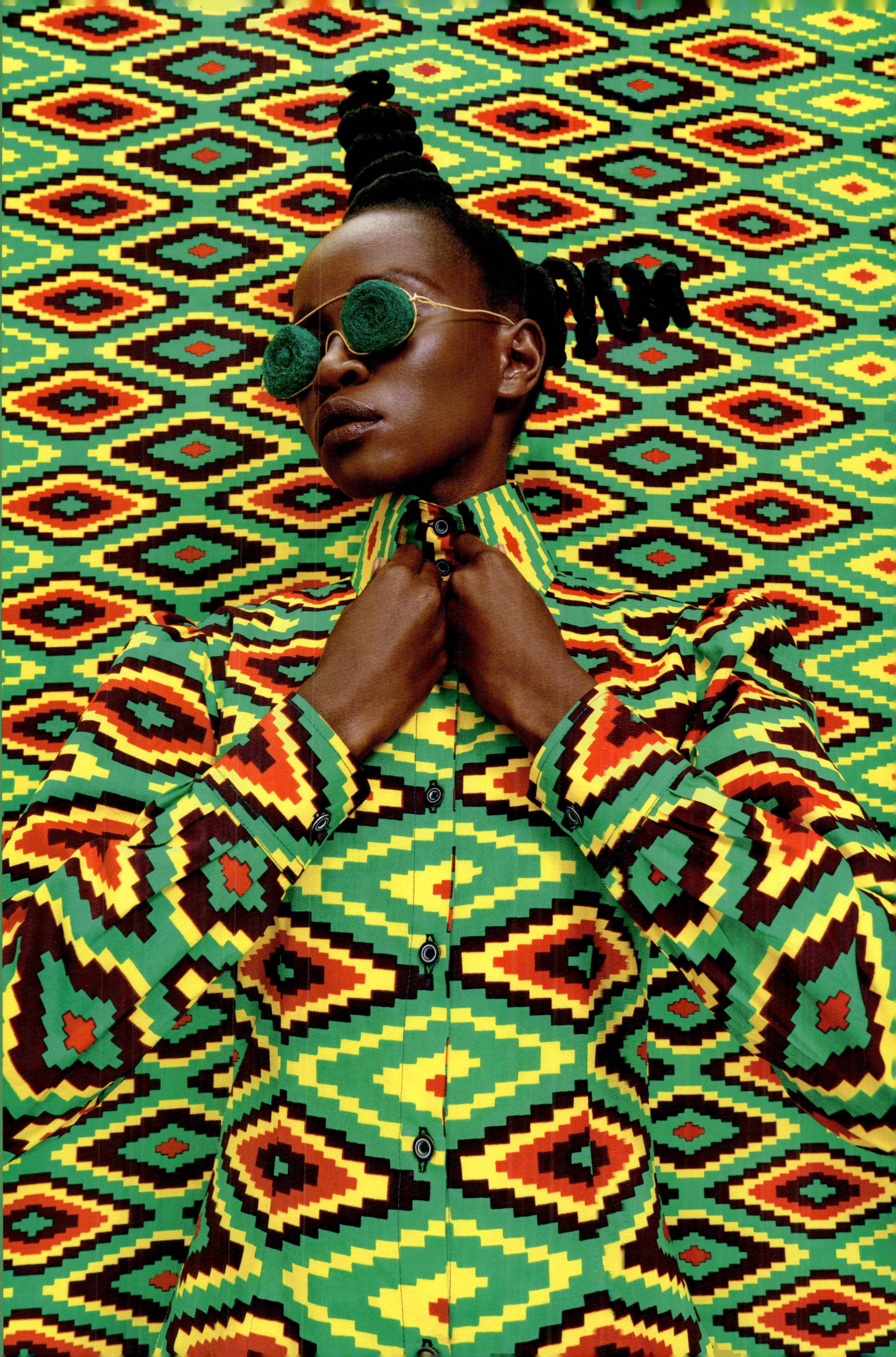

"If your vision is for a year plant wheat, if your vision is for a decade plant trees, and if your vision is for a lifetime plant people."

"Ikiwa maono yako ni ya mwaka mmoja, panda ngano, ikiwa maono yako ni ya muongo mmoja, panda miti, na ikiwa maono yako ni ya maisha yote, panda watu."

Like the rhythmic rise and fall of a cyclist's pedal, the angles within the print of Camo 33 are filled with bright movement. It is only fitting then, that the blue bursts of the eyewear's are actually the parts of a signature bicycle found in Kenya. This bicycle, known as the Black Mamba, is seen laden with towering piles of fresh bread, or bleating goats strapped to the back shelf, or elegant women perched daintily in sidesaddle, versatile in its usage. The African cyclists make it look effortless as they zip past cars during morning traffic, while in truth the Black Mamba bicycle is difficult to ride. It has no gears. The frame is sturdy. Yet it is the smooth transport to many in their morning commute and part of the vibrant heart of Kenya.

Eyewear constructed from bicycle cassettes.

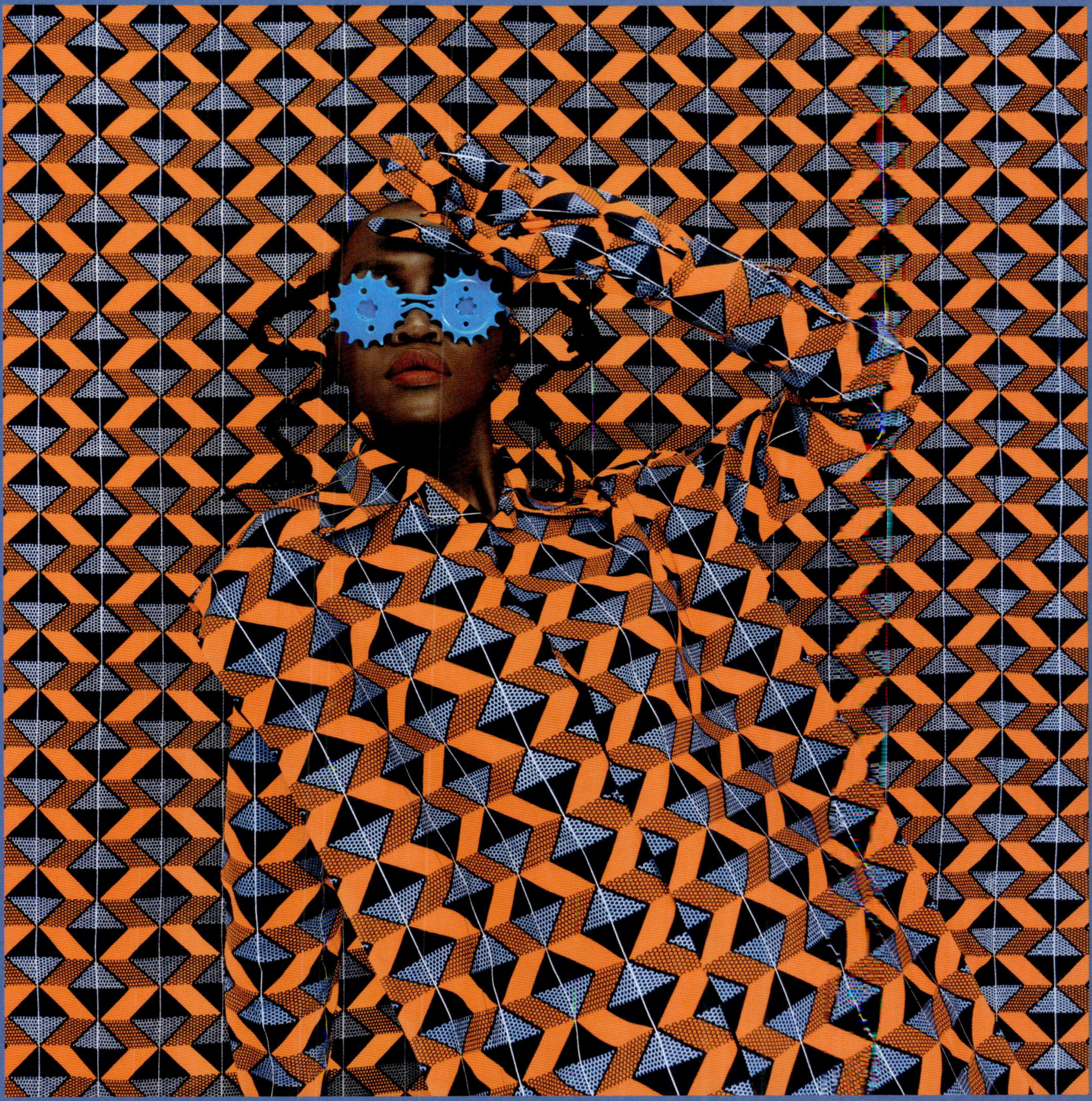

"The greatest truth is the simplest one."

"Ukweli mkuu hueleweka kwa urahisi."

The bursting loops of the African print of Camo 34 brings to mind the humble atom found in the deepest core of every human being. For this PHOTO 2022, Melbourne, Australia commission, Thandiwe sought to celebrate being human- the beauty of life in its various forms, whether its unseen depths, or the actions and emotions which we all carry. To her, the center of being human is the ability to feel, to experience, to internalize those experiences and turn them into the core of whomever we become- good or bad- as a person. It is the colors of life that remind us that we are human.

To quote BBC "But to be human is to be at the centre of our own universe, to experience life in all its colours and all its potential."

Eyewear constructed from candles

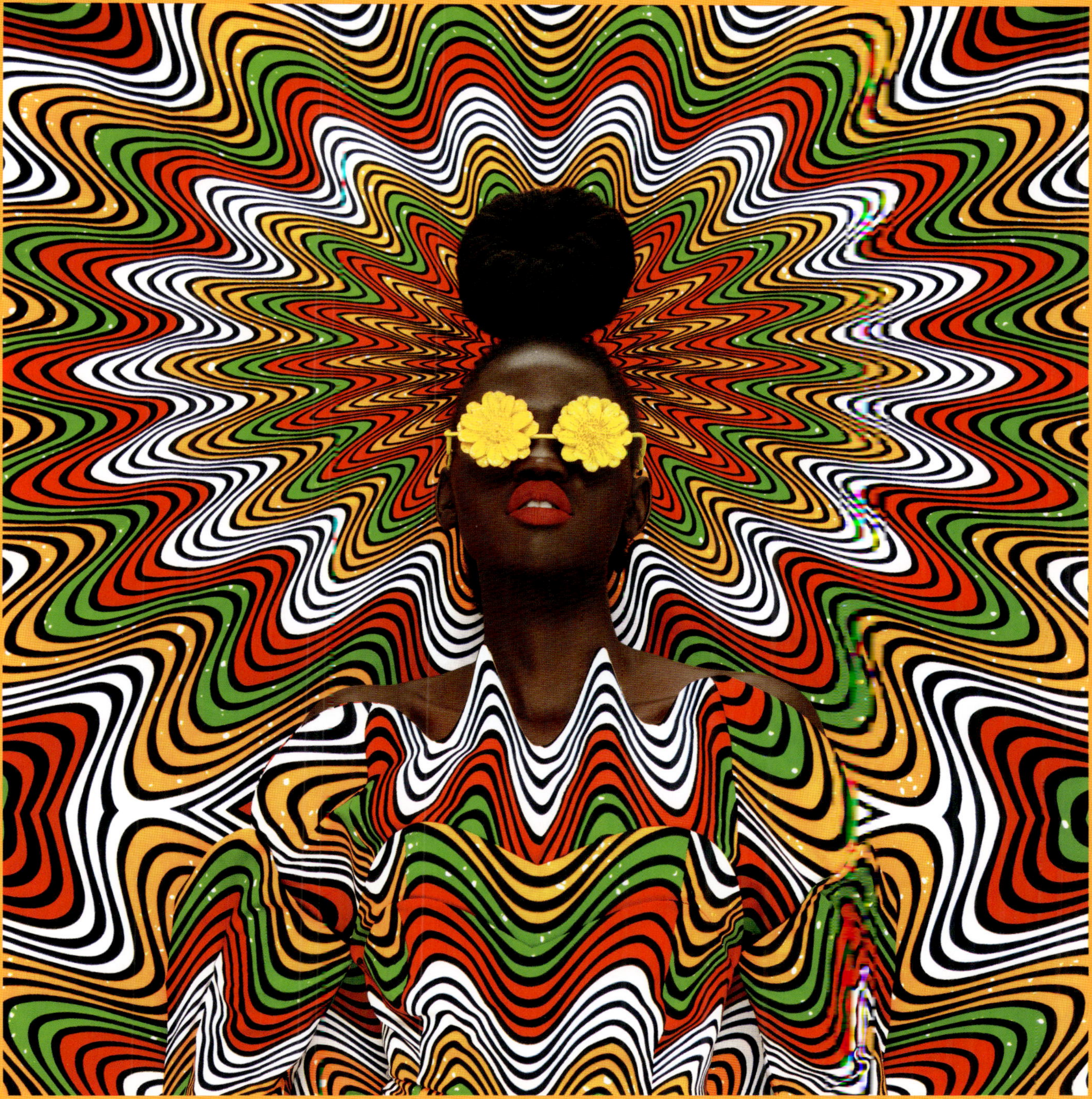

"Where you sit when you are old shows where you stood in youth."

"Utakapokaa kwa uzee huonyesha uliposimama kwa ujana."

Catching up on the latest African magazine or laughing with fellow salon-goers over one debate or another, hair parlours are a place of much needed recuperation and rejuvenation: if only for the hours it takes to create the perfect coiffure. Camo 35 celebrates Thandiwe's mother's beauty routine with a tribute to the highly fashionable hairstyle of the 90s—the Curly Kit. Within the lively atmosphere ladies gathered to catch up on the latest gossip, all while undergoing beautification. And oh, the patience it required! Hours spent meticulously setting locks with plastic rollers.

Thandiwe fondly recalls those precious moments of watching her mother in awe as she sat under the dryer, eagerly anticipating the grand reveal of her freshly permed tresses that shimmered gloriously in the sunlight. This work is testament to the stories woven within strands of hair.

Eyewear constructed from hair rollers.

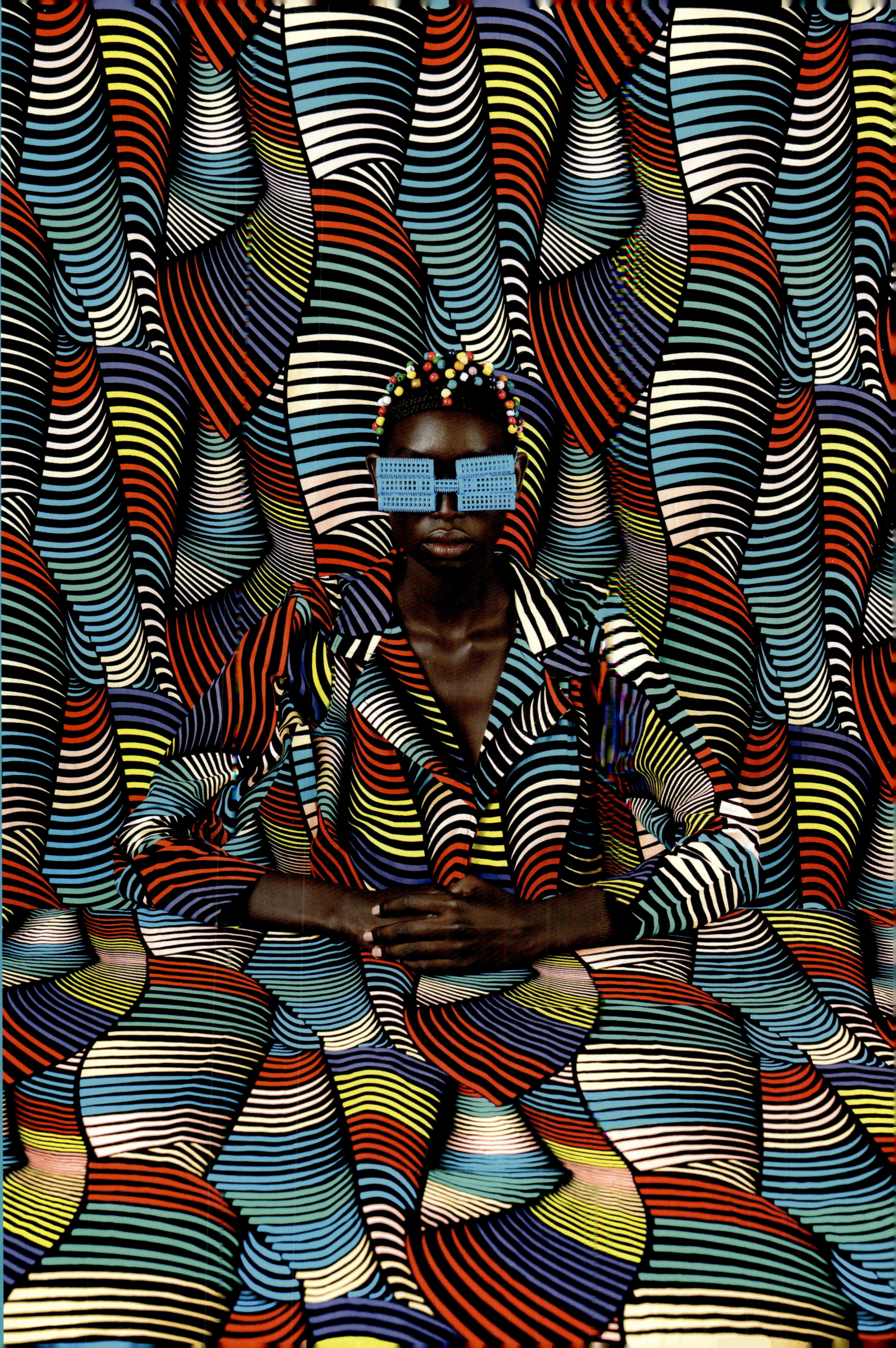

"A diamond does not lose its value due to lack of admiration."

"Almasi haipungui thamani kwa kukosa kutamaniwa."

No two African women's headwraps are ever the same–their beauty lies in their unique and personal touch. Each woman always adds her own flair and twist to the long strip of fabric coiled around her head. Headwraps were worn frequently by Thandiwe's mother, who would always drape the printed fabric in an elaborate design as she prepared for church, weddings or special events; transforming a humble piece of fabric into a beautiful piece of art. Every wrapping is a singular creation of twists, pinning and drape that can never be exactly replicated by its creator once she completes it.

A modern interpretation of this traditional African fashion piece, these works are a reminder that every time a woman puts on a headwrap, she adorns herself with the equivalent of a regal coronet; a crown for a queen.

Earrings constructed from bottle caps.

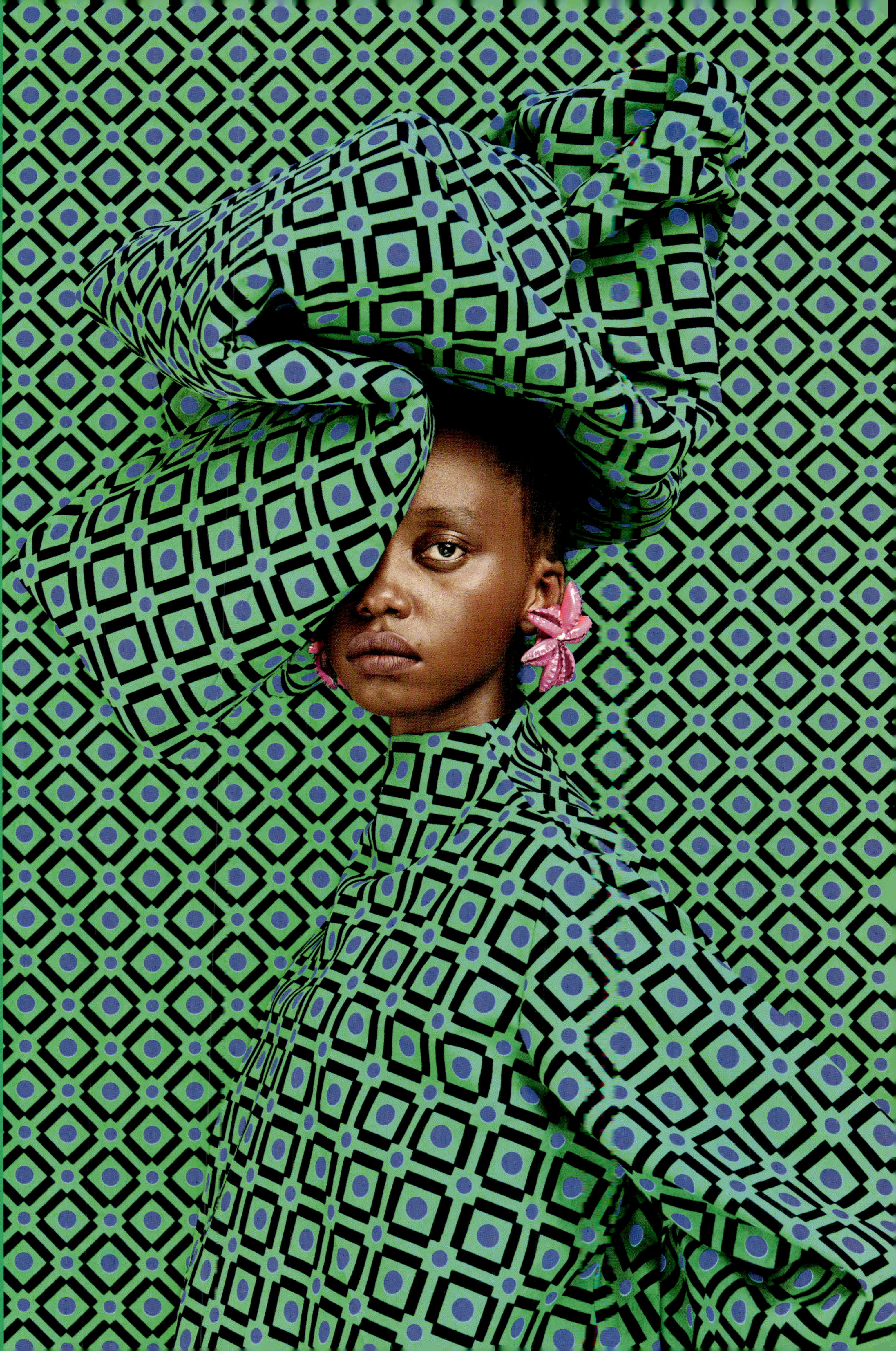

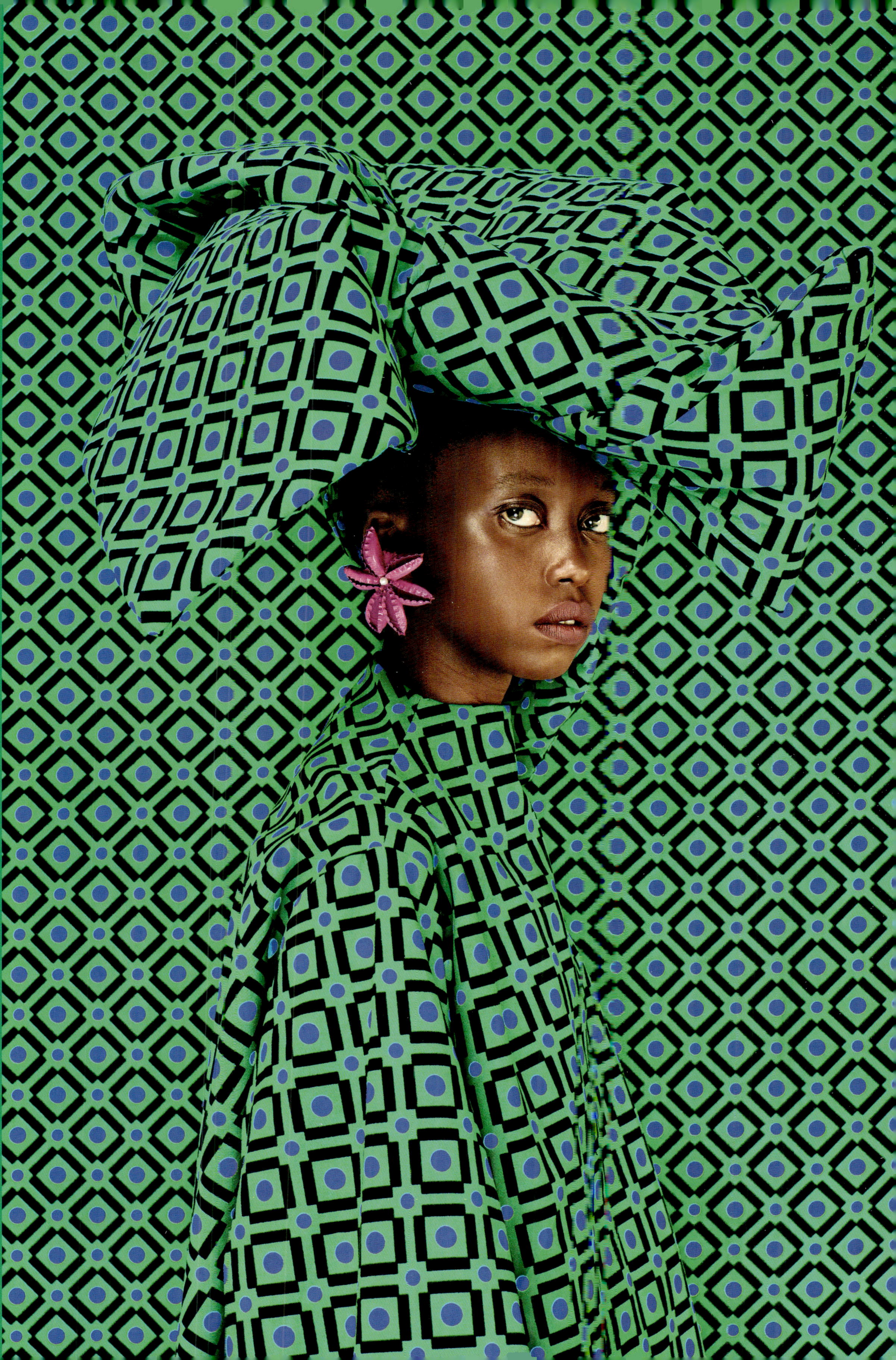

"When sleeping women wake, they move mountains."

"Wanawake waliyo lala waamkapo kutoka usingizini, wanahamisha milima."

If you drive on the streets of Nairobi, Kenya, you will see brightly painted mini buses with graffiti and flashing LED lights zooming past. These taxi minibuses are called 'Matatu' in Kiswahili, a cheeky name since every ride historically cost a mere 3 cents.

Sitting in a matatu means: subwoofers embedded into the seats making the booming bass so deep it shakes your bones, MTV music videos playing on tiny screens in the seat in front of you. Every matatu is a colorful reflection of its driver, with themes ranging from football to Lupita Nyong'o to world renowned celebrities embellishing the vehicle. Matatus are chameleons, always changing their decorative themes depending on the current opinion of the crew; a blank canvas for colorful expression. Inspired by the brake pedal of these minibuses, Camo 38 features chrome-plated eyewear that pays homage to the unique and dynamic spirit of these iconic vehicles.

Eyewear constructed from a lemon press.

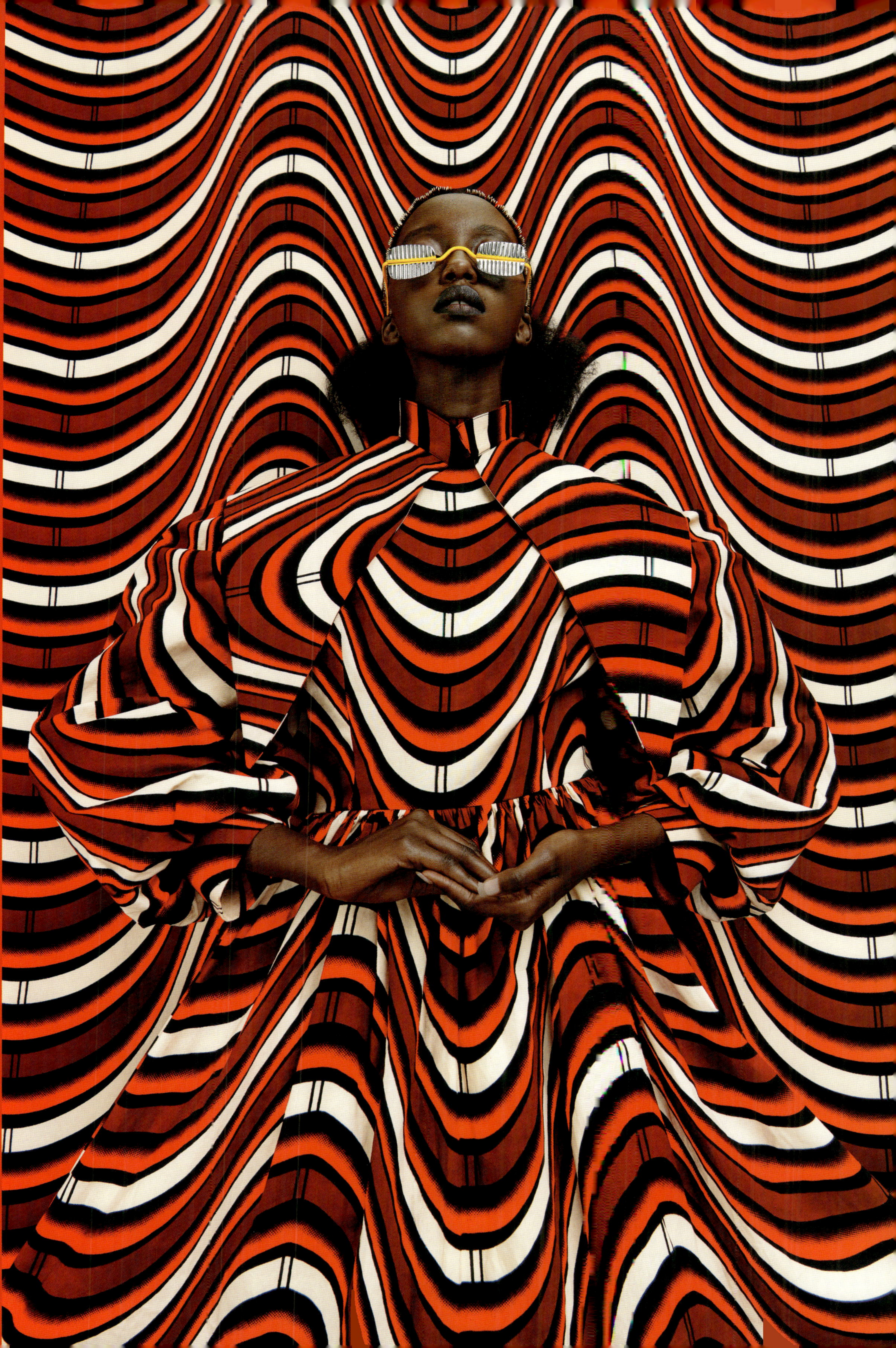

“A strong tree shall always grow from the roots and not the seeds.”

“Mti bora hukua kutoka kwa mizizi sio kwa mbegu.”

Within the larger message of Camo lies Thandiwe's aspiration to modernize history. She draws elements from Africa's past, reconstructed through her progressive lens to educate future generations.

A renewed appreciation for Himba traditional elements—two long braids and a shaven center worn by young Himba girls—is a poignant focal point of Camo 39. Thandiwe adds chunky African hair beads reimagined as sleek, Afrofuturistic glasses elegantly perched over the subject's eyes. Commonly made from wood, the beads now radiate a newfound gleam and enchantment, bridging the gap between the old and the new. Camo 39 examines and appreciates the beauty and significance of this heritage in a modern context.

Eyewear constructed from beads.

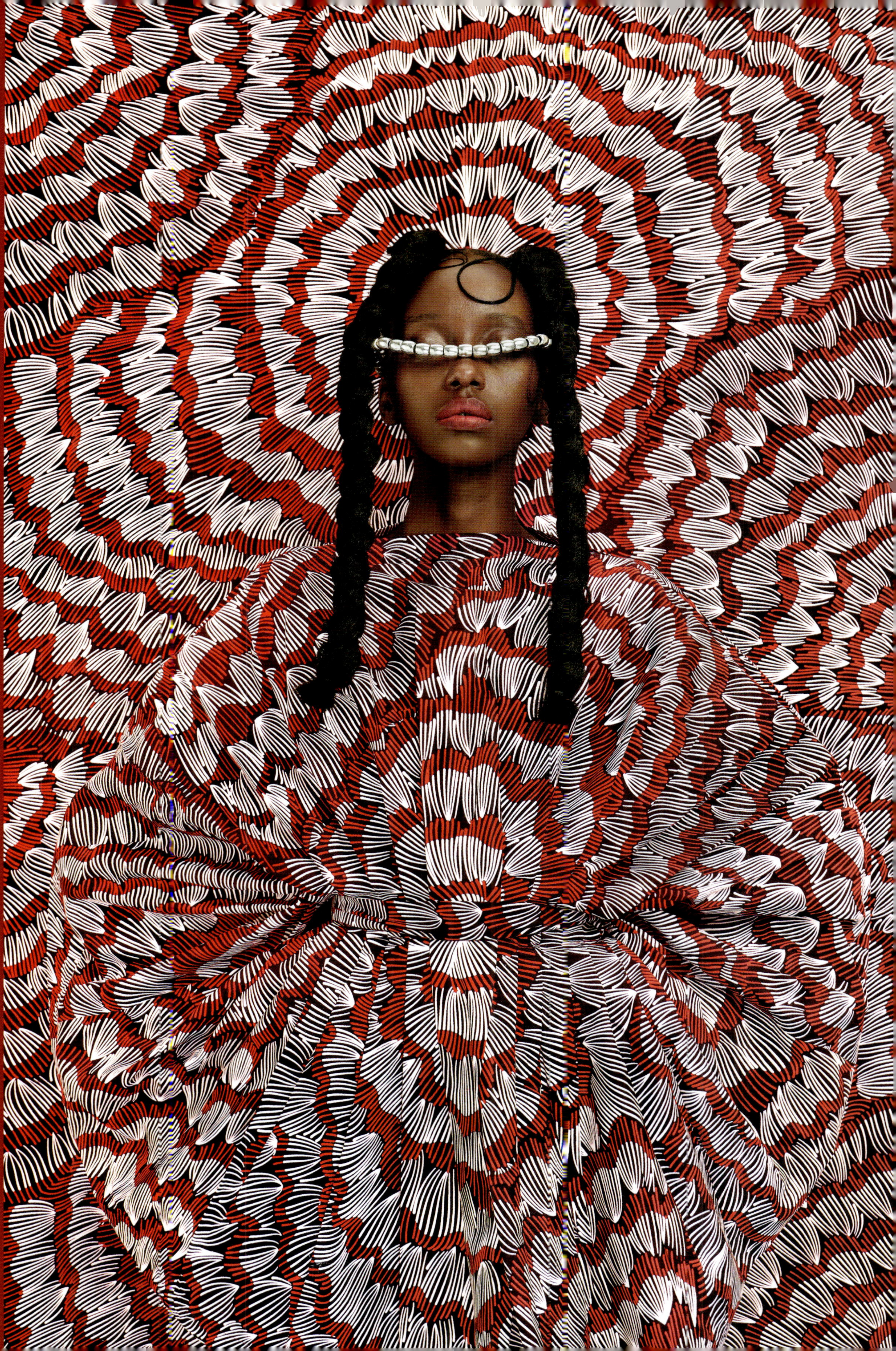

"Life without battle is life without victory."

"Maisha bila mapambano ni maisha bila ushindi."

Inspired by the looped fringing that adorned her uncle's car dashboard, this piece holds a special significance for Thandiwe. Each day at 4PM, her uncle's Toyota Corolla would rumble down the school driveway. Settling into the front seat, Thandiwe couldn't resist the temptation to run her fingers along the fringes, enjoying the sensation as they drove home.

These moments of play in the car as they wove through Nairobi's traffic add a touch of whimsy and nostalgia to the Camo series.

Eyewear constructed from fringe.

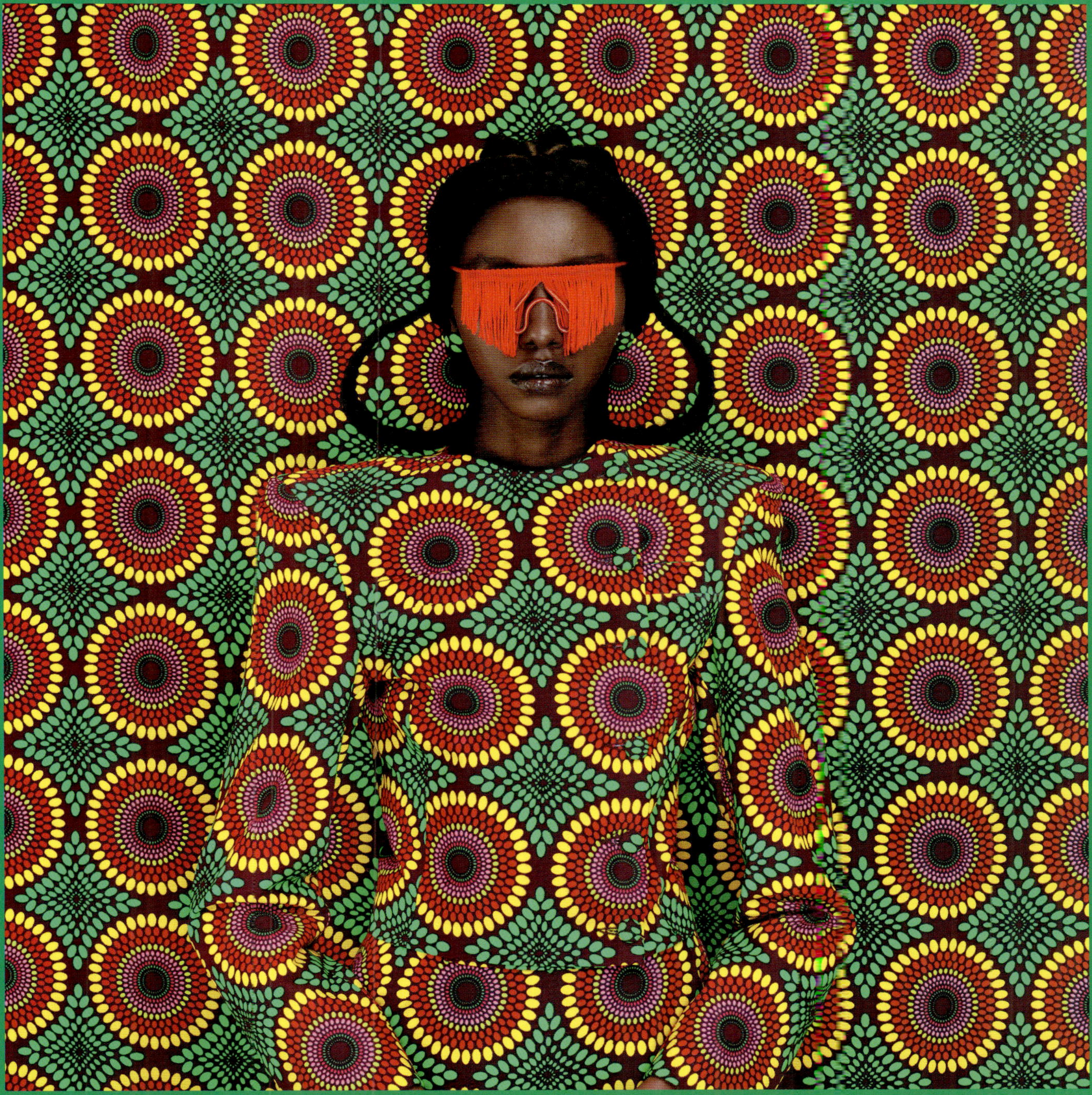

“A woman’s beauty is not hidden in her face.”

“Urembo wa mwanamke haufichwi usoni mwake.”

In Return of the Jedi, *Kenyan audiences always raise a cheer in the climax scene—not for Princess Leia or Luke Skywalker—but for Nien Nunb, voiced by Kipsang Rotich, as he speaks to his captain. His short sentence triggers uproarious laughter and delight among Kenyans as he cheekily asks a question in Kenya’s Kikuyu language. Little children and adults alike bask in the euphoria of hearing themselves in a distant Hollywood future, possibly for the first time.*

Camo 41 is a celebration of this emotional moment, as well as every woman who stands as a guardian and defender to those who rely on her, much like the heroic Princess Leia. Every woman can change a galaxy, shaping not only her own household but also the larger community. By standing up for what is right, she ensures the thriving of her family and the protection of her kin. With a visionary spirit, she allies with her community—and other Nien Nunbs—to reach for the stars, a beacon of hope for those around her.

Eyewear constructed from baking moulds.

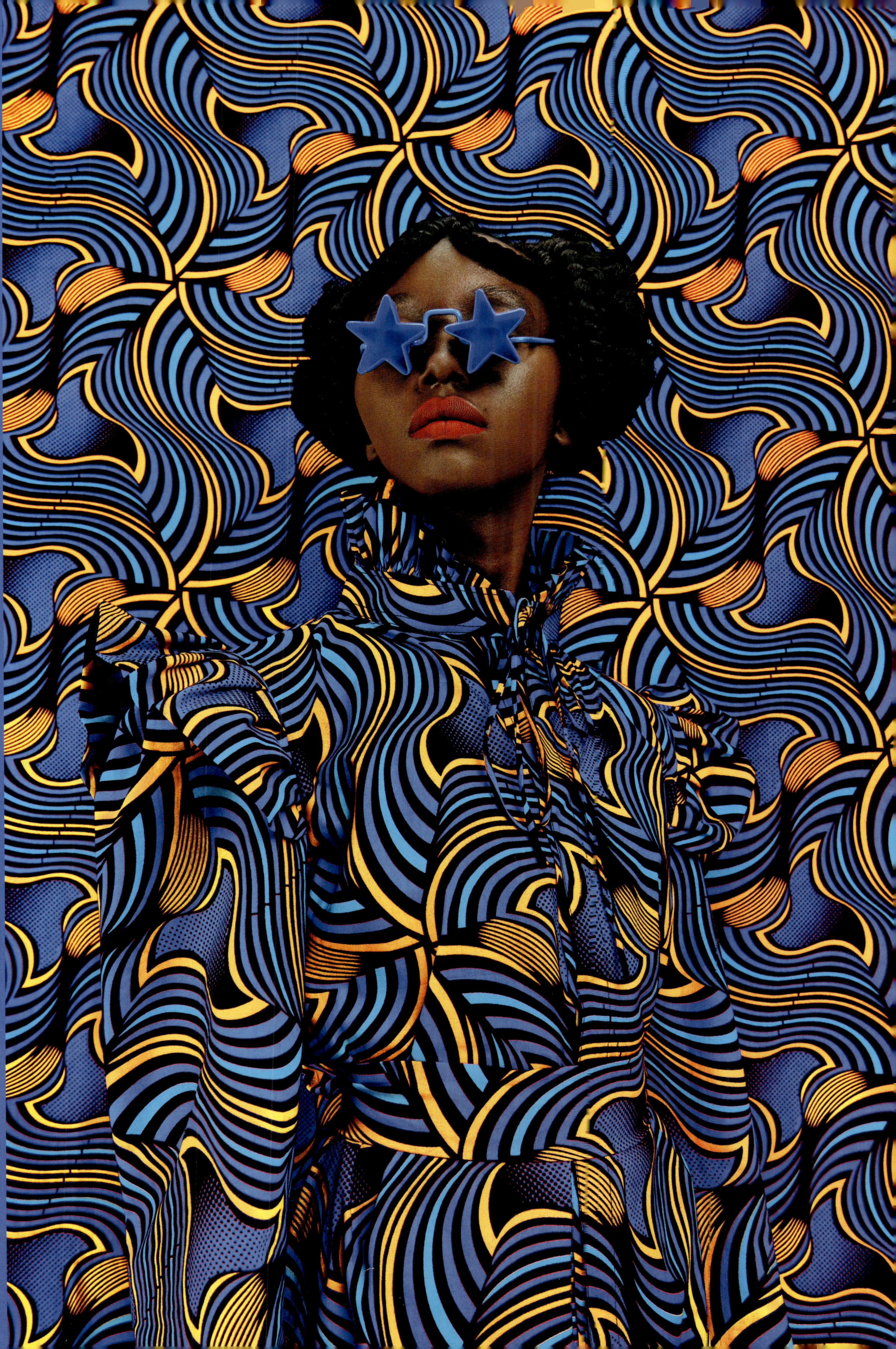

"Happiness is like a perfume, you cannot pour it all on others without allowing a few drops to fall on yourself."

"Furaha ni kama manukato, huwezi kuimimina yote kwa wengine bila kuruhusu matone machache yadondoke kwako mwenyewe."

In Kenyan culture it is customary for women to come together in the kitchen after a gathering, taking on the task of hand-washing piles of dishes. What can easily be a routine and mundane chore transforms into a beautiful moment filled with laughter and storytelling, where women reinforce their bonds. The simple act of washing dishes becomes a source of delight as they work collaboratively, embodying the African spirit of community.

Camo 42 celebrates these shared moments as it turns humble sink strainers into bright circles of joy.

Eyewear constructed from sink strainers.

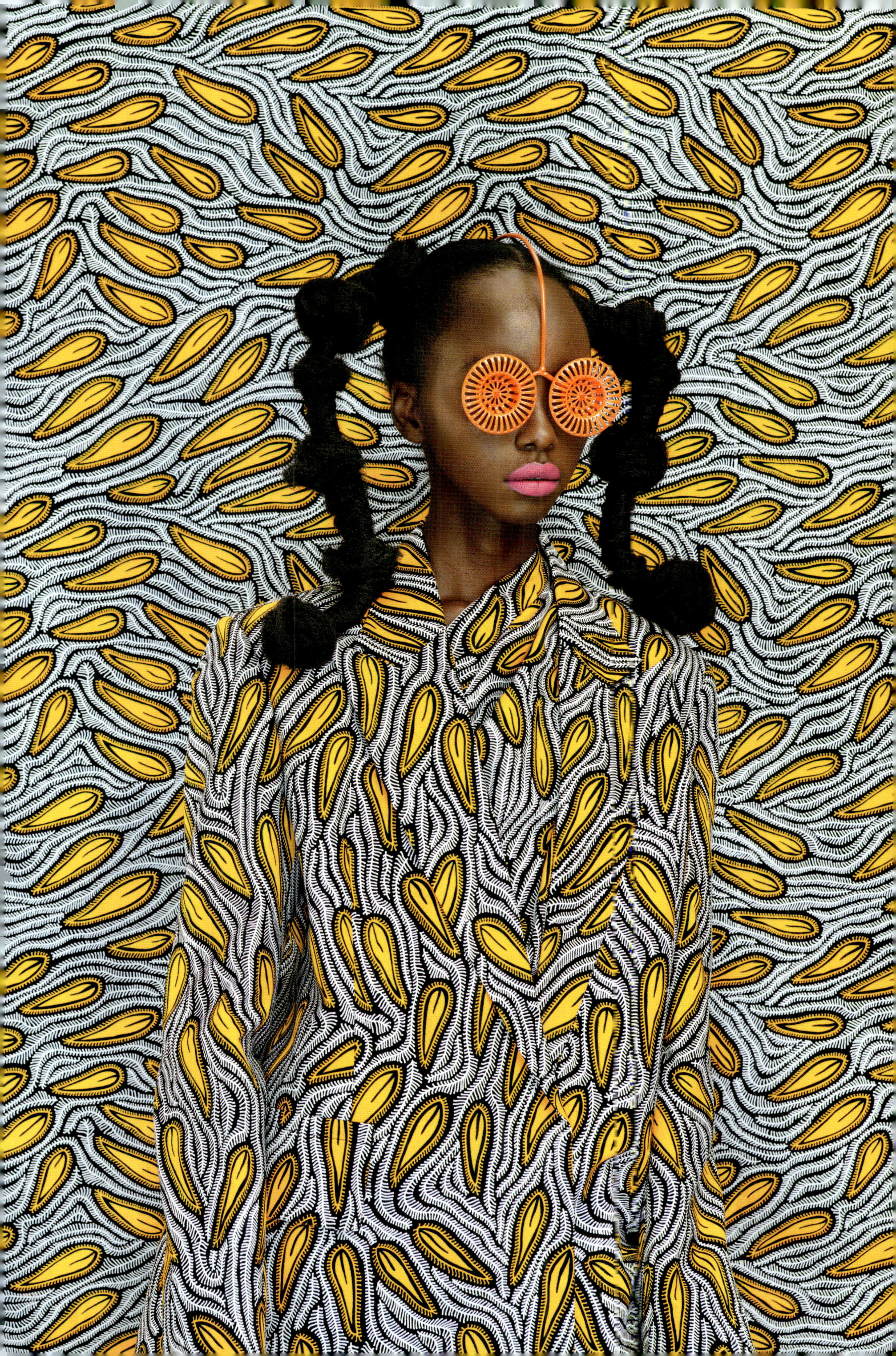

"However a stream flows, it doesn't forget its origin."

"Haijalishi umbali upi mto hutiririka, hausahau mwanzo wake."

In any good Kenyan school, a teacher is more than someone who relays information—they are a mentor, guide and sometimes disciplinarian who call out the best in their students. Thandiwe holds fond memories of her student days, diligently jotting down answers to questions from her study material, within a sun-dappled classroom. Constructed using two black-and-white beaded earrings as the base, paired with sections of the classic, global biro pen sprinting from the frames, Camo 43 represents the pursuit of academic achievement. A bright visual to the mentors, teachers, guides and synthesizers of knowledge. Camo 43 honors those whose knowledge and teaching makes navigating our world easier—the Dr. Joyce Nyairos and Dr. Awino Okechs of Kenya.

Eyewear constructed from Maasai earrings and pens.

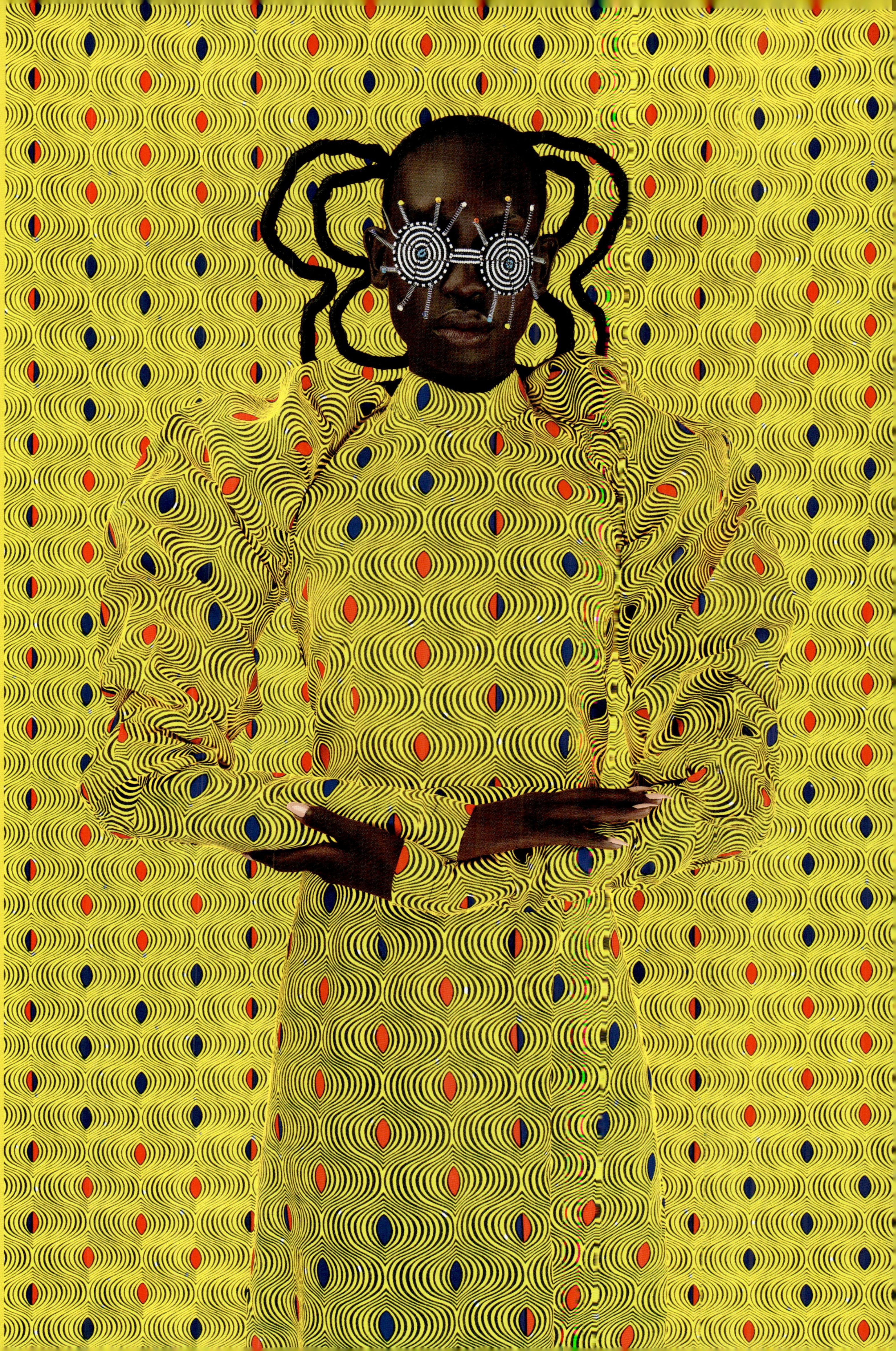

"Little by little, grow the bananas."

"Kidogo kidogo, hukuza ndizi."

Kenyan handymen hold a repertoire of many skills to solve their customer's problems, and always come to your door knowing a little bit of everything. This value addition makes them jacks of all trades who stand out from the competition, conjuring miracles from a myriad of objects. In the Kenyan version of Japanese Kintusgi, what is broken is fixed, what is lost reintegrated, repurposed instead of discarded.

The eyewear of Camo 44 combines jewellery and plumbing tape to create a unique celebration of this. The lens of the glasses made from the thin silicone tape that plumbers use to seal leaks in pipes and the ring of interlocking wires made from spring bangles that are hand coiled by Kenyan artisans in one of Nairobi's numerous open-air markets. Together the orange eyewear pops out in a fun, distinct way, similar to the often ingenious ministrations of plumbers.

While it may be a gamble whether their fixes will be helpful or destructive, functional or an eye-sore, Camo 44 celebrates the unique skills of Kenyan handymen.

Eyewear constructed from plumbing tape and metallic bangles.

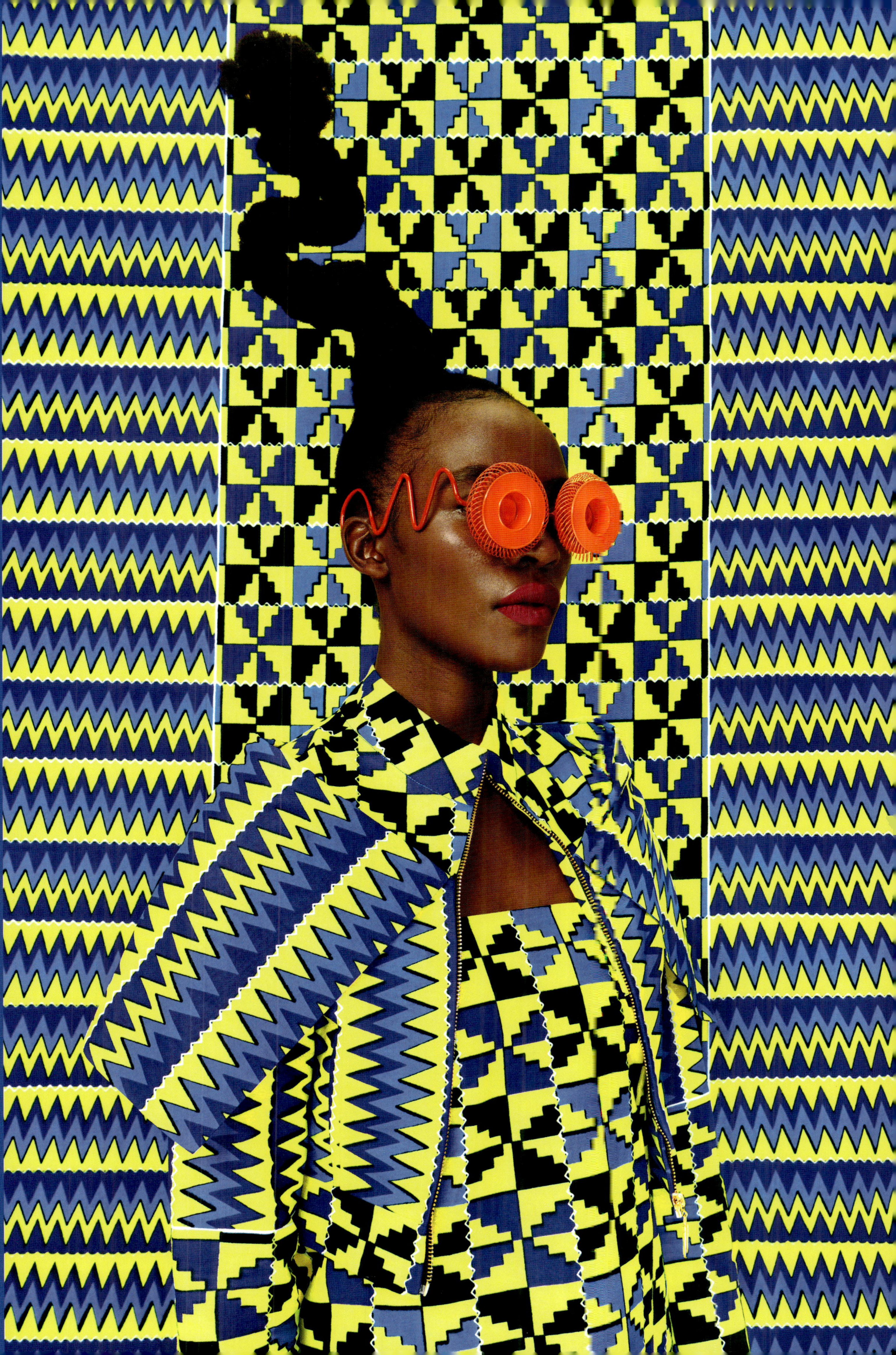

“When the powerful sit, they are none the weaker.”

“Mahodari wanapokaa hawawi na wadhaifu.”

Inspired by a photograph of her grandmother, Thandiwe reinterprets the distinctive blue headscarf of the Kenyan Women’s Guild, a renowned religious institution with a century-long history in the country, into her own houndstooth checkered delight. Identified by its blue headscarf wrapped around a member’s hair, the Kenyan Women’s Guild is a gathering of female community under the Presbyterian Church—a community that Thandiwe’s grandmother was a member of for many years.

In this black and white retelling, the materiality of the headscarf becomes a powerful symbol of unity, carrying the weight of ancestral wisdom and the pride of a vibrant heritage.

Eyewear constructed from hair clips.

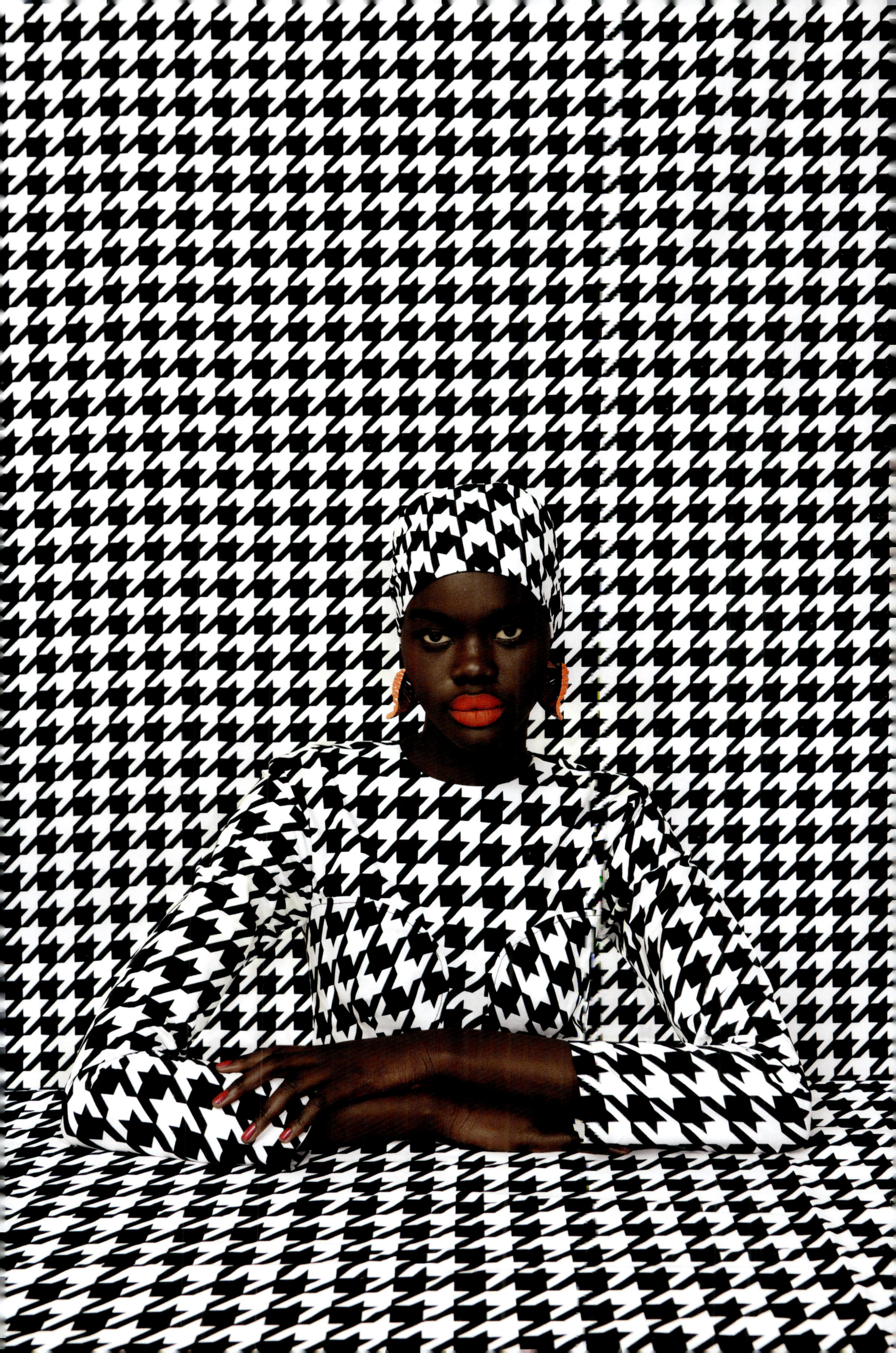

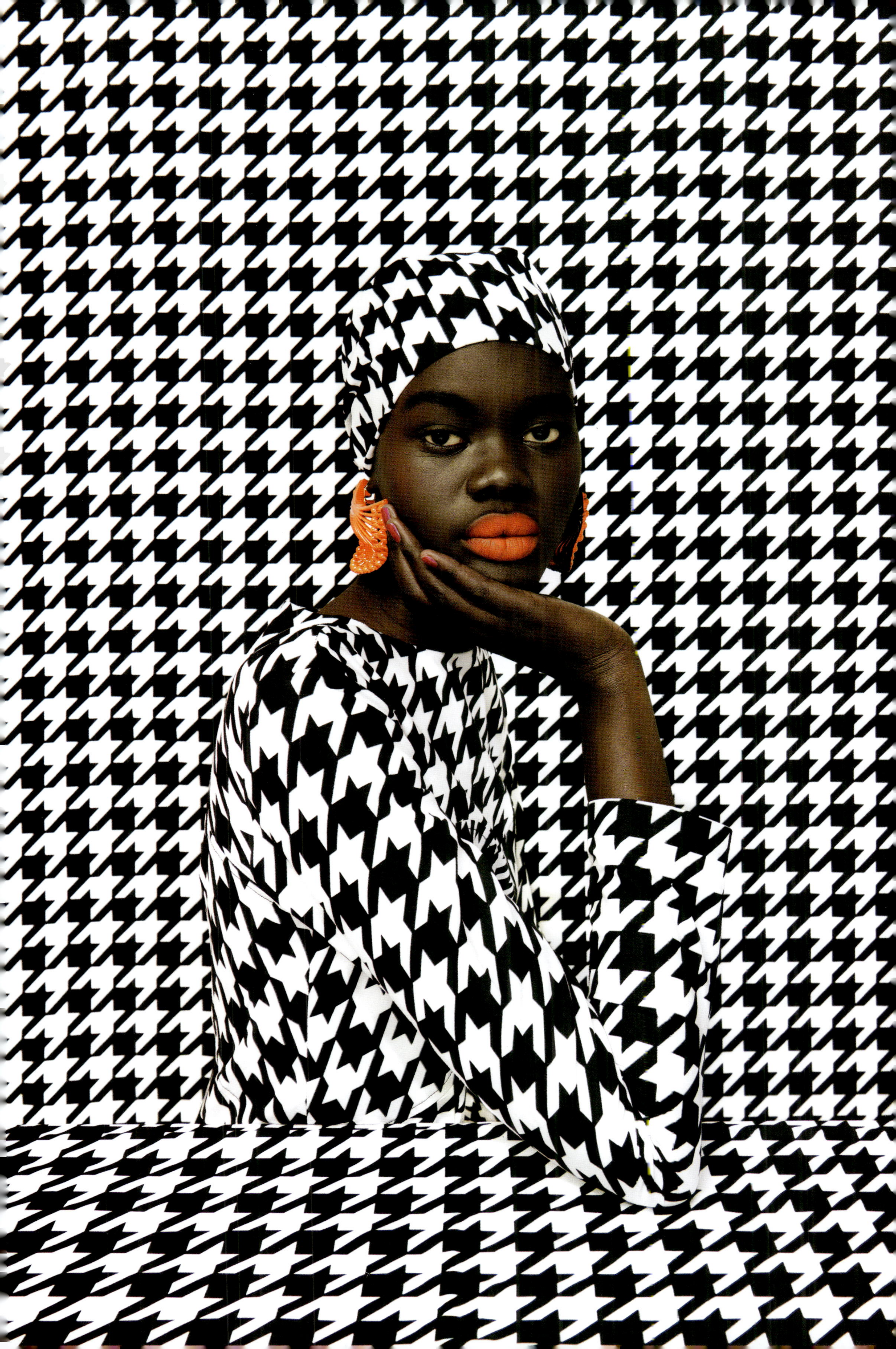

"It is not what you are called, but what you answer to."

"Sio unavyoitwa, bali ni unavyoviitikia.."

Kenyans are renowned for their innovative spirit, constantly finding creative solutions to everyday challenges using whatever resources are readily available. One such versatile item commonly utilized is low-cost nylon rope, easily obtainable from corner shops throughout the city. This rope serves as a clothesline for hanging laundry, or provides sturdy wrapping for cardboard boxes housing live chickens, or even acts as support for curtains in modest living rooms. It is the Kenyan lifestyle version of a completely versatile survival rope that is used for anything and everything, limited only by its users ingenuity.

In this particular instance, with nimble hands and an imaginative vision, Thandiwe skillfully wound a nylon rope around metal frames, meticulously fashioning them into colourful high fashion eyewear. The harmonious balance between form and function serves as a demonstration of the boundless possibilities of creativity.

Eyewear constructed from clothing line.

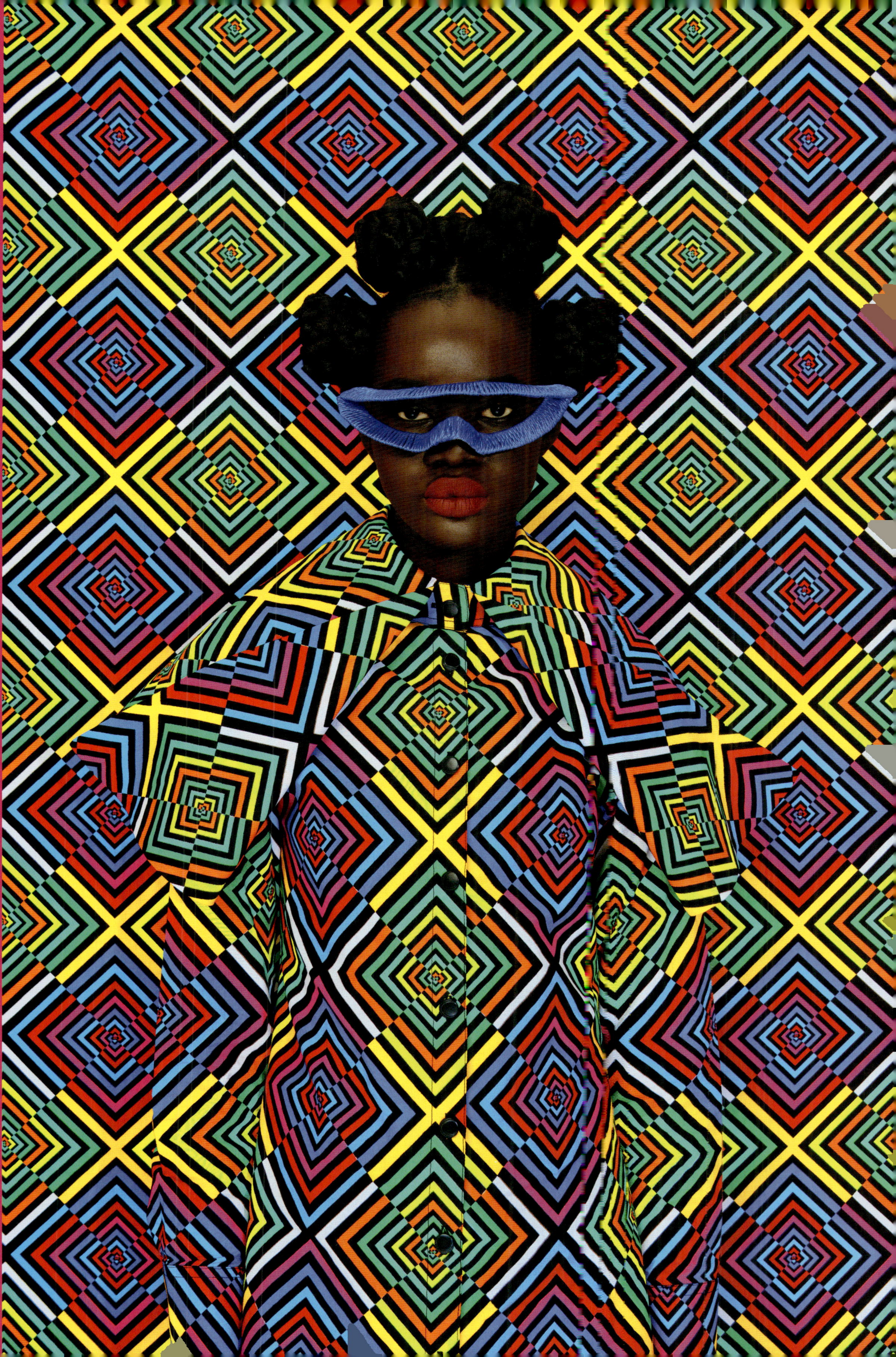

"Judge not your beauty by the number of people who look at you, but rather by the number of people who smile at you."

"Usipime urembo wako kwa idadi ya watu wanaokutazama ila kwa idadi ya wanaotabasamu wanapokuona."

The ability to dress impeccably is a skill possessed by every Kenyan woman, regardless of her budget. The presence of vibrant second-hand markets- particularly the well known Gikomba Market- is an absolute haven for fashion enthusiasts, offering a treasure trove of sartorial wonders.

Under the hot equatorial sun, bales of clothes are opened up for personal selection amidst the shouts of vendors. Within the labyrinthine aisles of Gikomba Market, one can embark on a thrilling fashion odyssey, where hidden gems await discovery. Here, haute couture aficionados and trendsetters alike can revel in the delight of finding unique pieces; shoes, handbags, belts, sunglasses, that breathe new life into their personal style narratives.

During her childhood, Thandiwe and her friends spent countless hours wandering through the market, often using their hard-earned pocket money to purchase stylish sunglasses for a mere one hundred Kenyan shillings (1$). These sunglasses provided a fashionable relief from the bright sun. It was within this vibrant Gikomba marketplace that Thandiwe sentimentally acquired the sunglasses featured in Camo 47, adding to their unique story and connection to her memories.

Eyewear constructed from sunglasses.

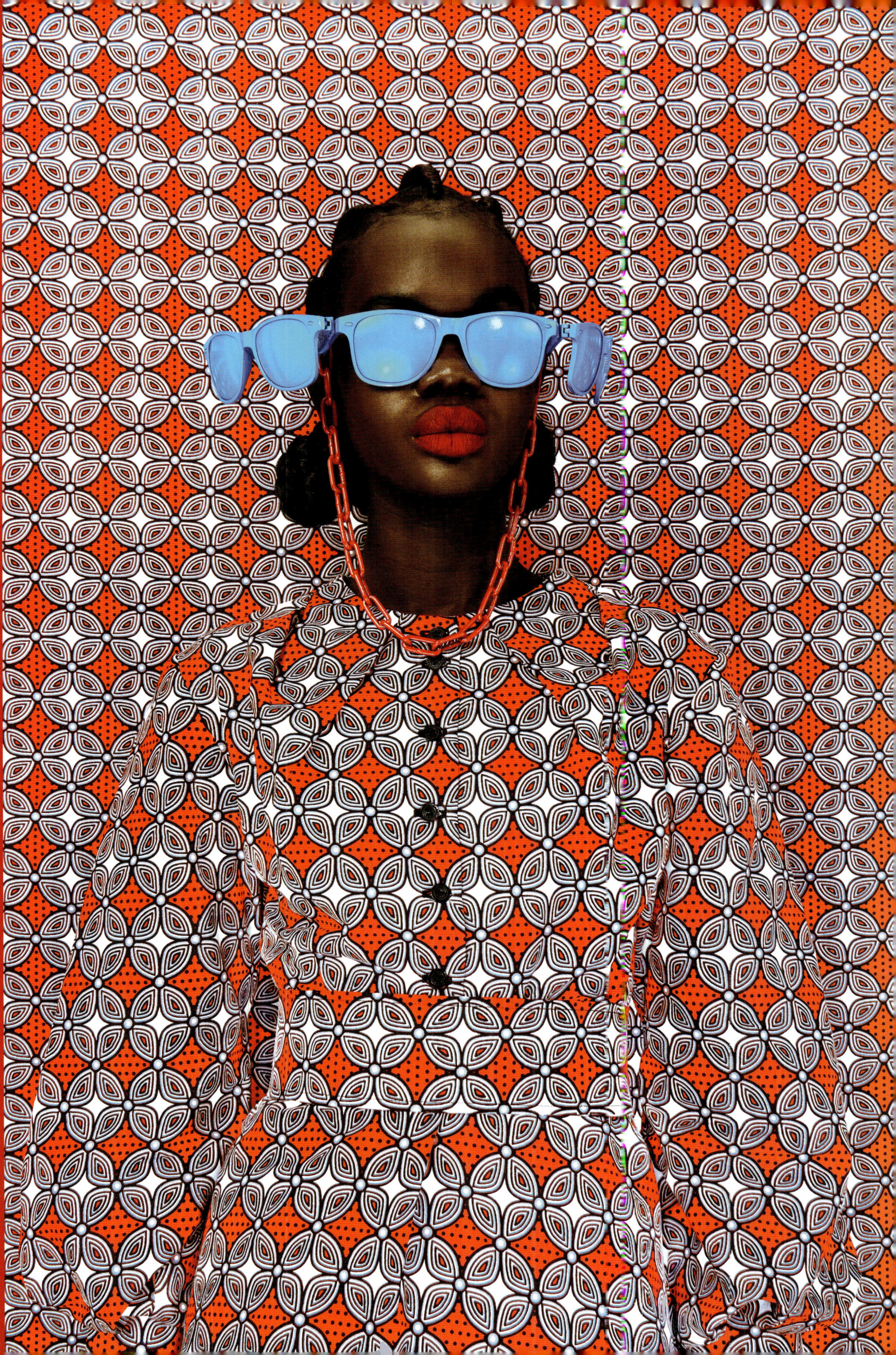

"He who has people is richer than he who has money."

"Aliye na watu ni tajiri kuliko aliye na pesa."

A wedding holds a special place as one of the greatest moments in a woman's life. In African culture, this celebration involves her entire community coming together to honor and support her through a multitude of kind acts. These myriad of services climax into a great party—and a party is never complete without good African food!

In a creative display that captures the elegance and couture of the bride, Camo 48 reimagines plastic spoons commonly found at Kenyan weddings. The sunburst of eyewear symbolizes the culinary delights, and communal bond shared by the bride and her loved ones on this momentous day.

Eyewear constructed from plastic spoons.

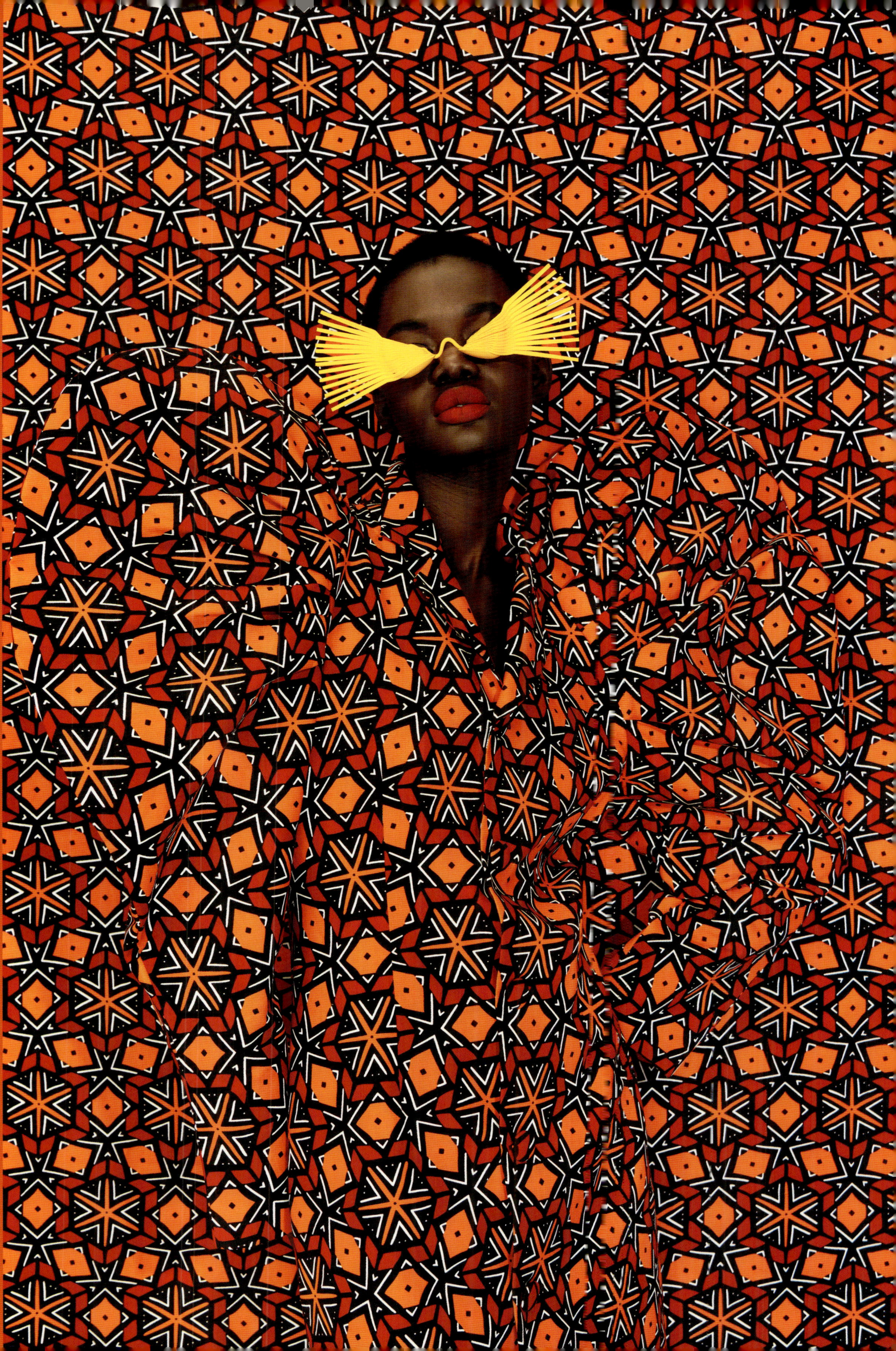

“Mother is God number two.”

“Mama ni kama mungu wa pili.”

Reimagining a toddler’s squeaky toy as striking eyewear, Camo 49 celebrates motherhood with a playful twist. This cheeky eyewear is a reminder of the energy and enthusiasm that toddlers bring to life- easily bouncing from one wall to the other during play- and the invested caregivers who love and keep up with them. Raising a child is a monumental task that extends far beyond the scope of a single mother’s efforts. It takes a village to raise a healthy, happy child. Adoptive aunties, sisters, grandmothers, and teachers form an interconnected web of support, working hand in hand to raise children with joy, understanding, and unconditional love.

Within this harmonious village, the sanctity of motherhood transcends biological bonds, encompassing the boundless compassion and care provided by the extended community.

Eyewear constructed from squeaky toys.

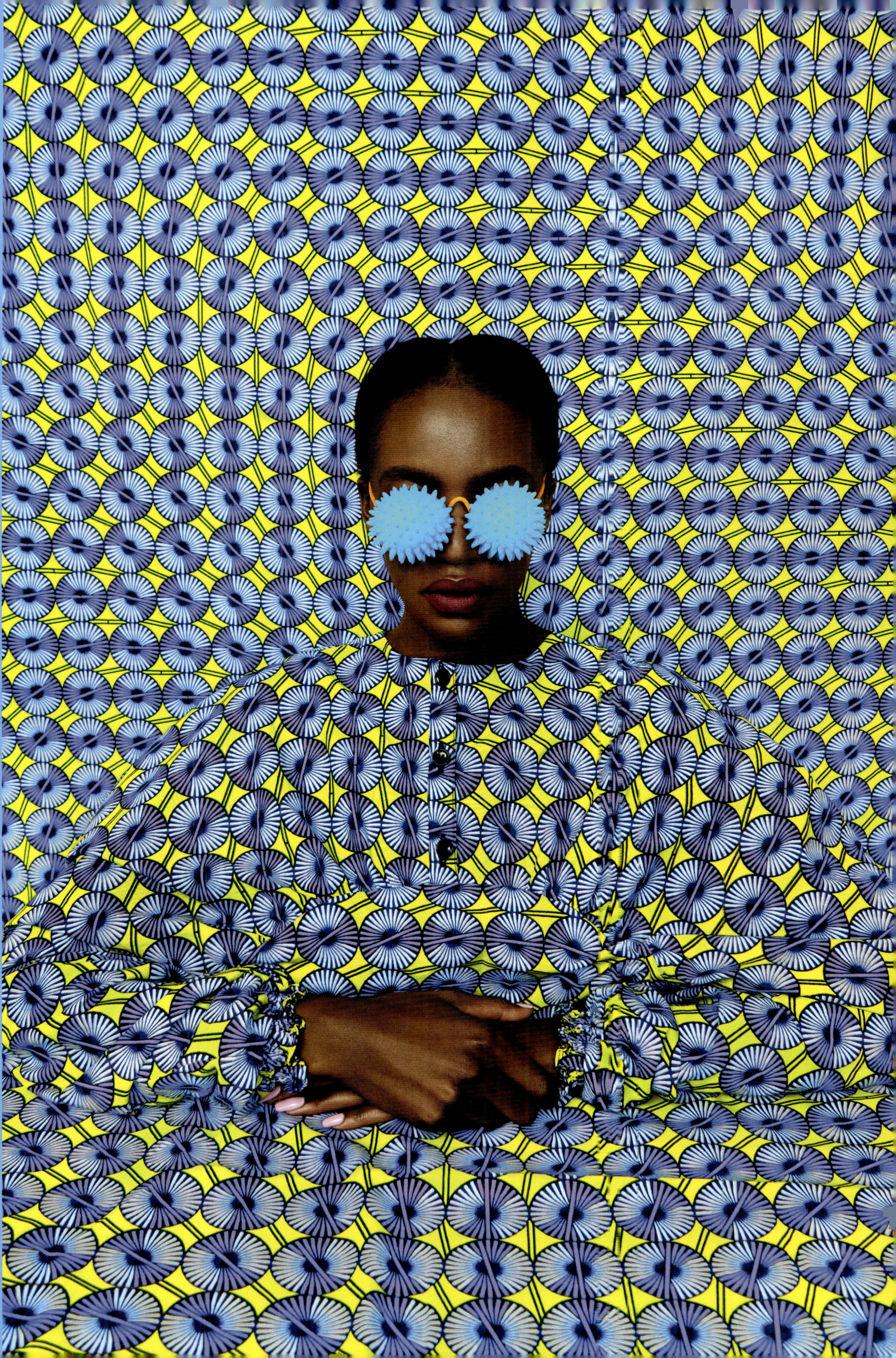

"A tree cannot stand without roots."

"Mti halistawi bila mizizi."

The beauty of a confident woman and her self-assurance is accentuated by a distinct symbol of achievement—a ribbon rosette adorning the eyewear.

Thandiwe's lens becomes a portal through which the strength and grace of a confident woman shine radiantly. A celebration of the praiseworthy achievements of a woman who has found her unwavering belief in her own ability to shine. Through this inner exploration, she casts aside doubts and societal expectations, reaching the place within herself where she firmly validates her own abilities allowing herself to fully blossom.

Eyewear constructed from award ribbons.

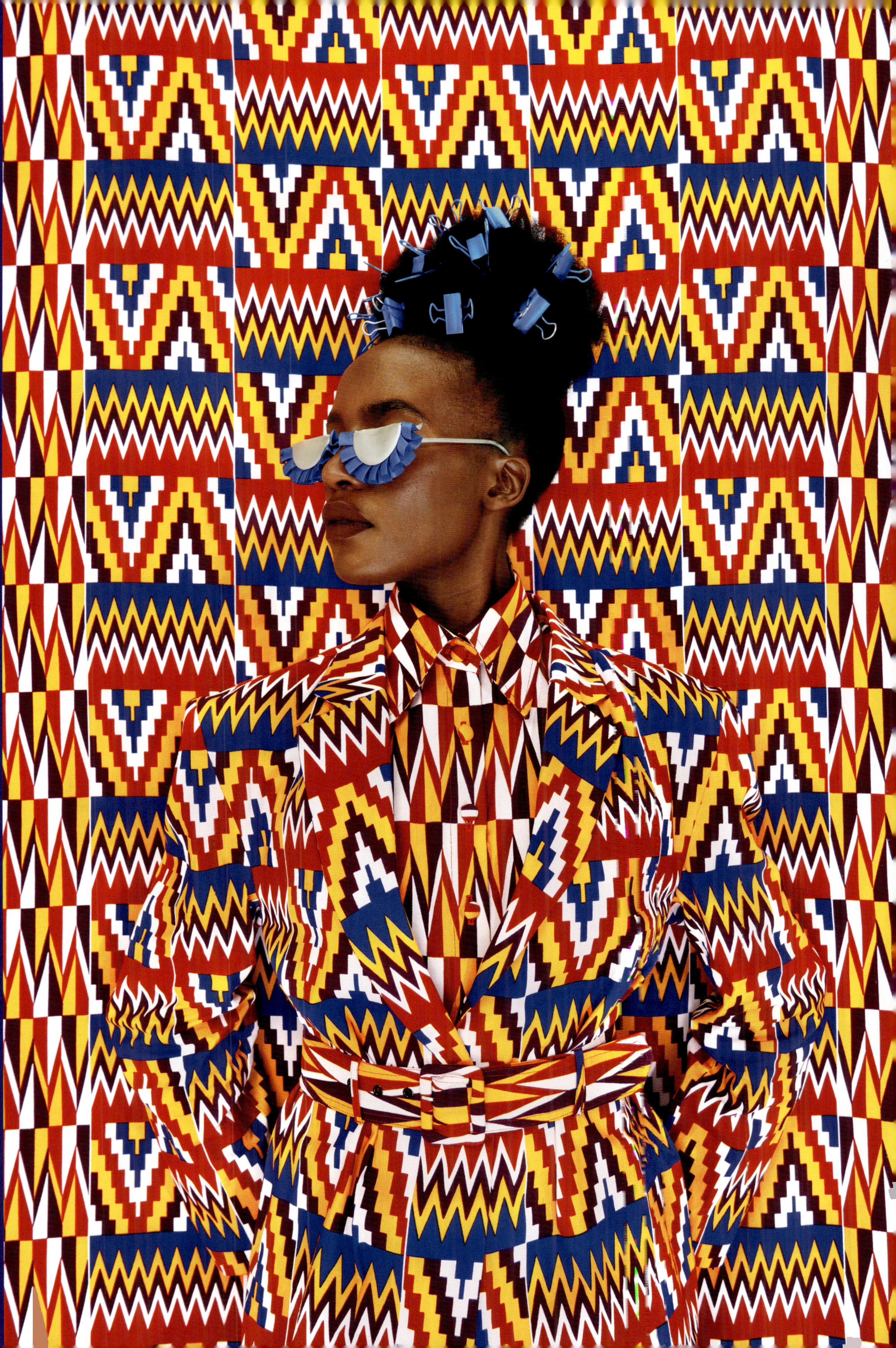

“Wisdom outweighs strength.”

“Hekima ina uzito kuliko nguvu.”

There is a power in her eyes. Camo 51 is a visual homage to the leadership of women whose unwavering gaze and inner resilience guide communities without a word.

The pins in the subject’s hair are a symbol of the duality of women’s lives, being unshaken leaders both in their homes and at the workplace. It requires an inner resilience to lead others without being distracted by external noise, and with a steadfast focus on the ultimate goal- yet many times this masterful balance they hold is overlooked by society. Camo 51 honors and celebrate this unique form of leadership and its strength and wisdom, which often goes unnoticed or unappreciated.

Hair accessories made from safety pins.

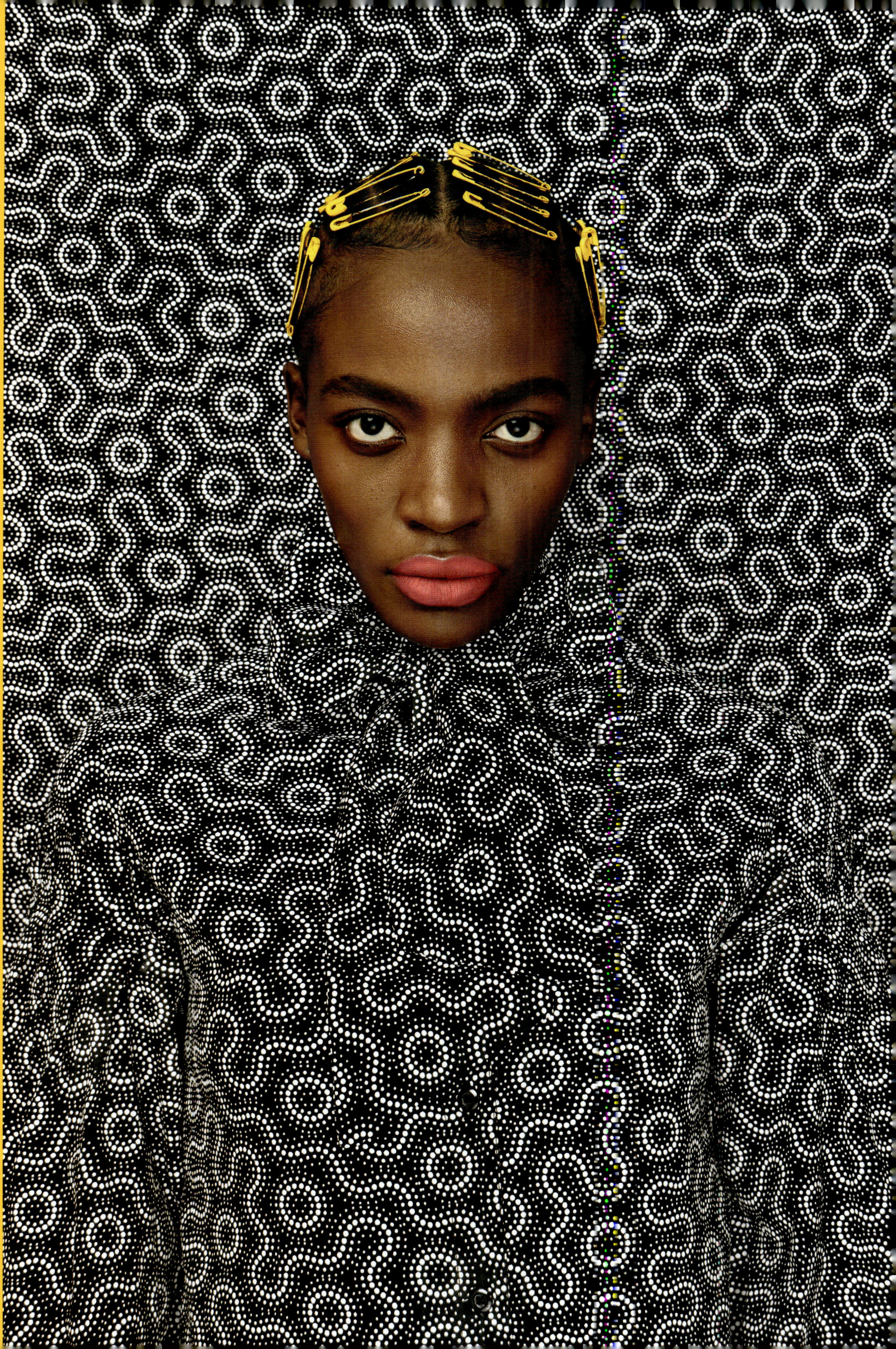

"If there is no enemy within, the enemy outside can do us no harm."

"Pasipokuwa na adui wa ndani, adui wa nje hawezi kutudhuru."

Every woman must fight an internal battle to love herself and see herself as beautiful against the ever shifting standards of beauty defined by the world. The most precious gift a woman can give herself is treasuring her body even as the beauty standards around her inevitably shift, enabling her to navigate The Tempest of conformity with grace.

If she remains unshaken in her self-affirmation then like a beacon in the sea, she is a grounding ray of light that gracefully defies the unattainable standards surging against her. By simply being herself, her inner beauty is akin to a tower of strength that remains unyielding in the face of a raging windstorm.

Eyewear constructed from torches.

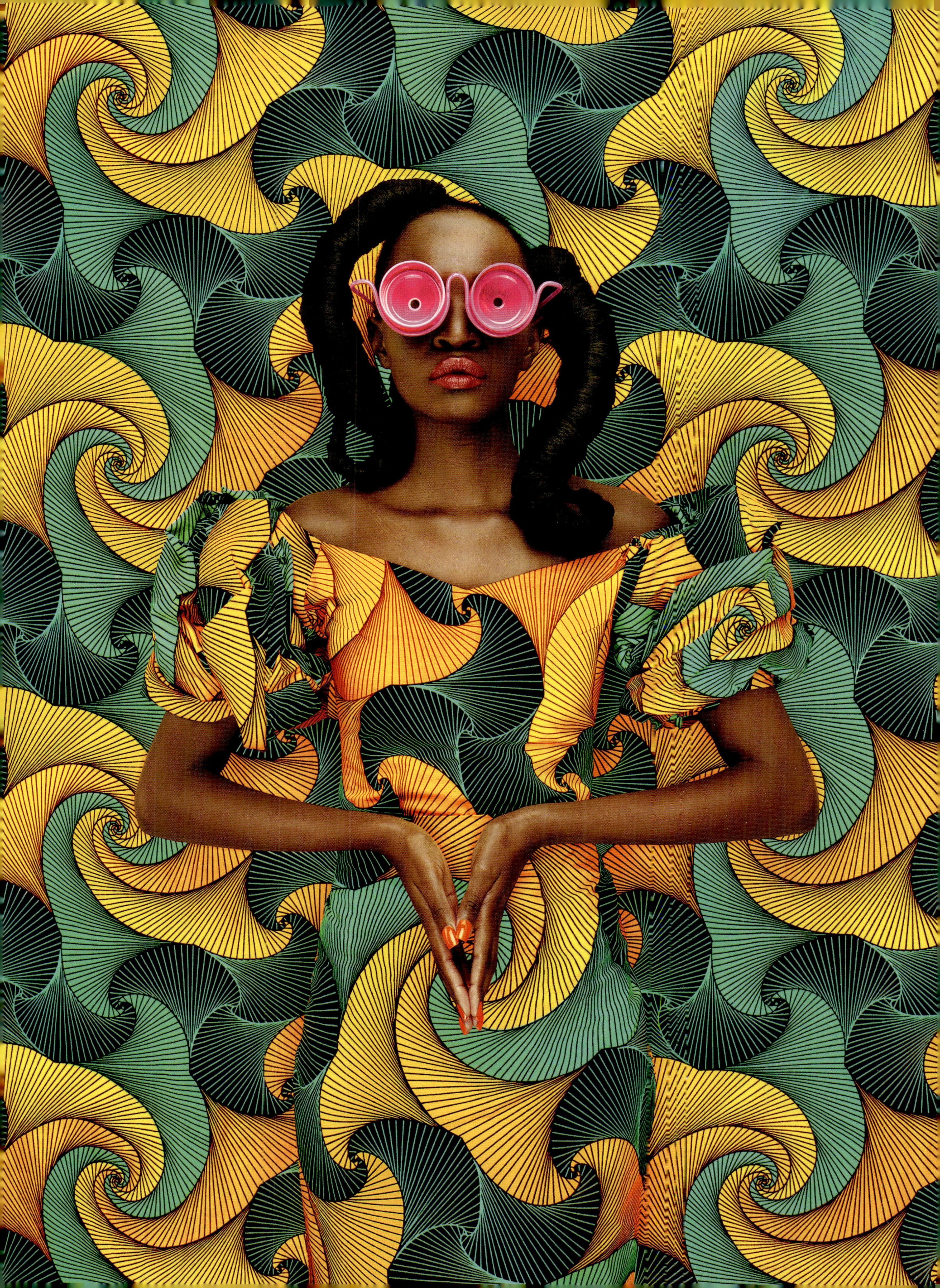

“Every bird flies with its own wings.”

“Kila ndege hupaa na mbawa zake.”

Sunday mornings in Kenya herald a vibrant procession of impeccably dressed women, who delight in wearing their best pieces and elaborate hairdos to church. Sidewalks become Sunday catwalks as each woman revels in the opportunity to showcase herself as an African beauty queen.

The boldness of prints, intricate hairstyles, skillfully applied makeup, and alluring fragrances culminate into a beautiful tapestry of diversity and color. Each Sunday best becomes a celebration of not just personal style, but also a reflection of the beauty found within the community. No woman outshines another; each one a winning personality contributing to the collective splendor of the occasion.

Eyewear constructed from cocktail strainers.

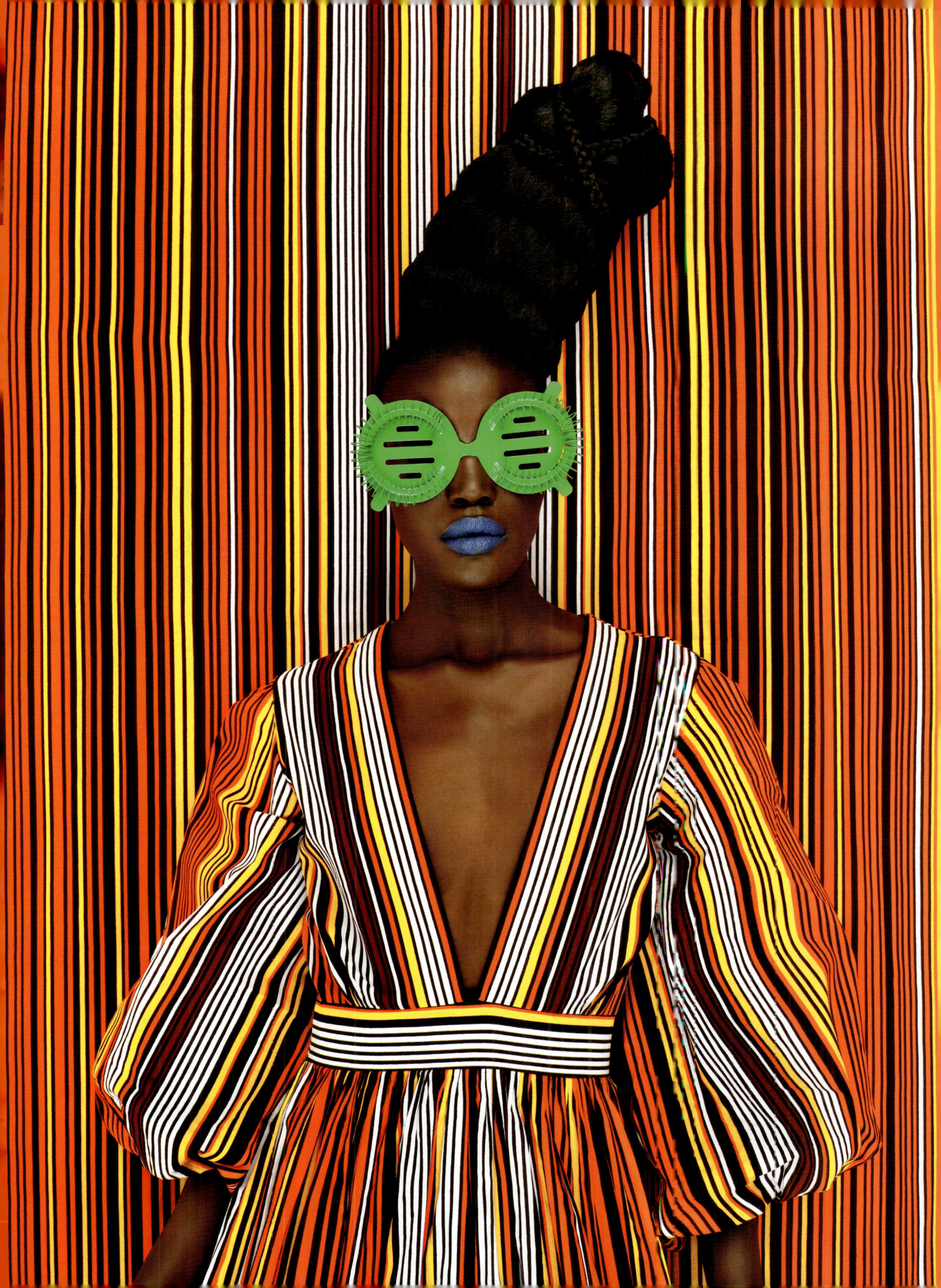

“Without effort no harvest will be abundant.”

“Bila jitihada, mavuno hayatakuwa tele..”

The hair of a Kenyan woman is her canvas for self expression. She can change her look week to week based on her mood, important events on her calendar or inspiration from one of the numerous gifted hairstylists she knows. Just like fashion, Kenyan hairstyles go through trends- though some looks remain timeless classics. The versatile box braid, the sleek shoulder-length straight weave and the tight ring curls popular amongst older Aunties are just a few of the common favorites.

One hairstyle to the next can be as different as night and day. Cornrows, weaves, adding beads, threading or splashes of color are a few possibilities—all that limits each woman is her imagination. A walk down Nairobi’s streets becomes a visual delight of smartly dressed women embracing their creativity and confidently asserting their individuality.

Eyewear constructed from cookie molds.

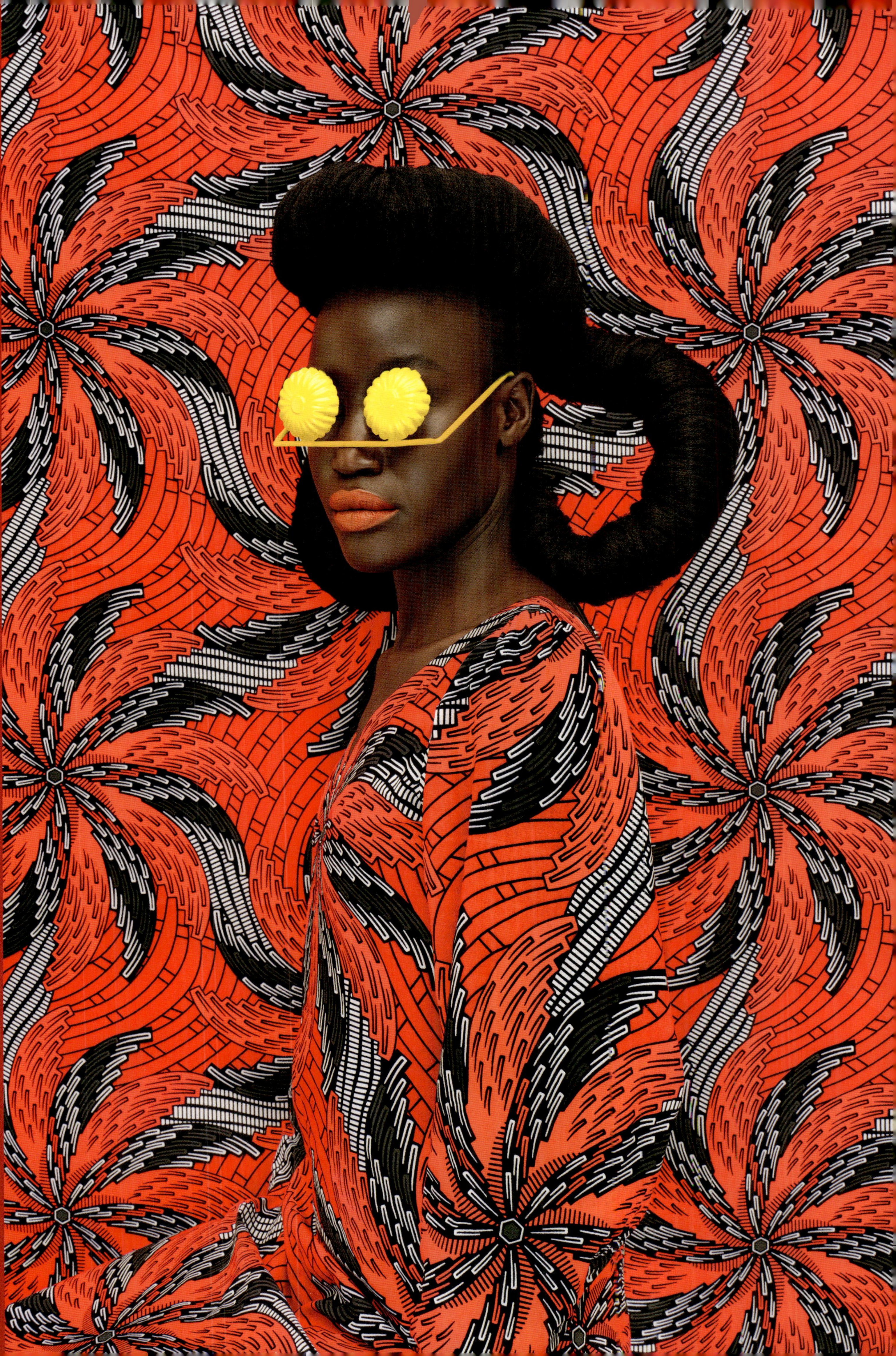

"When your sister does your hair, you do not need a mirror."

"Dadako akikusuka nywele huhitaji kioo."

In Africa, women empower each other by freely giving a helping hand or word of advice when needed. When a woman goes to get her hair done, she sits at the heart of a semicircle of women who all braid her hair. While they plait, she relies on the honesty and affirmation of the other clients around her as they collectively decide on hair length, colour or styling.

Under the baking African sun women commune; laughing together as each offers her best ideas towards the hairstyle. Empowerment becomes an uplifting collaboration between women. Strangers quickly become friends over the simple act of helping each other look their best. The connection forged in these moments goes beyond mere hairstyling; it exemplifies the strength and support that African women consistently extend to each other, creating a network of encouragement and togetherness.

Eyewear constructed from sewing thread.

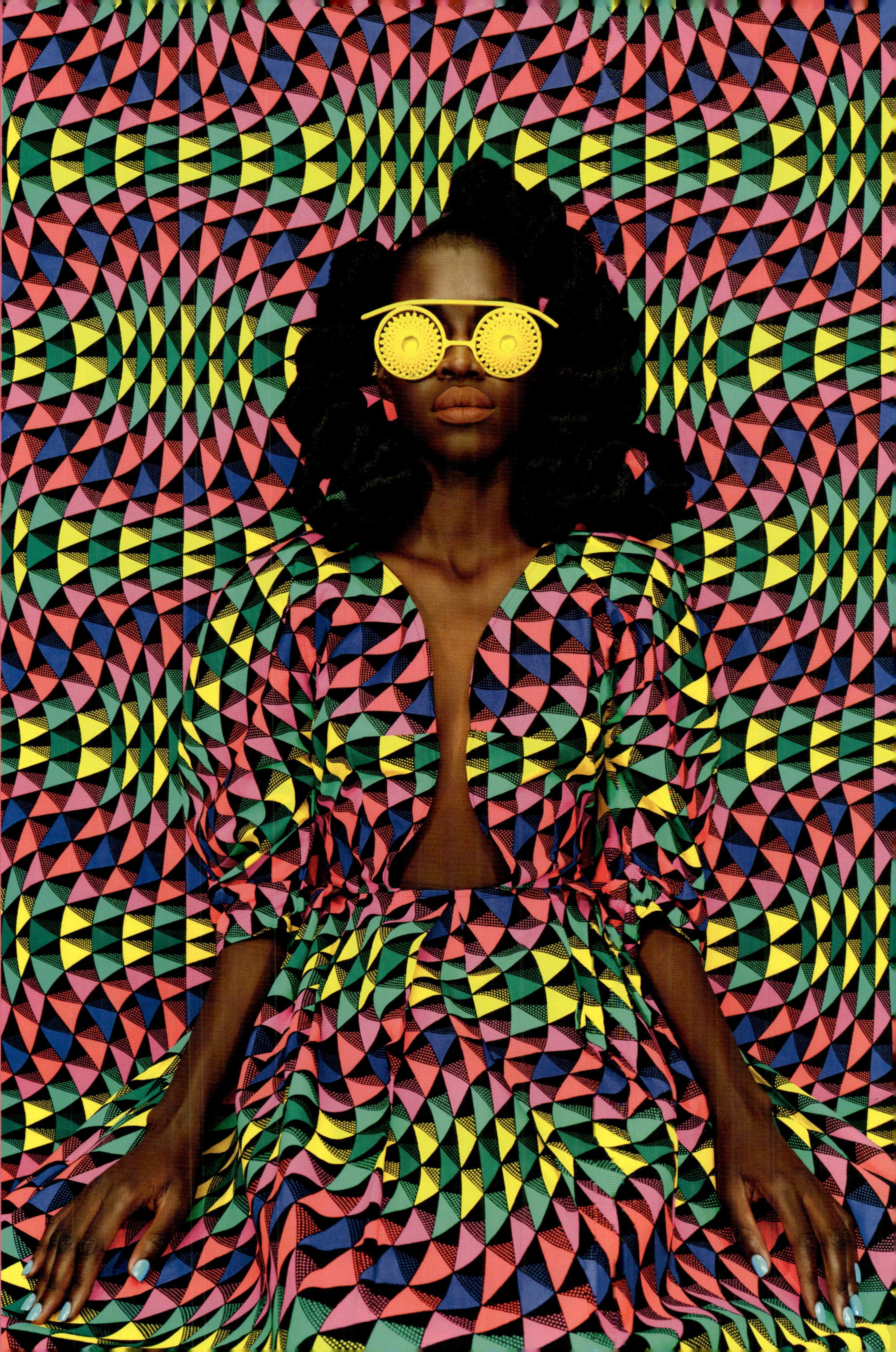

"You must act as if it is impossible to fail."

"Lazima utende kana kwamba haiwezekani kushindwa."

Africa boasts a rich history of female leadership—from queens and female chiefs to strong political leaders, all of whom have left behind successful legacies.

Female pharaohs, such as Cleopatra and Nefertiti ruled ancient Egypt. Queen Nzinga, the warrior queen, commanded an army composed almost entirely of women and was a fierce barrier against enslavement of her Congolese people. In Kenya, Chief Wangu defied societal norms, becoming the only female tribal leader during the fight for independence in a time when the position was held exclusively by men.

Her Everlasting Legacy honours all these African female leaders of the ages, whose long-lasting impact have shaped the collective heritage of the continent and became the centre points of African legacy. Their contributions inspire generations to come, serving as an inspiring highlight to the strength and leadership capabilities of women.

Eyewear constructed from hair combs.

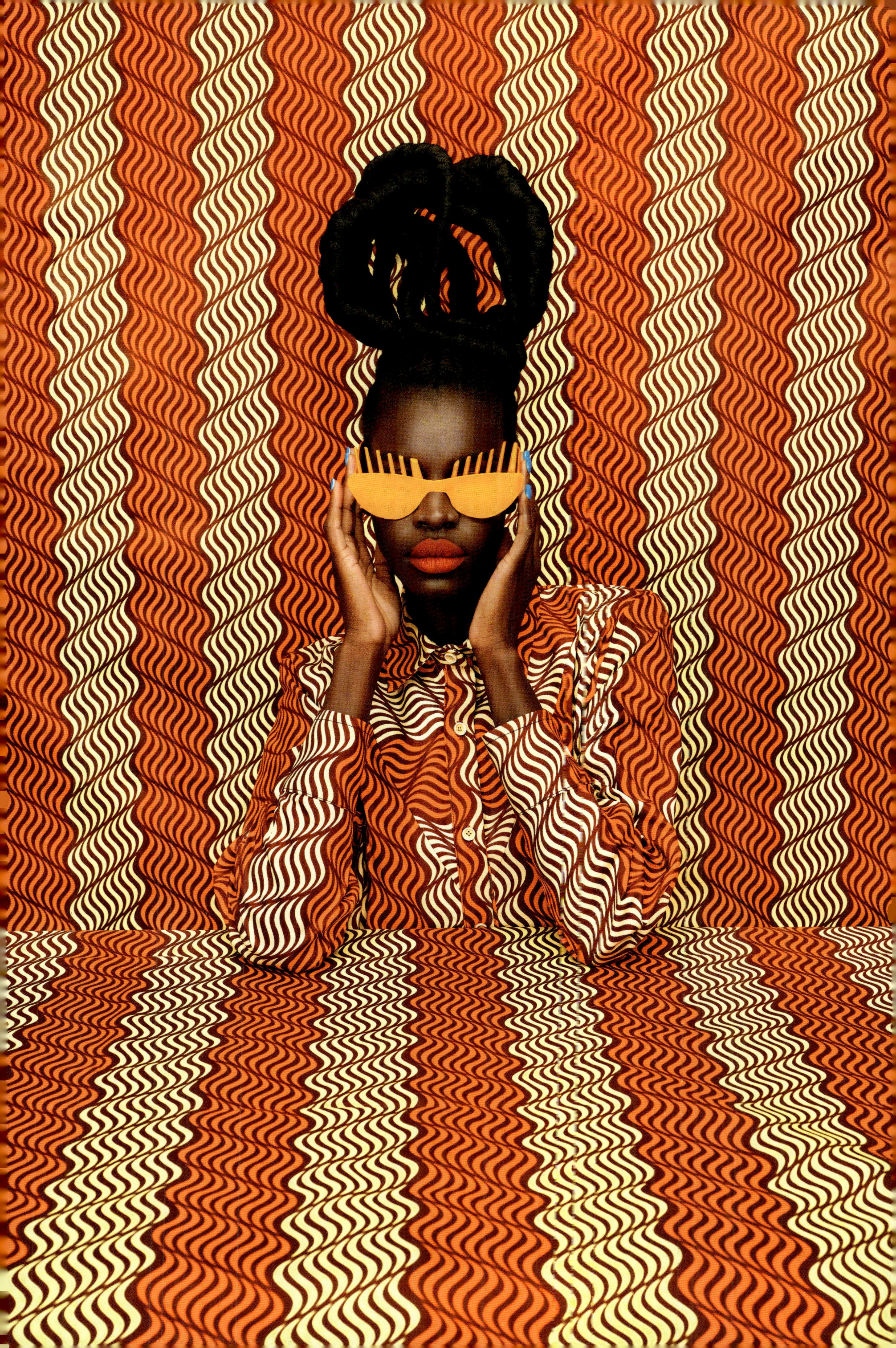

"Happiness is not perfected until it is shared."

"Furaha haikamiliki mpaka inapoenezwa."

Everyone's mother is a Master Chef, whipping up recipes filled with love that form core memories of home. Women are masters of the kitchen, using their recipes to bring their families and communities together. Chopping, frying and dishwashing become a symphony of love, and the final dish a masterpiece. With each meticulously prepared recipe, a mother's tender touch transforms simple ingredients into a symphony of comfort, warmth, and nourishment.

The kitchen is not just where unique flavors and aromas are born, but also where generations connect, sharing recipes, talents, and the essence of their culture. Gathering around a home-cooked meal is a special moment that evokes the importance of being together.

Eyewear constructed from gas stove hobbs.

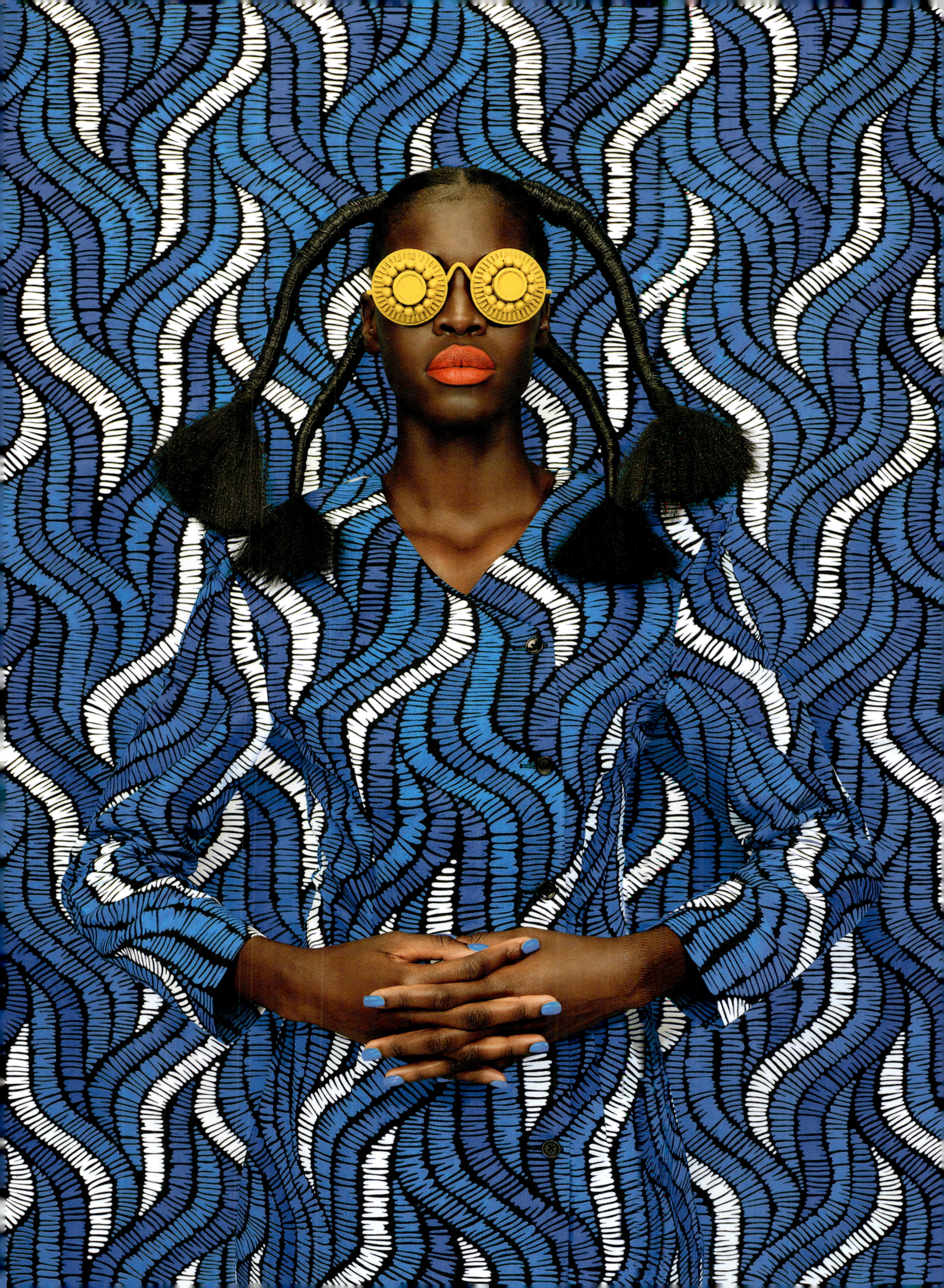

"A great leader is an ordinary person with extraordinary wisdom."

"Kiongozi mkuu ni mtu wa kawaida aliye na hekima ya isiyo ya kawaida."

A woman possesses an noteworthy gift—the foresight to understand how her actions today can shape the future. She has the remarkable ability to recognize what needs to be done in the present to preserve tomorrow. With her insightful vision, she can identify and safeguard what is truly precious, leaving a lasting impact that reverberates across generations.

Kenyan conservationist Wangari Maathai was a true champion of this long-term perception; she fought for a single tree so that her children and grandchildren could walk in a Kenyan forest.

Eyewear constructed from hair clips.

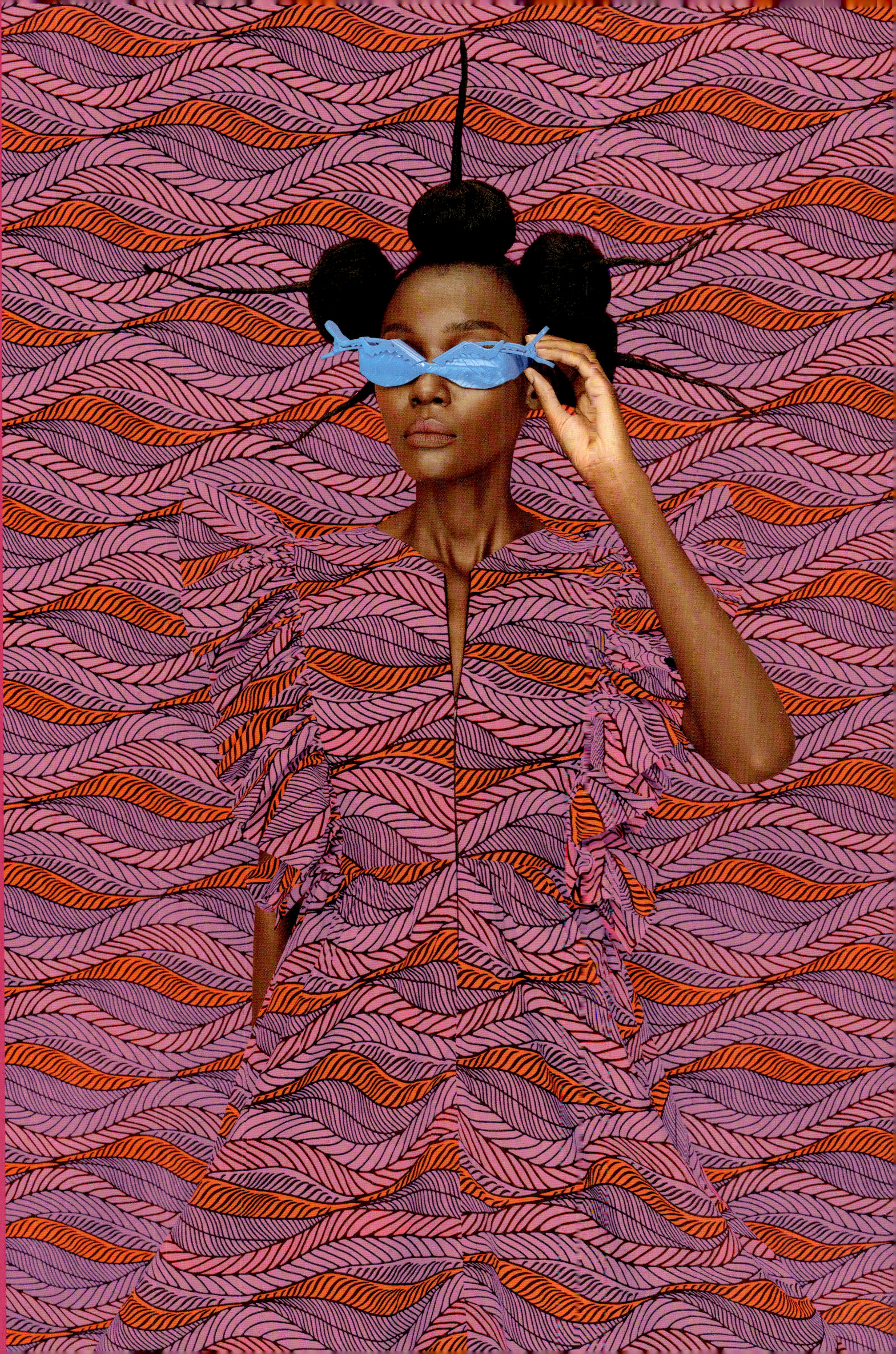

"He who loves, loves you with your dirt."

"Akupendaye anakupenda na uchafu wako."

School holidays are a time where many Kenyan children travel to the countryside to bond with extended family and learn of their treasured culture. More than just a sneak-peek into their parents' upbringing, each grandchild has a chance to soak in their mother-tongue and enjoy fun-filled escapades with their grandparents.

During these long awaited breaks, Thandiwe would often spend adventure filled time at her maternal grandmother's home, where her mischievous side came alive. Many an afternoon was spent playing with the prized rotary dial phone—even though she knew she shouldn't. When not making imaginary calls, she sat under the watchful eye of her beloved grandmother devouring large, juicy watermelon slices.

Eyewear constructed from dial phone cord.

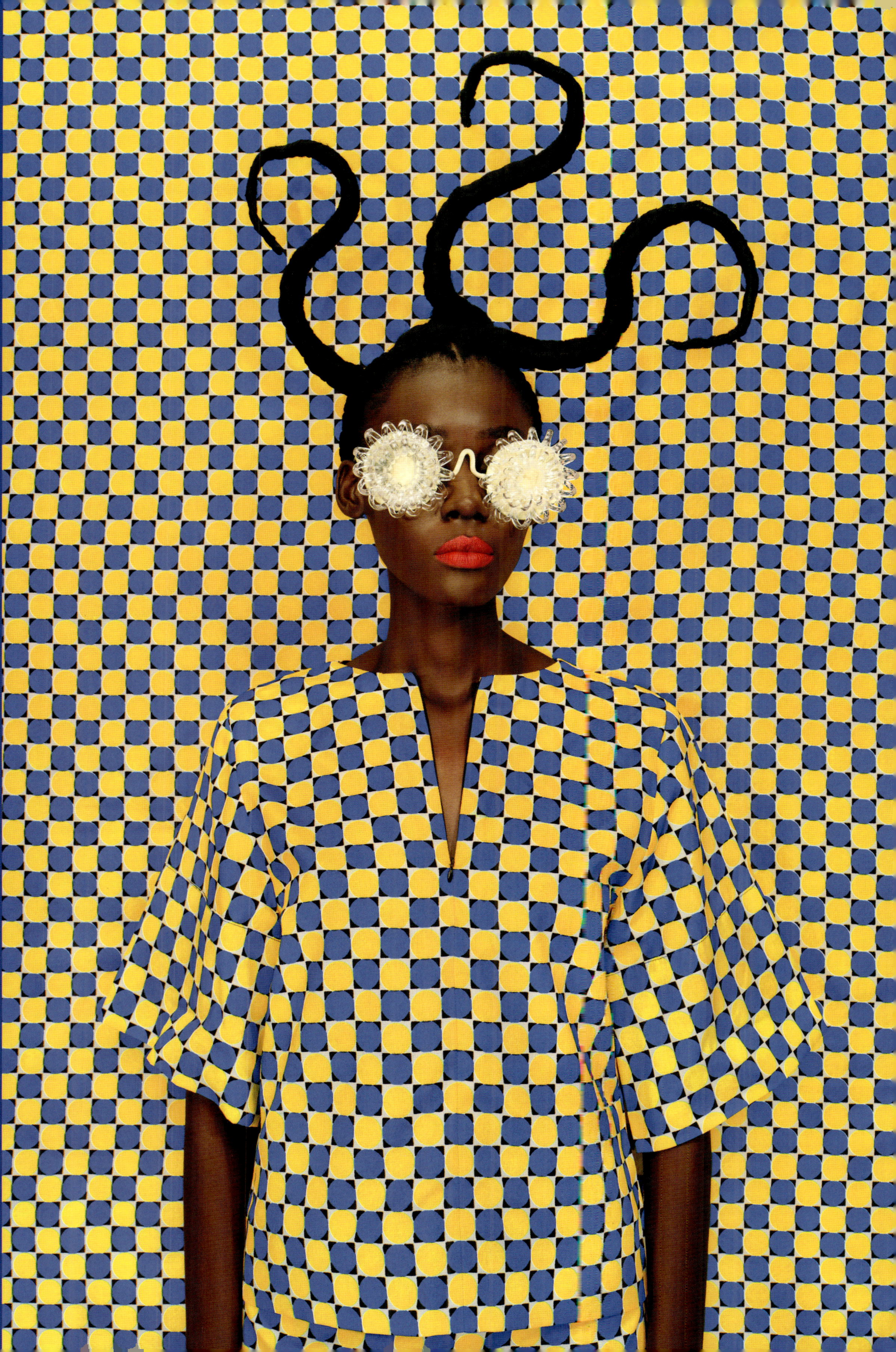

"A person is a person because of other people."

"Mtu ni mtu kwa sababu ya watu wengine."

Every Kenyan woman's secret weapon is her personal tailor. A woman's tailor is a hidden advantage she fiercely guards, whispering it only to her closest friends. For it is her tailor who lets her know when the newest fabric stock is available so that she can get the first pick and design a bespoke dress.

Seamstresses not only construct beautiful creations, but become image consultants- convincing their clients to try new looks or bolder details. A flattering cut, perfect pattern alignment and neat stitching are the hallmarks of a masterful creation coveted by others.

In her own creative process Thandiwe instinctively participates in this cultural practice. Designing the garments worn by her subjects, she collaborates closely with her own Secret Weapon, her tailors, to bring those custom pieces to life. Every Camo print is marked by precision and intentionality as she chronicles the ever evolving journey of African beauty.

Eyewear constructed from spools of thread.

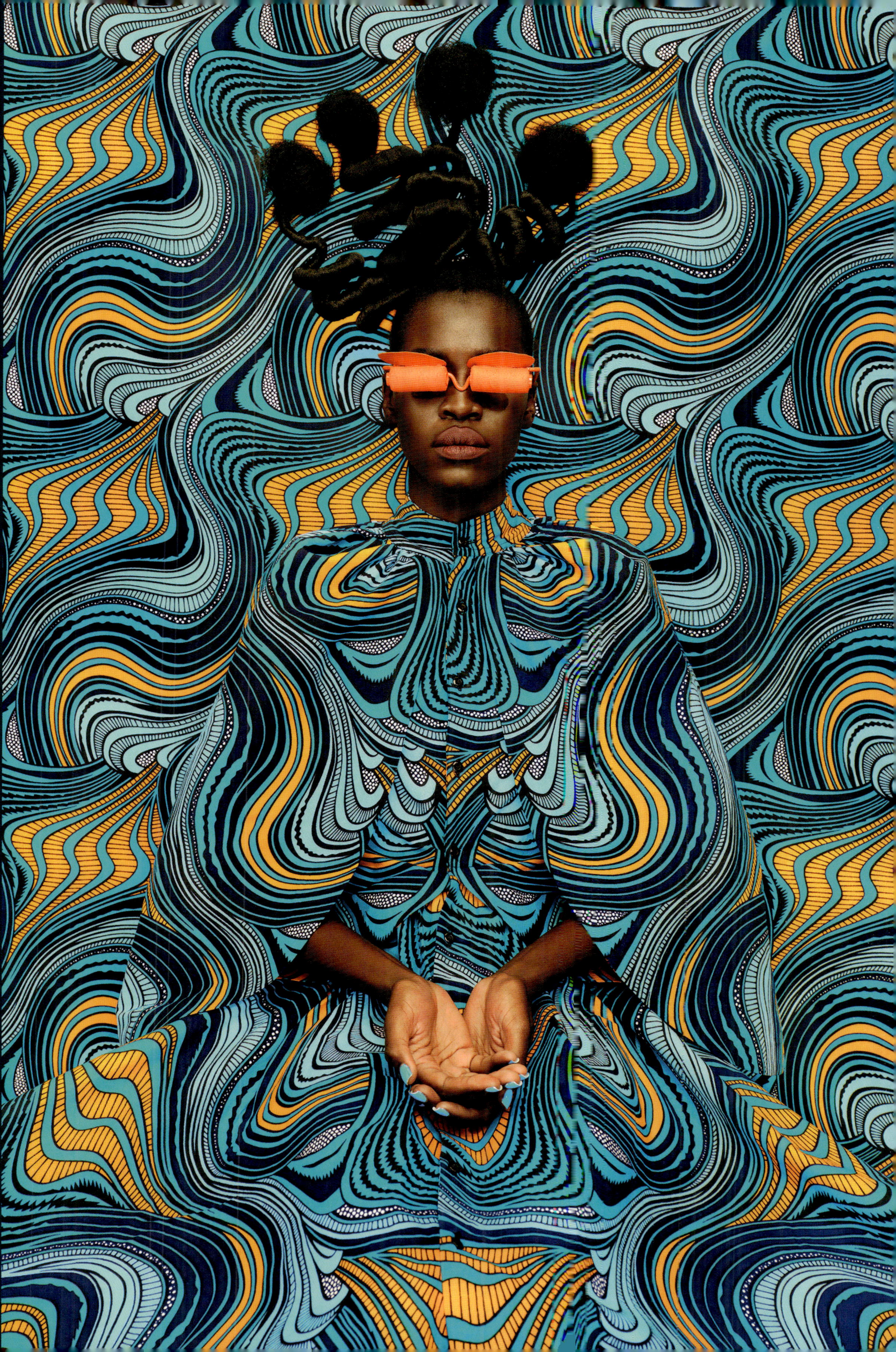

"A man cannot sit down alone to plan for prosperity."

"Mwanaume hawezi kukaa pekee yake na kupanga mafanikio."

It is often overlooked in society that a woman's contribution can extend far beyond the limits imposed upon her; that her mind holds a wealth of untapped potential. In numerous cultures women have historically been encouraged to conform to predefined roles- yet there is a rising chorus of voices challenging this cultural camouflage.

Within the vibrant realm of Camo, Thandiwe boldly expresses her own journey as a woman pushing against the constraints of a conservative culture, all framed by her distinct prints and innovative eyewear as she amplifies her voice and experiences through her lens.

Eyewear constructed from nail files.

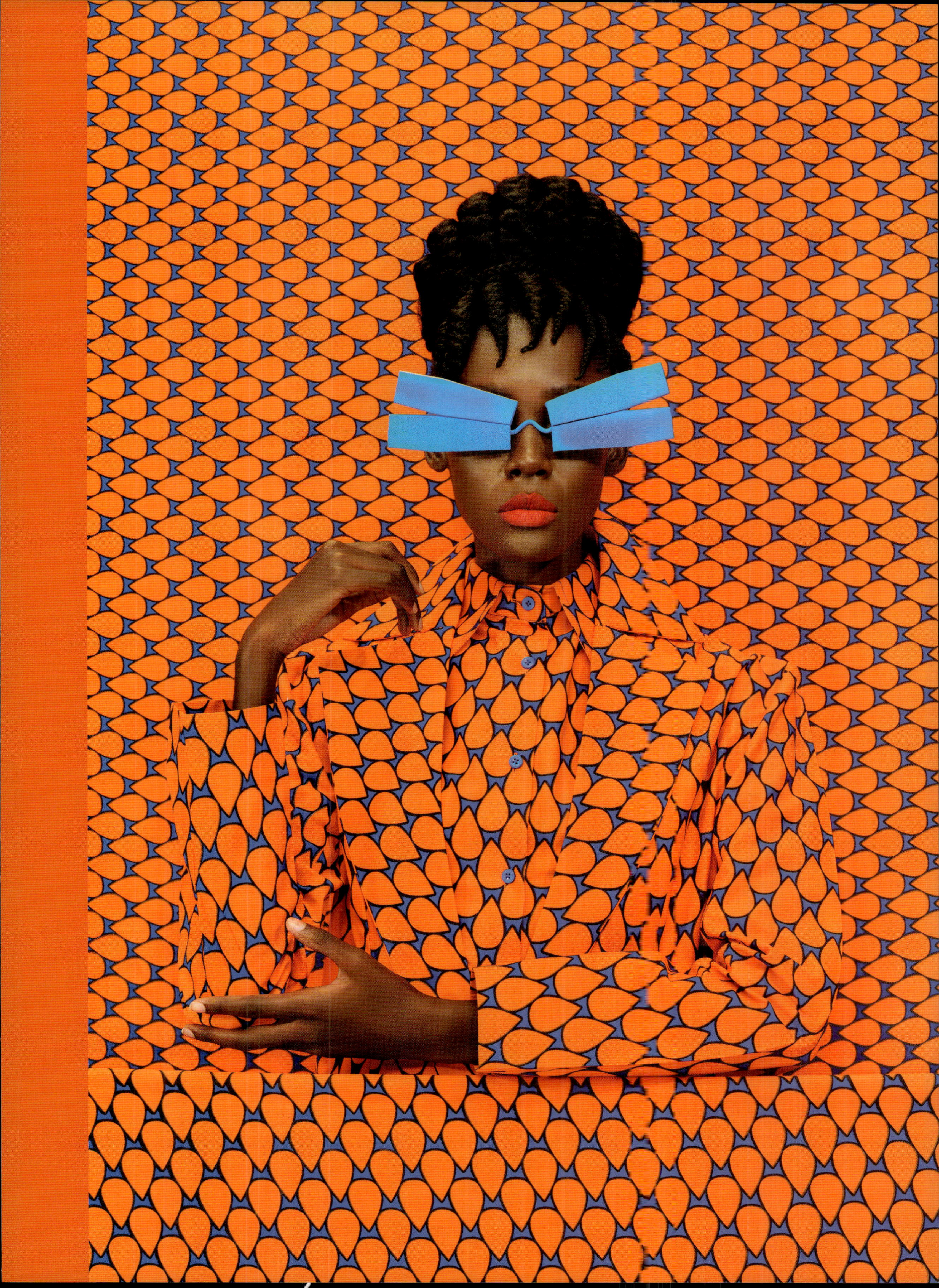

“Women are part of the origin of life’s big mystery on earth; they know the secret of a good life.”

“Wanawake wamebaini fumbo la asili ya ulimwengu, wanajua siri ya maisha mazuri.”

The essence of life lies in its wonder, and a sense of optimism transforms its challenges from difficulty to opportunity. Just like a rolled up paper becomes a pinwheel, a woman who approaches life’s surprises with this mindset will always have hope no matter what she faces.

Kenyan women exemplify the practical ability to embrace what may initially seem like limitations and instead transform them into boundless possibilities. From this place of wonder, they are able to perceive new avenues and potential even in the face of adversity.

Eyewear constructed from faucets.

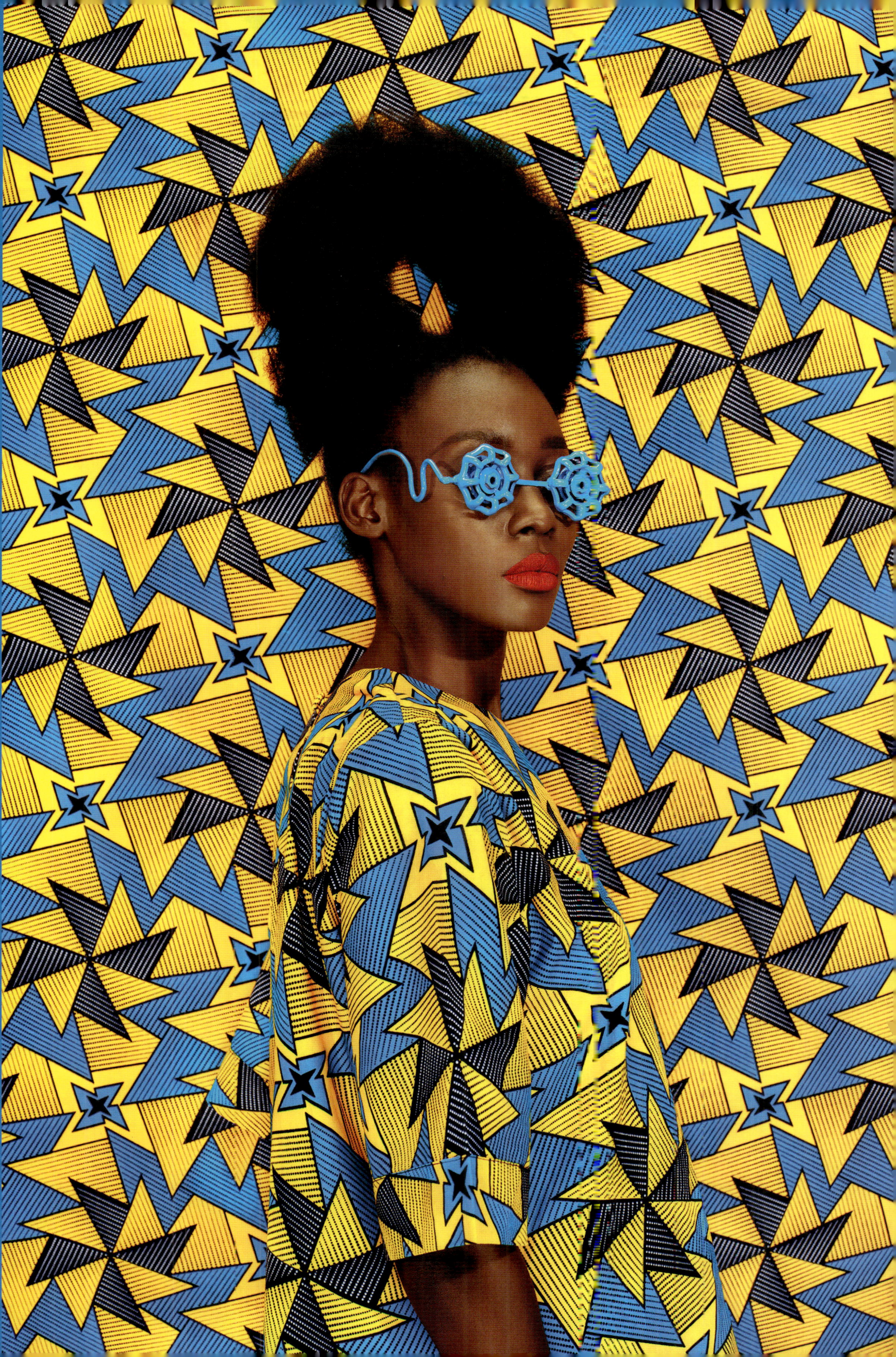

"Where there is love, there is no darkness."

"Penye upendo hapana giza."

Making the unseen, seen is a gift carried by all women. They are able to bring into focus the possibility in things easily dismissed; solve problems by creatively using everyday items and exercise their gift to pass on comfort and life to those they care for. Kenyan women are known for being able to face difficult realities and unearth innovative solutions from the simple resources before them.

By taking often invisible tissue rolls and bringing them to the forefront of the viewer's gaze, I See You celebrates this resourcefulness and ingenuity.

Eyewear constructed from tissue rolls.

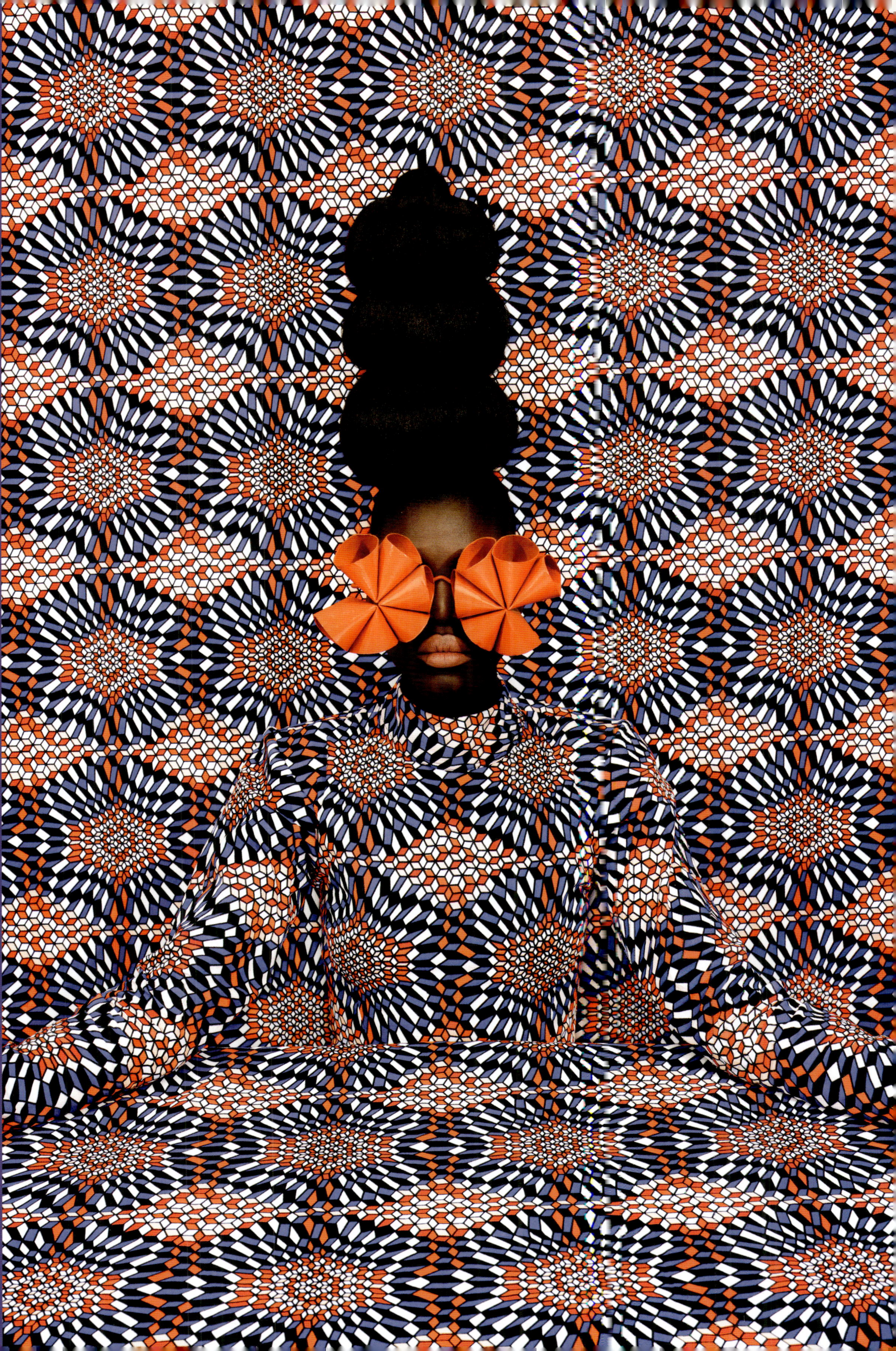

"A little rain each day will fill the rivers to overflowing."

"Rasharasha za mvua kila siku zitajaza mito ifurike."

Every woman is a precious rarity, crafted for so much more than she acknowledges of herself. Despite this reality, there is a shared blindness among women preventing them from seeing the true beauty they possess.

Through the journey of Camo, Thandiwe has cultivated the habit of seeing the extraordinary from the ordinary-reimagining shoe polish tins into stunning bursts of sunshine. This habit can be transferred from eyewear to womanhood. Every woman has it within herself to shift her self perception; seeing beyond her 'ordinary' and instead refocusing on the extraordinary within her.

Eyewear constructed from shoe polish and hair bands.

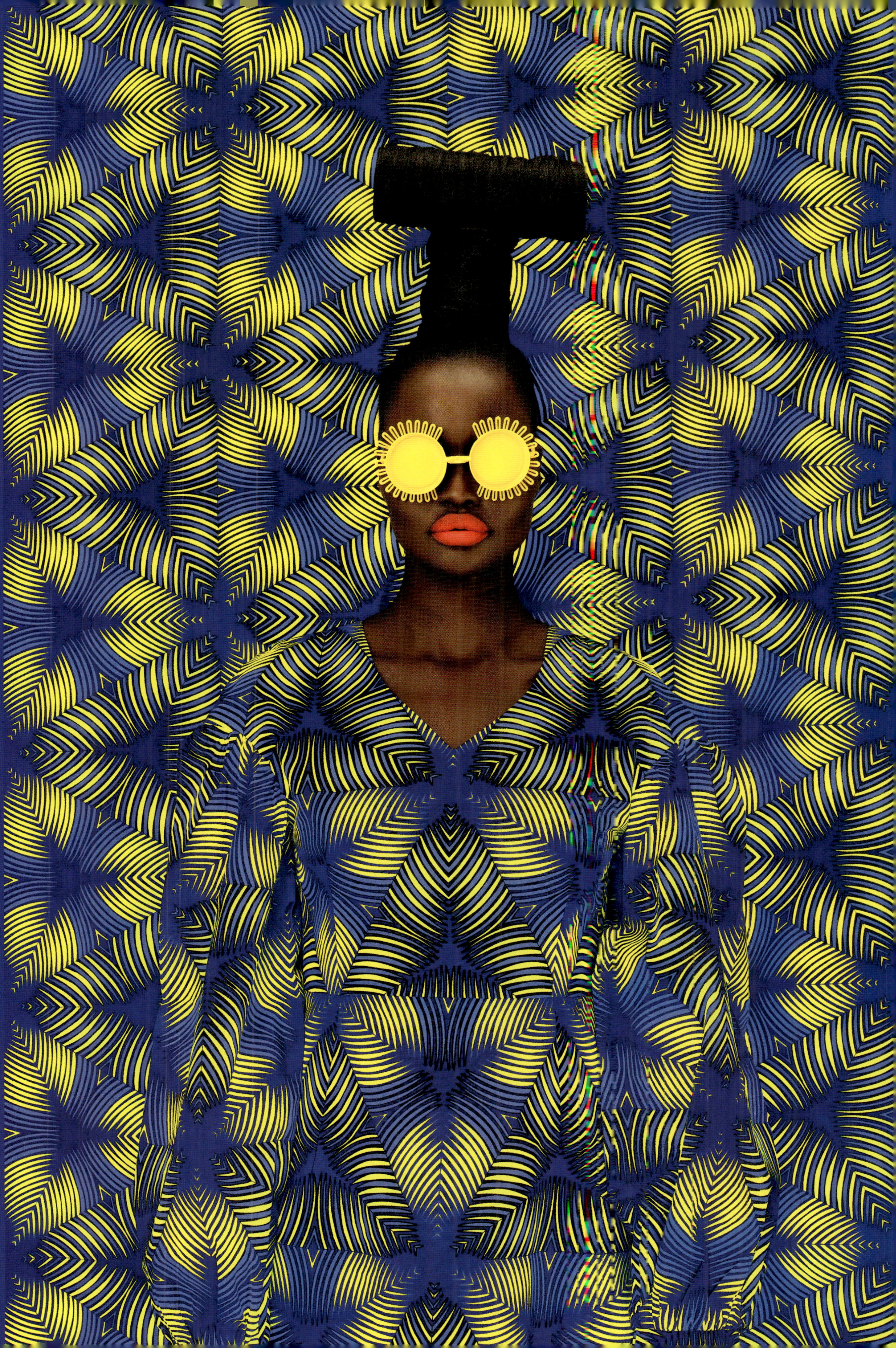

"The words of the elders do not lock all the doors; they leave the right door open."

"Hekima ya wazee haifungi milango yote;bali huacha milango ifaayo wazi."

Kenya embodies the essence of storytelling, where the rich tapestry of the past is handed down through spoken words and melodic songs. Women are perpetual orator; reliving memories and sharing history with those they love. Their enlightened voices fill homes, schools, institutions and gatherings as their wisdom weaves its way into the very fabric of culture.

This storytelling not only preserves cherished wisdom but also imparts invaluable life lessons to younger generations. What is shared by these women transcends mere tales; it is a priceless heritage that gains strength and significance with each retelling, ensuring that the experiences of past generations continue to resonate and guide future ones.

Eyewear constructed from plastic ruler.

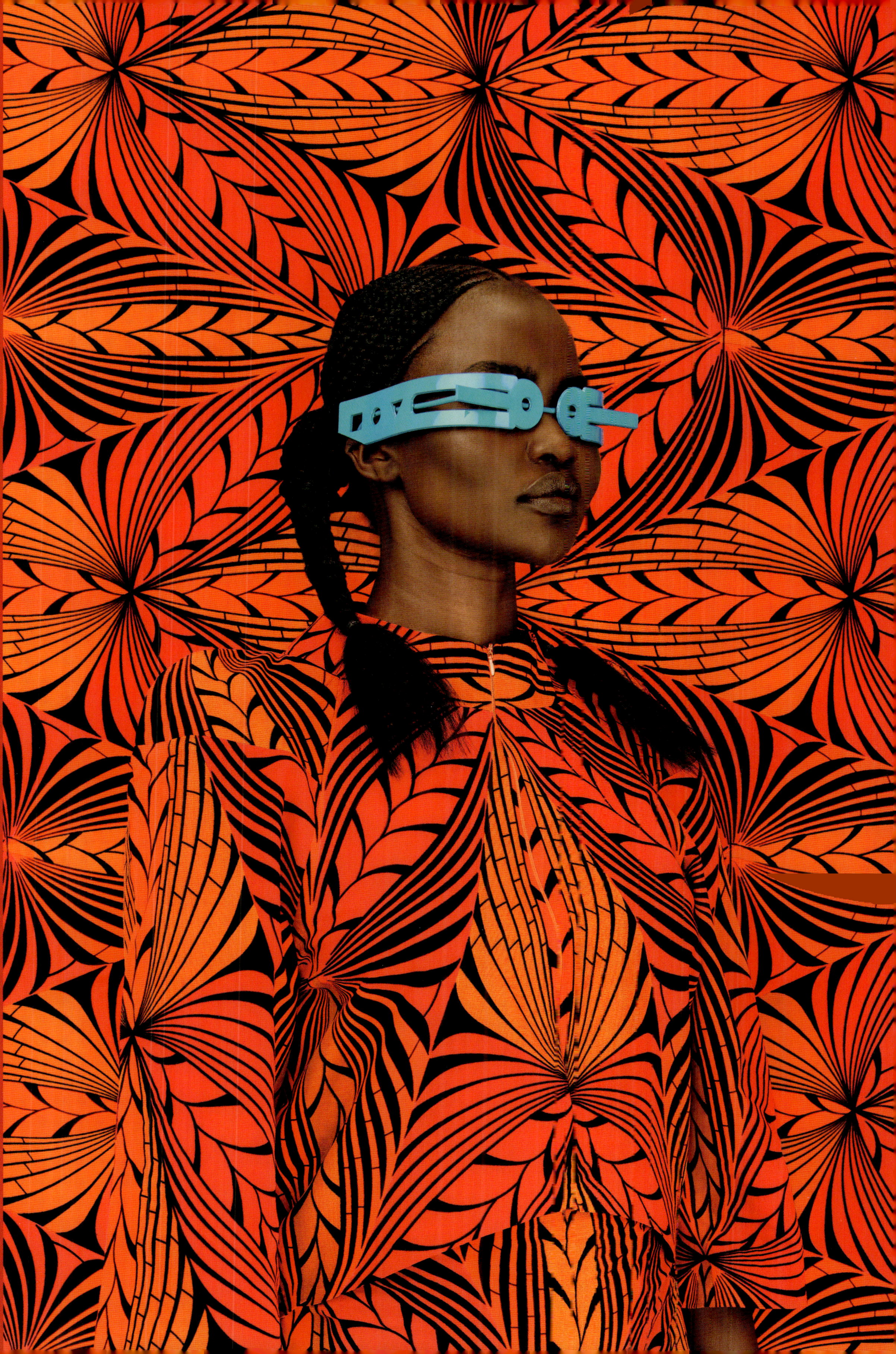

"Friendship doubles joy and halves grief."

"Urafiki hufanya furaha maradufu na huzuni kuwa nusu."

Every woman is a vessel, carrying within her a wealth of affirmation, encouragement, and wisdom that other women have poured into her. These women, her sisters, born out of the bonds of true friendship, understand the song of her heart, embracing and accepting its melody but also adding their own harmony to call her home when she is lost.

The unwavering presence and support of these friends become the solid foundation of their bond. And as she journeys through life, her friendships run deep, flowing like streams of love from diverse sources, merging together to create a beautiful ocean of community.

Eyewear constructed from plastic bottle tops.

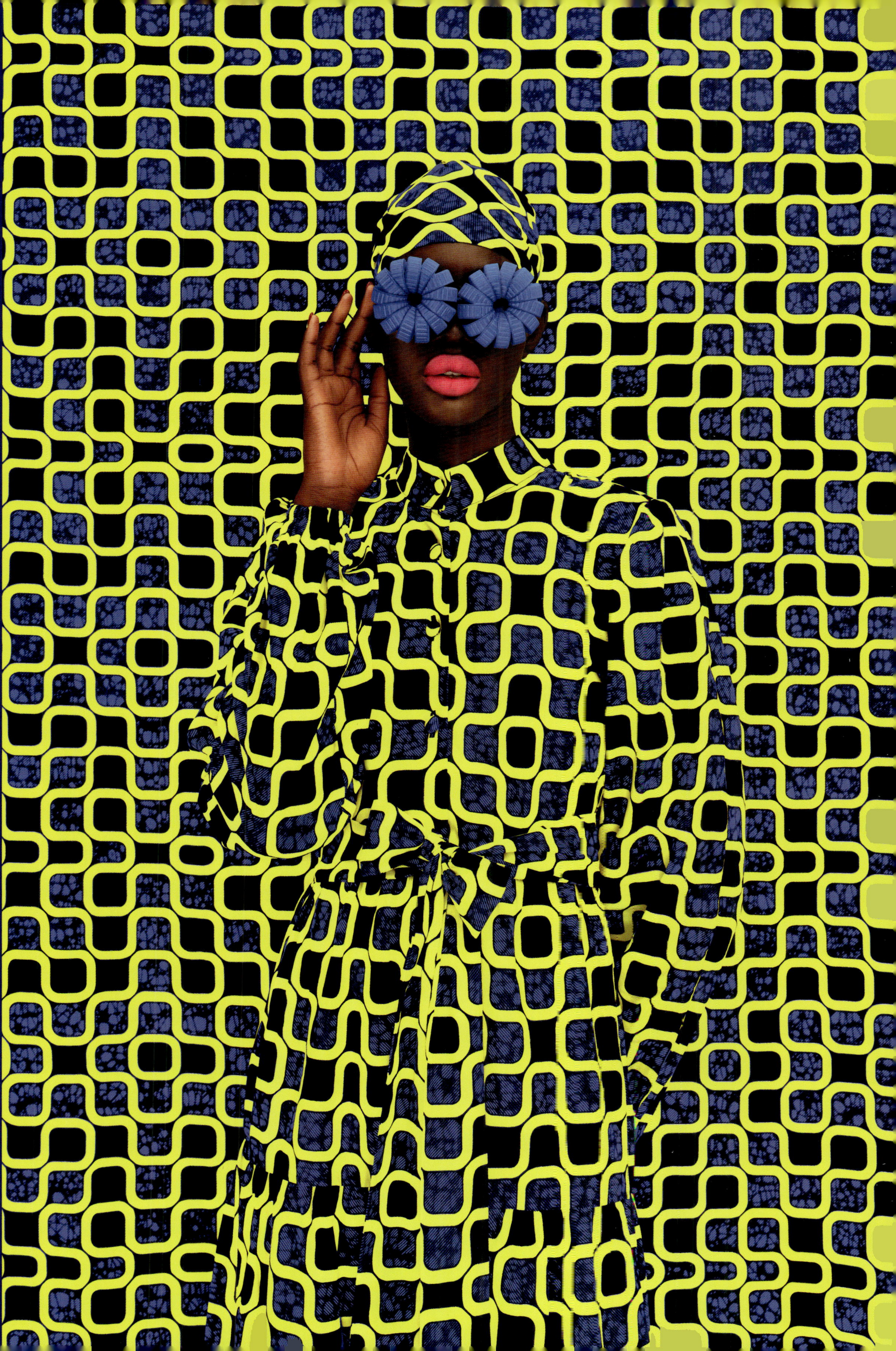

"Sticks in a bundle are unbreakable."

"Vijiti kwenye kifungo havivunjiki."

Within communal culture, a beautiful concept called the "circle of care" emerges as women gracefully journey through the chapters of life. Younger women tend to older women taking on more responsibilities as they live out the selflessness their predecessors carried. Rooted in intentional acts of love, this cycle knows no familial boundaries and flourishes within adopted relationships.

The cycle of nurturing and support serves as a system for cultural preservation. The intergenerational exchange of care is an unending gift passed from woman to woman.

Eyewear constructed from muffin cups.

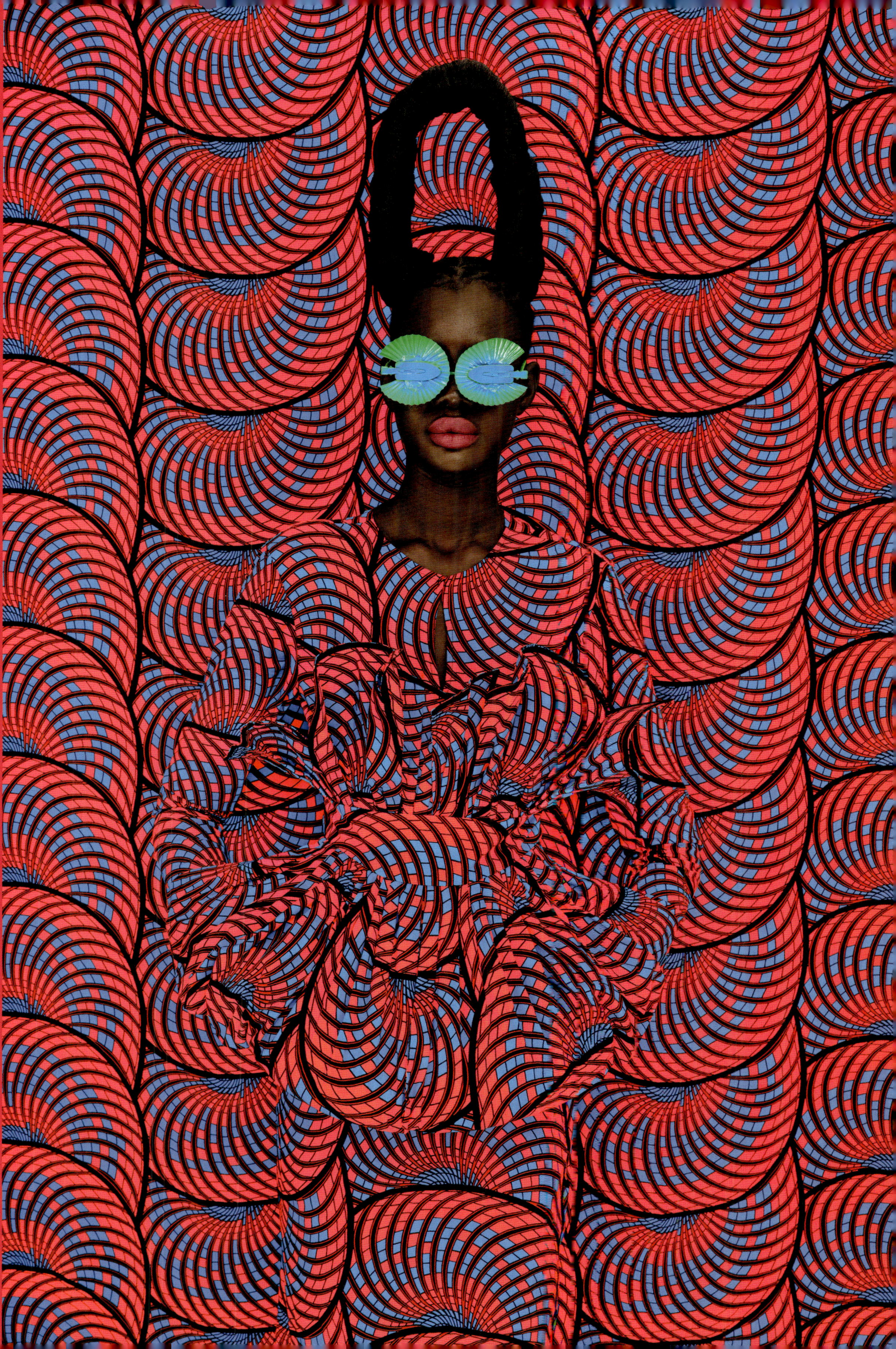

"One tree cannot be a forest."

"Mti mmoja hauwezi kuwa msitu."

At the core of womanhood lies a profound connection to the art of singing. When a woman joins in song, she finds solace and harmony within the collective creating a note that transcends the boundaries of self. It is the very essence that reverberates through her being, shaping her identity as she unites with others in a resounding symphony.

In song, a community finds language for its deepest emotions. Women's collective voices, on behalf of their community, lift up both the joys and pains that limited words cannot fully describe.

Eyewear constructed from speakers.

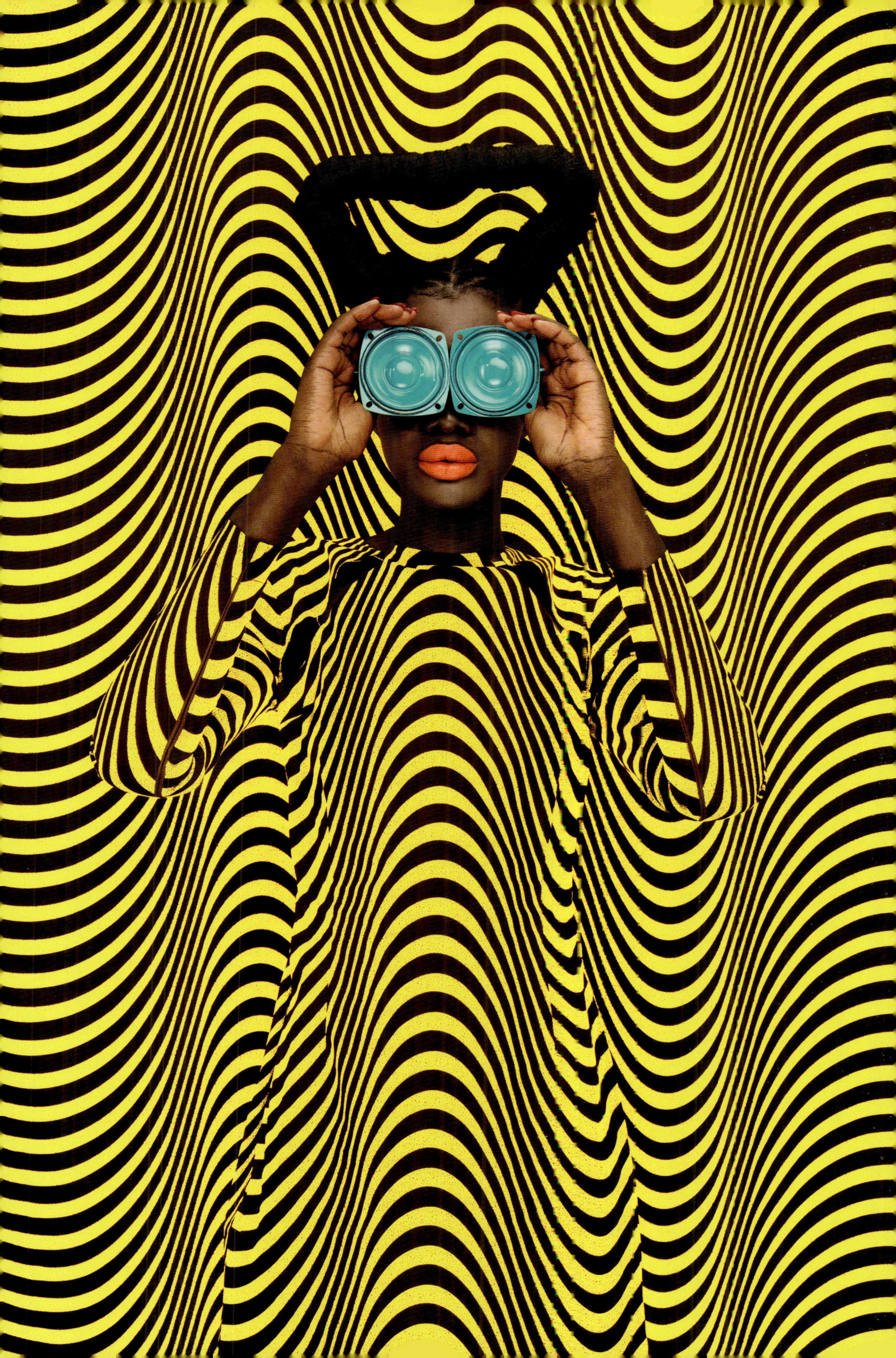

“I am because you are.”

“Nipo kwa kuwa wewe upo.”

African Youth have skillfully blended Western modernism and African tradition into a culture of their own. They have blended strains of different elements, gleaned through digital exposure, into their inherited customs. Like the joining of hands this merging of two seemingly opposing worlds has enabled them to create a unique hybrid of culture: their New Africa.

More than just a look, it is a heartfelt philosophy lived out in vivid African reality. Exploring with other African artists of these times, Thandiwe interweaves science fiction, fantasy, and Afro-diasporic cultures to reimagining them with colourful distinction. This new way of life glistens, radiating enchantment within the realm of Afrofuturism.

Eyewear constructed from pegs.

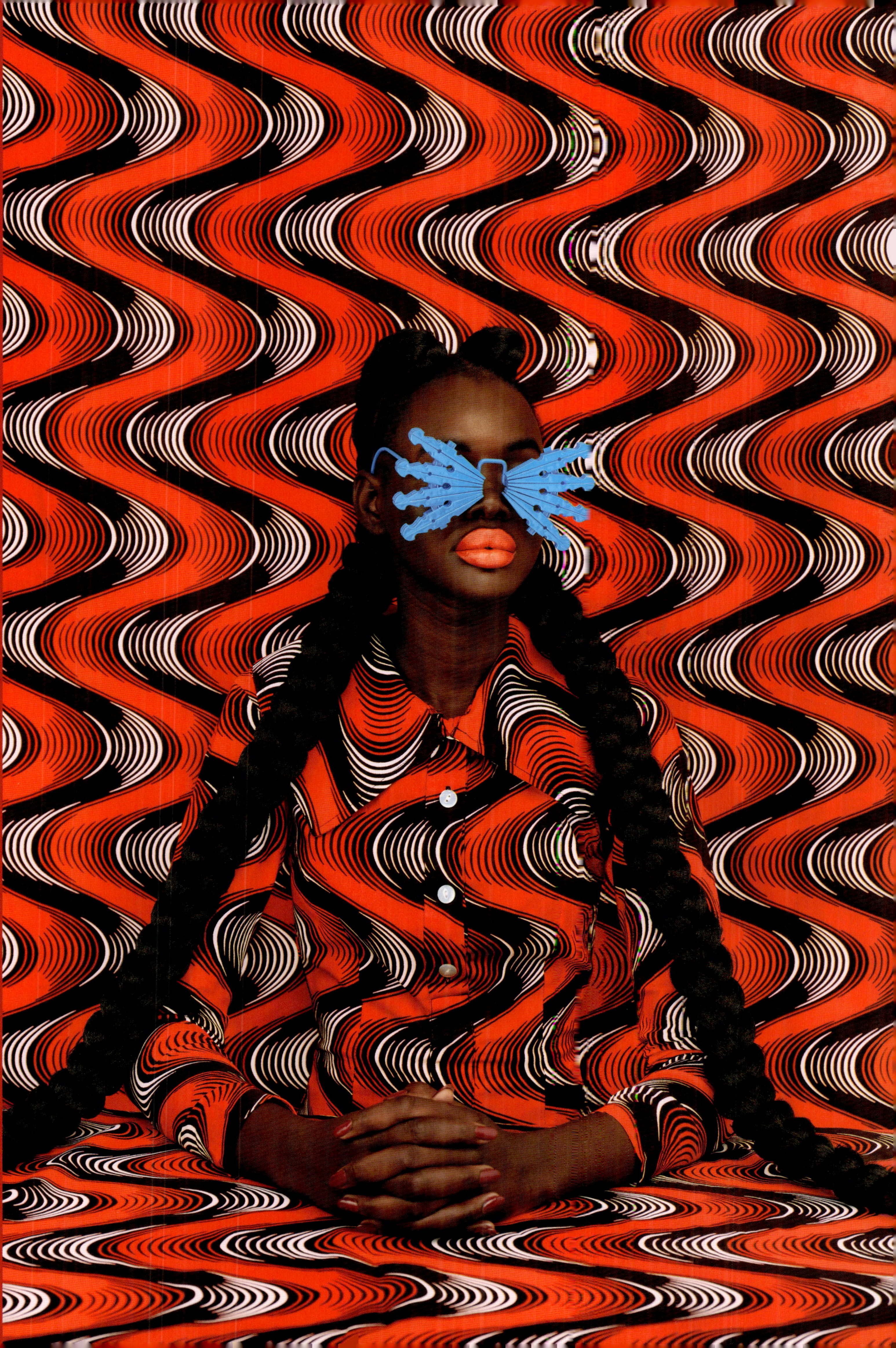

“A joyful woman is a beautiful woman.”

“Mwanamke mwenye furaha ni mwanamke mrembo.”

Echoes of women's laughter can often be heard resonating all over gatherings in Kenya. It is the high-pitched delight of reconnecting with old friends after weeks, days, or even just hours apart, the exuberance expressed when complimenting each other's outfits or the gleeful cackle that spills forth when juicy gossip is shared.

Where women gather, laughter lives. Etched into the core of womanhood, it is a sound that emotes joys, pleasures and victories with playful abandon, momentarily lifting the weight of heavy burdens. Solace and a sense of camaraderie are found in the midst of shared laughter, faces become a radiant canvas of unadulterated delight raising spirits beyond present circumstances.

As women laugh together, their eyes sparkle with renewed vitality and their souls resonate with the euphoria of collective memories being revisited. It is with laughter that a contagious sense of positivity and hope is nourished.

Eyewear constructed from graters.

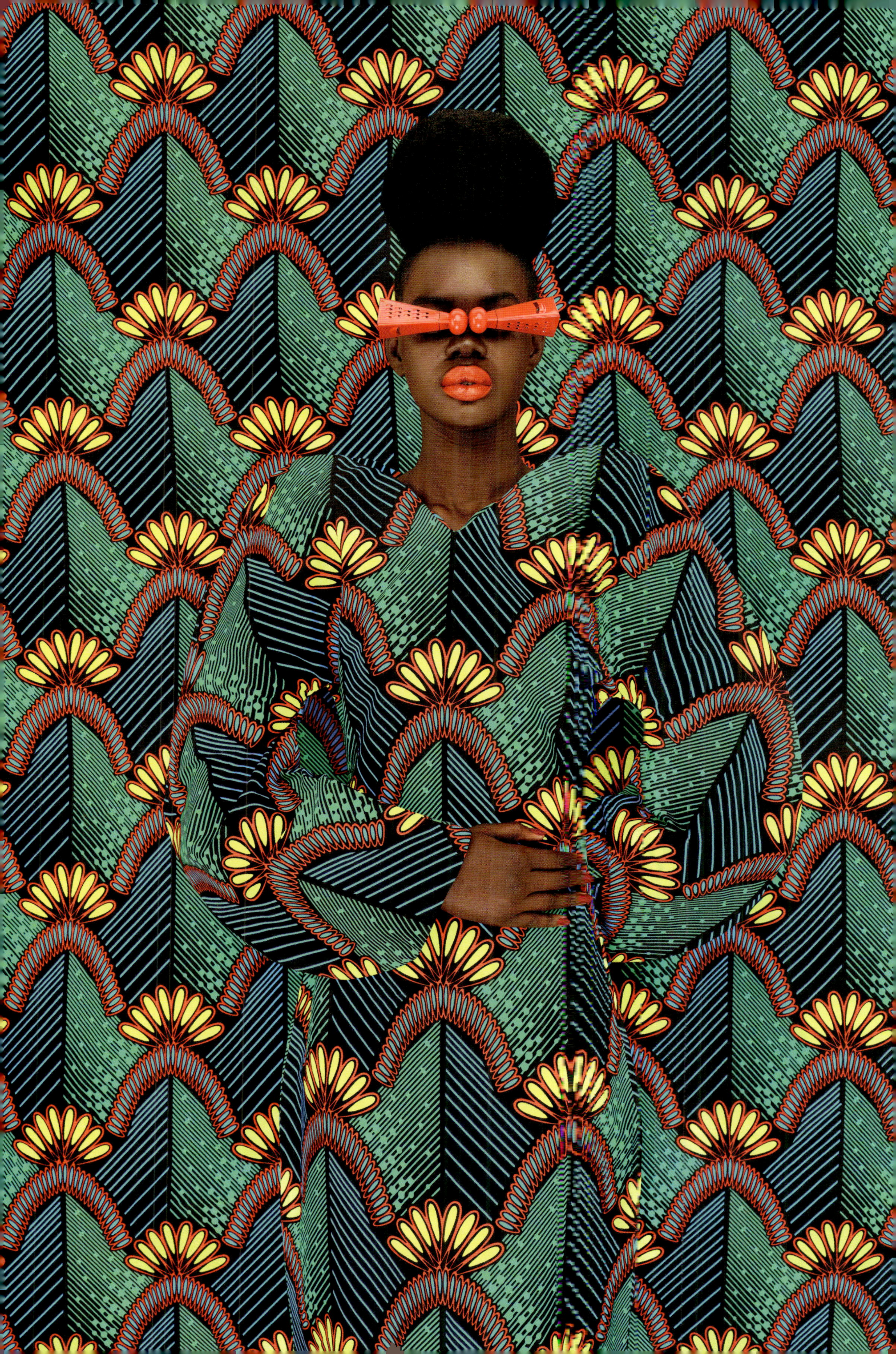

"A man's face shows what is in his heart."

"Uso wa mtu hudhihirisha yaliyo moyoni mwake."

A woman is a living masterpiece, her presence alone can transform the world around her. Her radiant smile has the ability to effortlessly dismantle what separates and create a space of connection and unity. Her eyes, like shimmering pools of kindness, speak compassion and understanding. Every line on her face, whether the delicate imprints of time like crow's feet or etchings of joy woven through laughter lines, are exquisite marks of experiences, immortalized.

The true masterpieces that grace our world, every woman's face tells a story as individual as the soul it belongs to. Their universal consistency of compassion and strength revealed with a closer look, only become more striking against the contrasting backdrop of a broken world.

Eyewear constructed from nails.

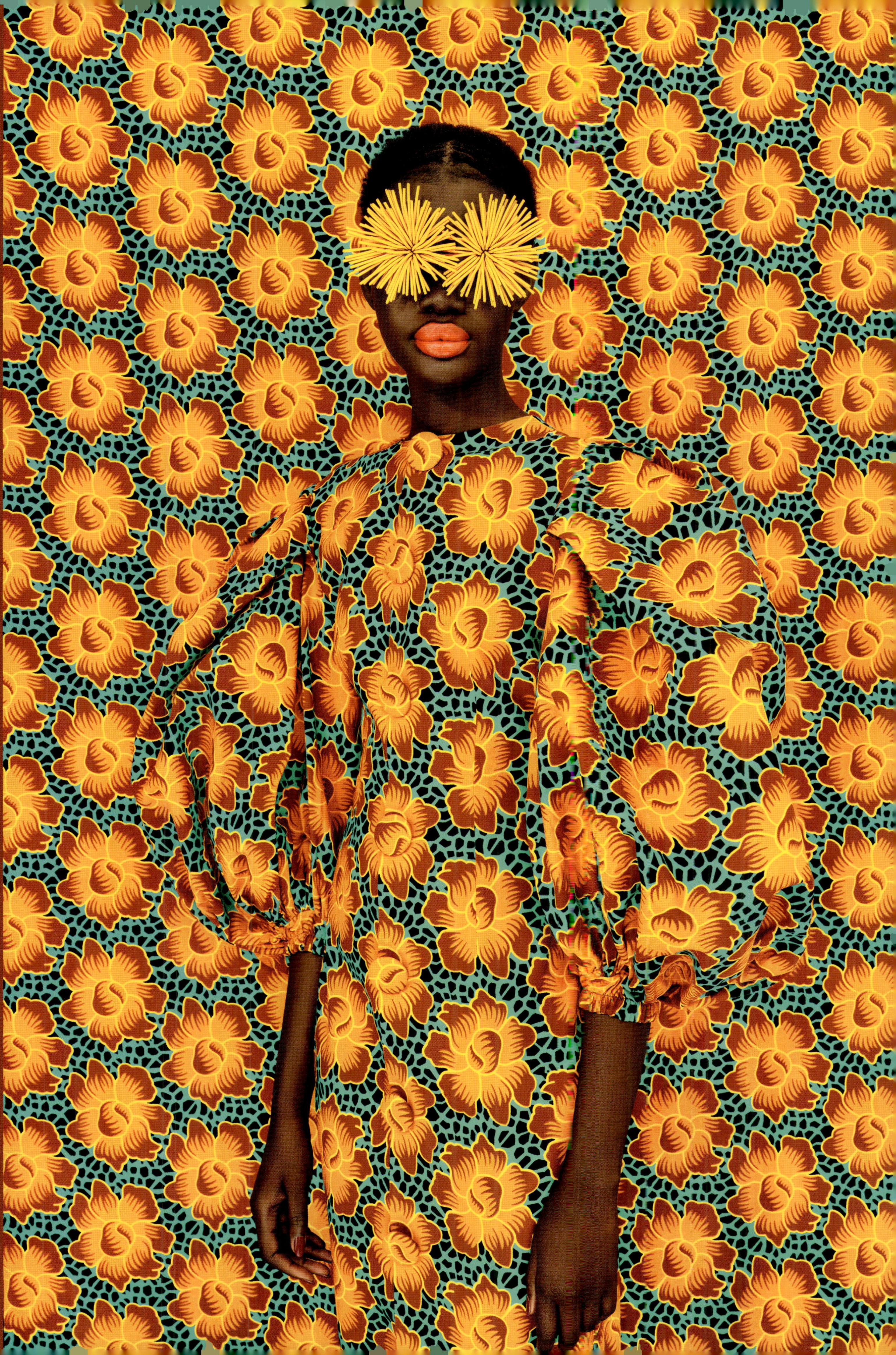

“It is not length of life, but depth of life.”

“Si urefu wa maisha, bali undani wa maisha.”

Like the hidden treasures that lie deep beneath the surface of an ocean, womanhood holds within it sweetness and wonder that go far beyond what meets the eye. From the tender years of girlhood, where innocence dances hand in hand with curiosity, to the onset of adolescence, which ushers in a world of transformation and self-discovery, the journey unfolds through an array of changes.

By embracing the full spectrum within each evolution, there is a joy to be discovered in these new seasons. Womanhood is a ever shifting dance with the ebb and flow of life; a true dive into the ever-changing nature of growth.

Eyewear constructed from bottle openers.

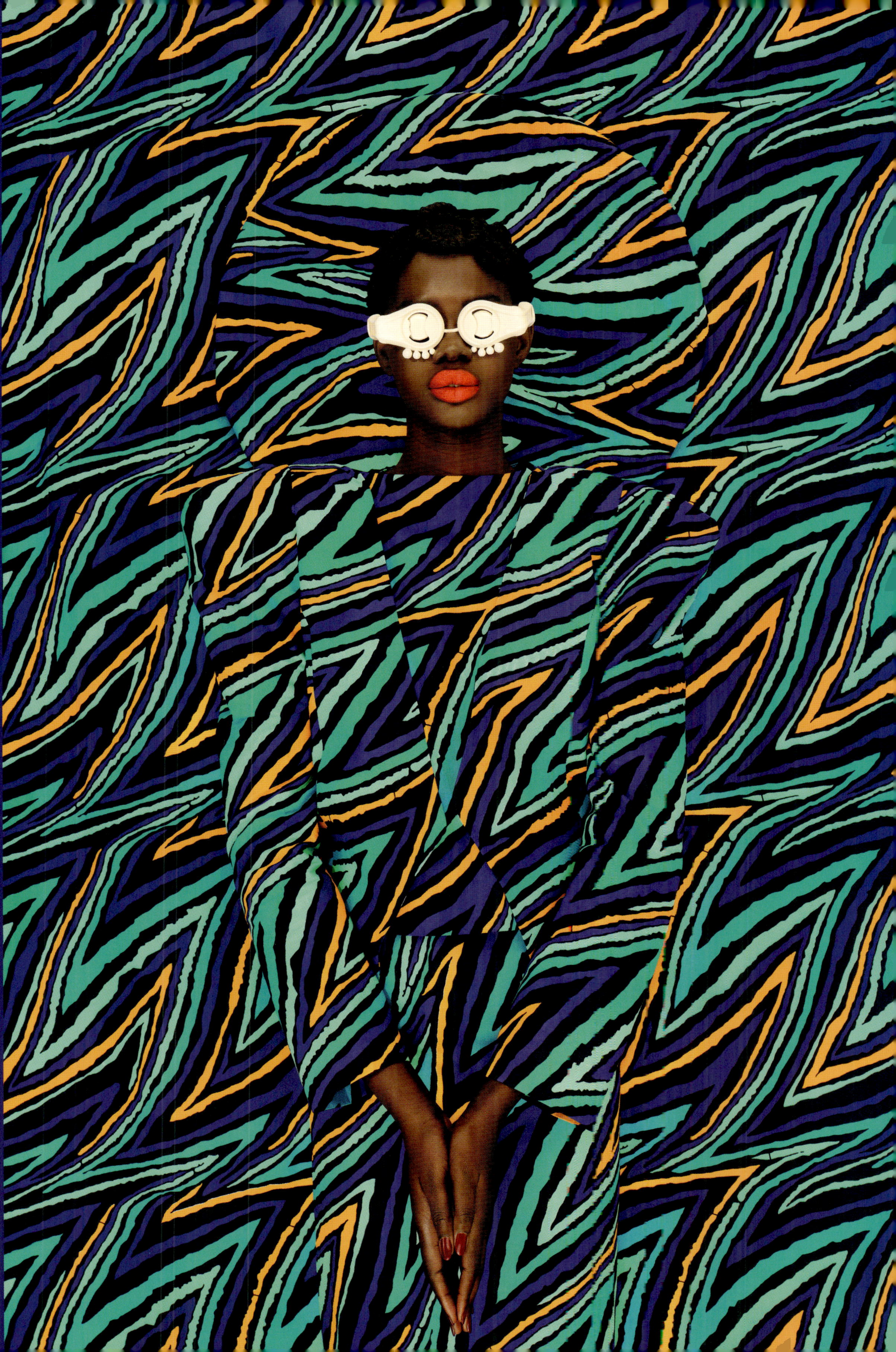

"Great fires erupt from tiny sparks."

"Mioto mikubwa huzuka kutoka cheche ndogo."

In society, there is often a great emphasis placed on outward displays of strength, particularly traditionally masculine expressions. Strength alone is not enough for lasting success; true strength is fortified by wisdom and insight. It is an open secret that the man may be the head of the household, but the woman is its heartbeat. From her discernment a family is equipped to face the outside world. Her sage advice on maneuvering conflict, the soothing heat of a favourite meal on a bad day, her encouraging words as new ventures are pursued, the critical support of a woman is an essential ingredient of success.

Eyewear constructed from wooden cooking spoons and nuts.

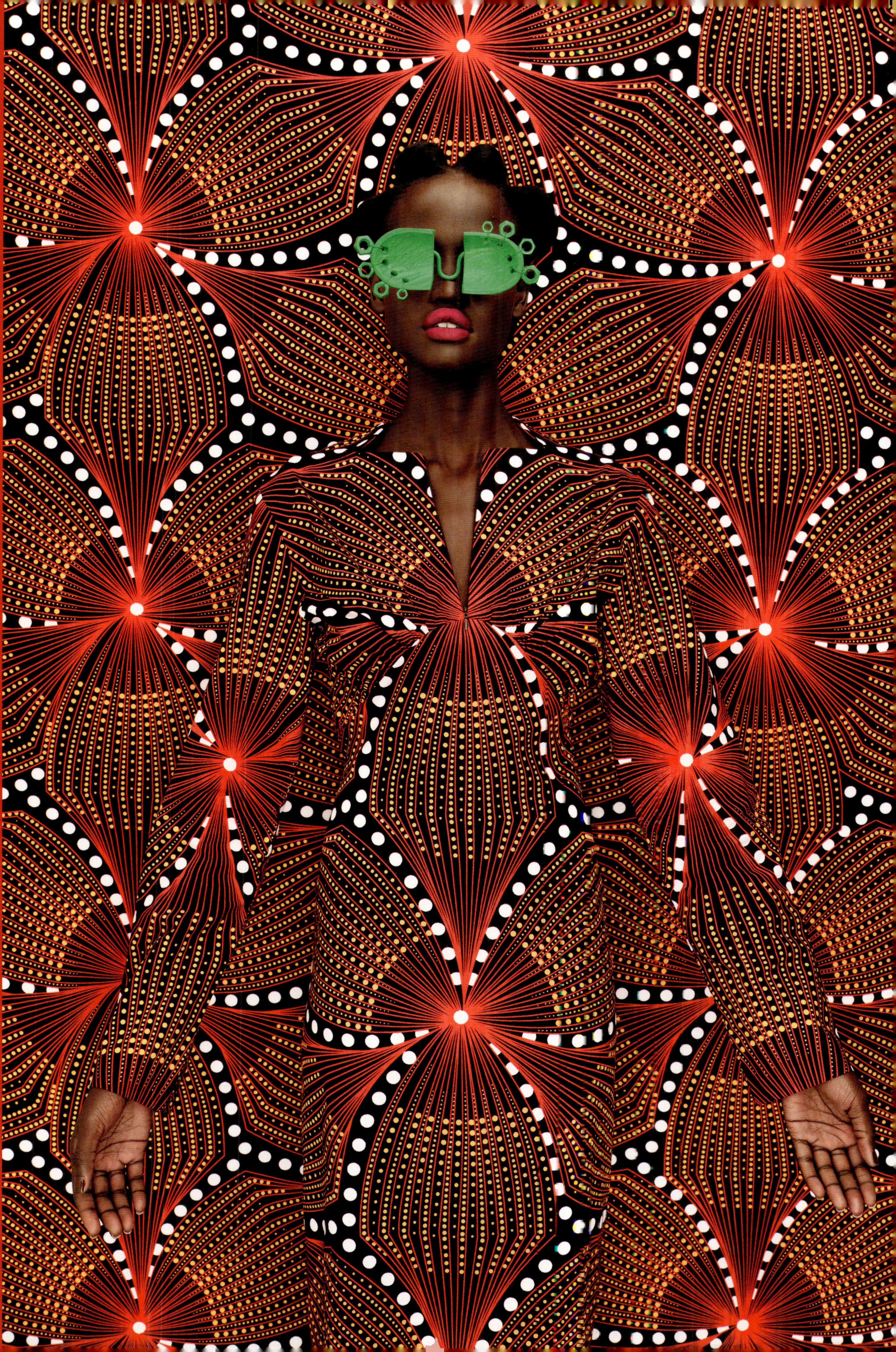

“Don’t count the many times a man falls but those times he rises up.”

“Usihesabu mara ngapi mtu huanguka lakini hesabu mara ngapi husimama tena.

It takes a courageous woman to welcome the depth and meaning that mistakes add to her life. They uncover the layers of true self and trigger her journey towards authenticity. She doesn’t need to have all the answers, but instead a teachable spirit: to try, to improve, and to learn.

Embracing imperfection turns stumbling blocks into stepping stones unlocking her power to rise above self doubt. Through her spirit, open to improvement and growth, a beautiful totem of wisdom and transformation unfolds.

Eyewear constructed from erasers.

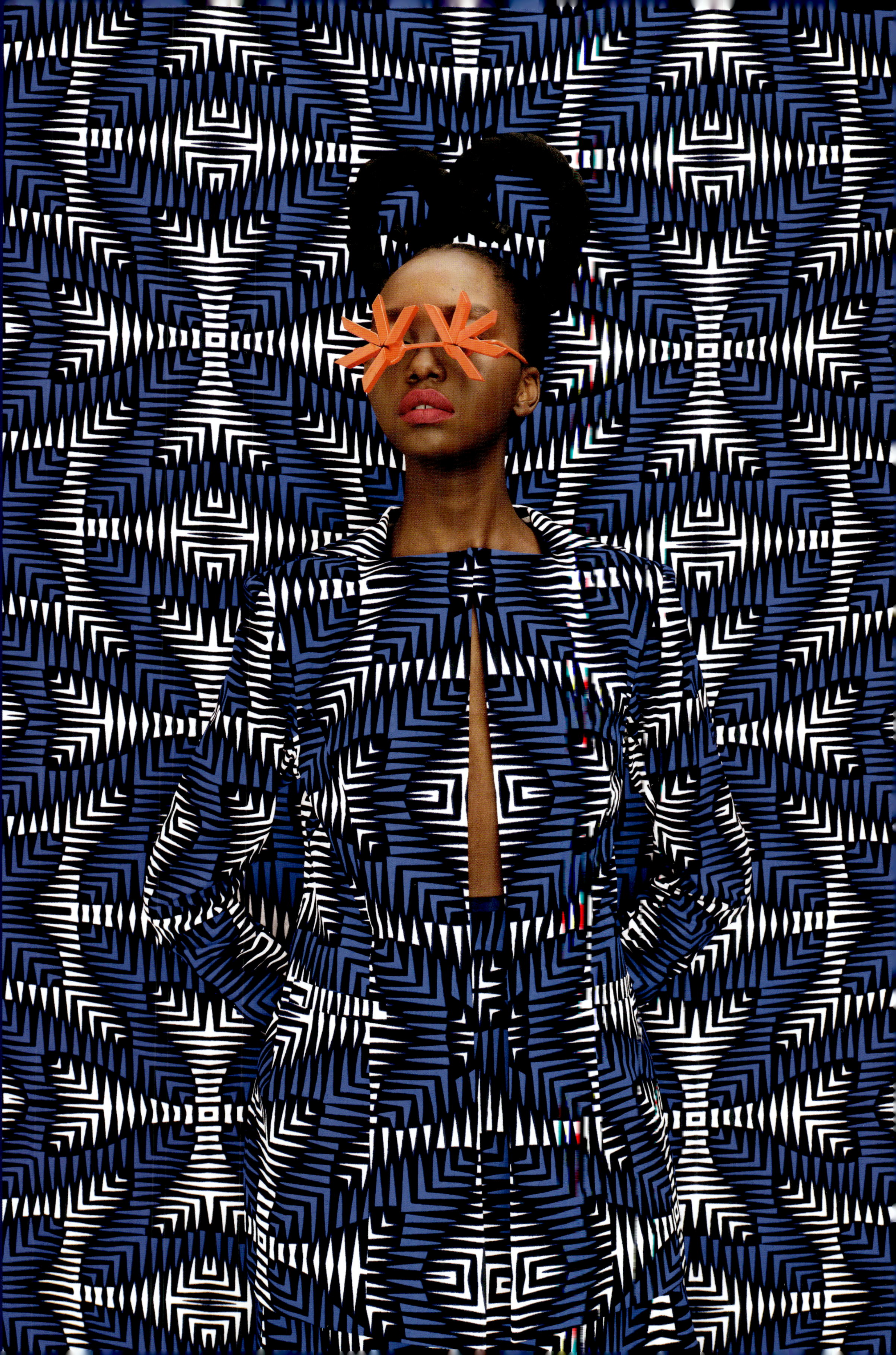

"Being blind doesn't mean one cannot dream or imagine."

"Kipofu pia huota na hufikiri."

A woman's dreams know no boundaries, transcending the limitations imposed by a society determined to define her. Victorious Dreams salutes the brave women, who fearlessly venture beyond the boundaries. They champion the spirit of visionaries, steadfastly charting their own course and inspiring others to do the same.

The awe-inspiring journeys of Faith Kipyegon and Allyson Felix transcend mere athletic achievement and have become global symbols of empowerment. Through unwavering determination, Faith Kipyegon has shattered multiple world records, while Allyson Felix fearlessly broke through barriers while experiencing the transformative journey of motherhood. These resounding victories are not just personal triumphs, but instead are catalysts to women of all walks of life, inspiring them to pursue their own personal victory and contribute to a future where a woman's dreams are boundless, unrestricted, and gloriously fulfilled.

Eyewear constructed from sieves.

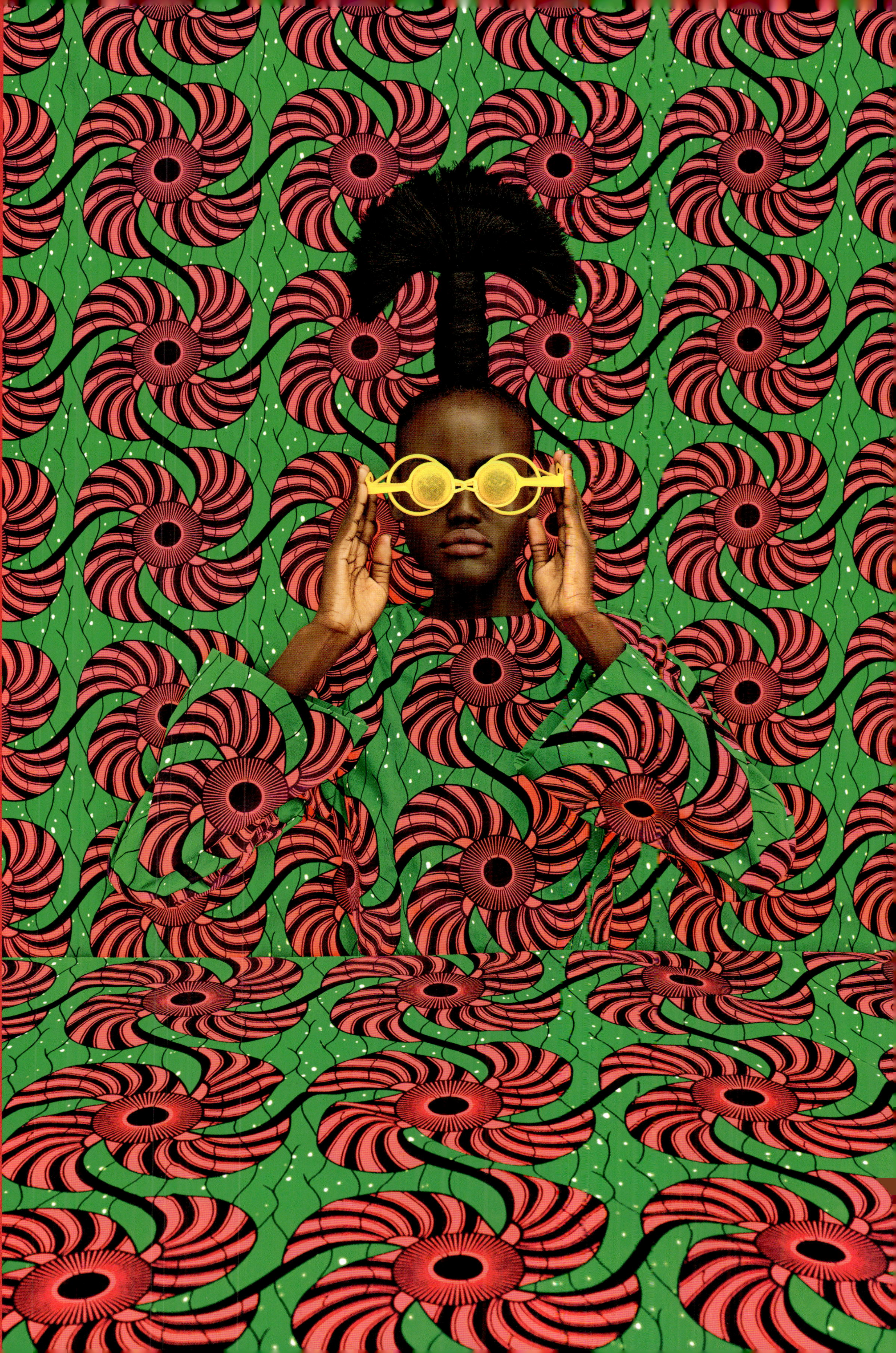

"You cannot beat a drum with one finger."

"Kidole kimoja hakipigi ngoma."

One of the greatest delights of being a woman is the countless options for self expression. Whether it is the playful abandon of dancing, the boldness of red lipstick, the loud warmth of a squeal of delight or the cathartic release of tears, women have many languages to vocalize their innermost feelings.

Spices in the feast of expression, these creative languages enliven interactions, offering cultural nuances. In the Kikuyu tribe of Kenya, it is the women's ululations, a jubilant vocal expression bursting forth from their lips, that informs the entire community of their newest member's gender. They perform a distinctive sequence—four repetitions for a girl and five repetitions for a boy, creating an audible celebration.

A myriad of sounds, dress and many other languages paint a picture of the inner world of a woman.

Eyewear constructed from door hinges.

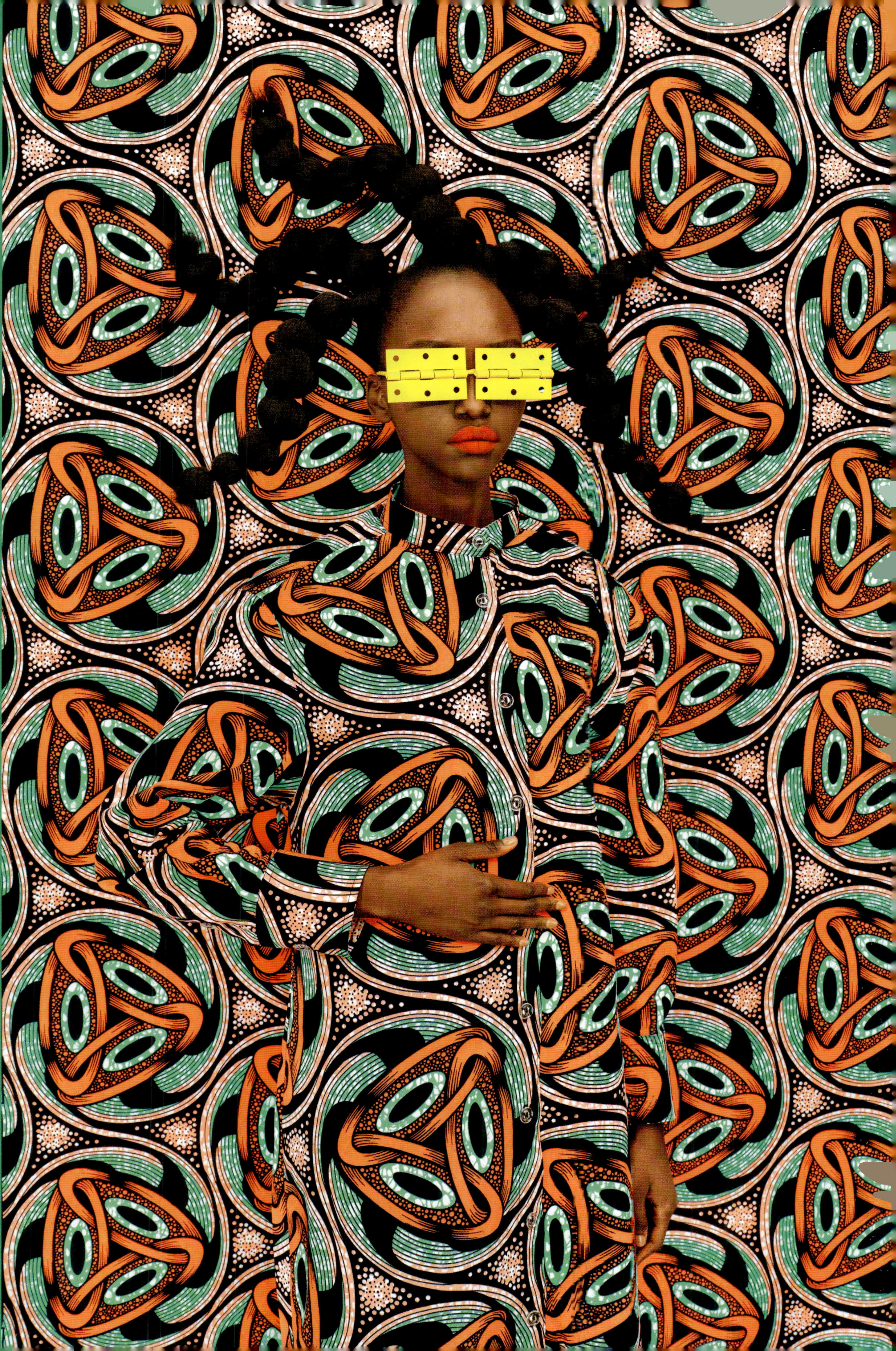

"When the roots are deep, there is no reason to fear the wind."

"Mizizi yenye kina haina hofu ya upepo."

Throughout the centuries, women have championed the winds of change. The present 21st century has heralded an unprecedented momentum towards battling the stereotypes of womanhood. In the midst of this cultural crossroad, a new woman has emerged—one who gracefully balances the realms of tradition and modernity. It takes discernment to navigate this new world and daily, African women sail above tradition to embrace the winds that propel them forward.

This change is especially evident in Kenya, where women have began to transcended traditional roles. Travelling through Nairobi could mean riding past a female construction worker, industriously reshaping the Nairobi skyline in her vibrant yellow hard hat. Public vehicles have been customarily driven by men, but in the bustling city, you might catch a glimpse of a woman behind the steering wheel of a matatu—a Kenyan taxi minibus. If luck is on your side, you may witness a female makanga—the Kenyan equivalent of a bus conductor—confidently herding her passengers onto the fast moving vehicle.

If pressed for time, you might even clutch at the shoulders of a female bodaboda rider as you move at hyperspeed on the back of her public transport motorbike maneuvering through crowded streets and congested traffic.

Eyewear constructed from sewing pin circles.

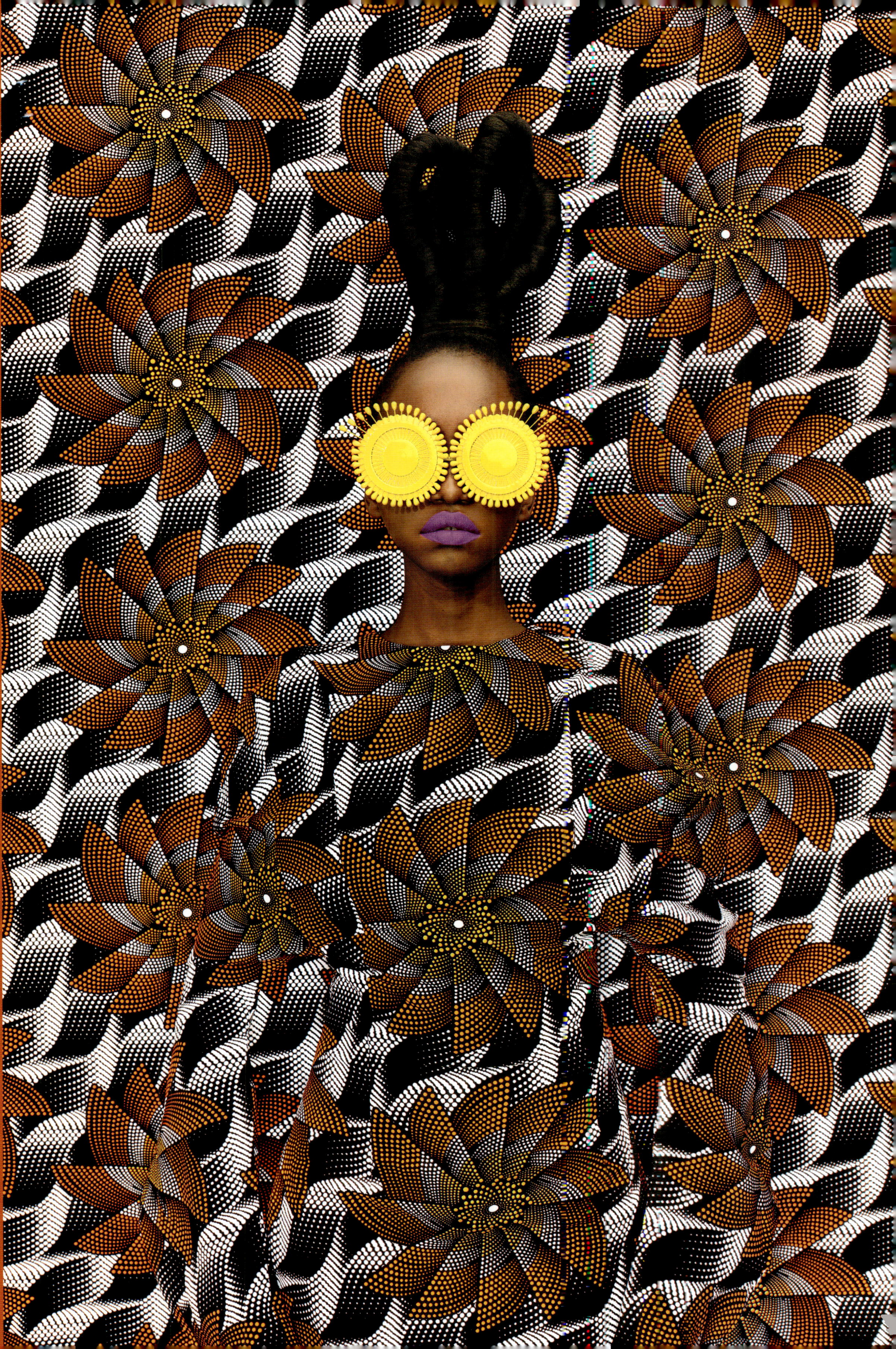

"The sky is wide enough for two birds to fly without their wings touching."

"Upana wa anga waruhusu ndege wawili kupaa bila mabawa yao kuguzana."

In many cultures, there is a strong emphasis on women prioritizing their roles as mothers and caregivers above all else. Historically, respect and status in society was measured by the number of children she had, if any.

In Kenya, this identity runs so deep that even in dress, a woman is linked to her children. Sunday afternoons bring the heartwarming sight of families, little ones in tow, dressed in meticulously curated outfits perfectly matched with the fabric of their mother's. They are guided towards gatherings where mothers take the opportunity to parade them before cooing relatives and acquaintances alike.

However, womanhood goes beyond the boundaries of motherhood, even with all its delights. It encompasses a wide range of experiences, identities, and relationships—the many dimensions that shape a woman. Her complete and perfect whole is drawn from these varied aspects coming together.

Eyewear constructed from door stoppers.

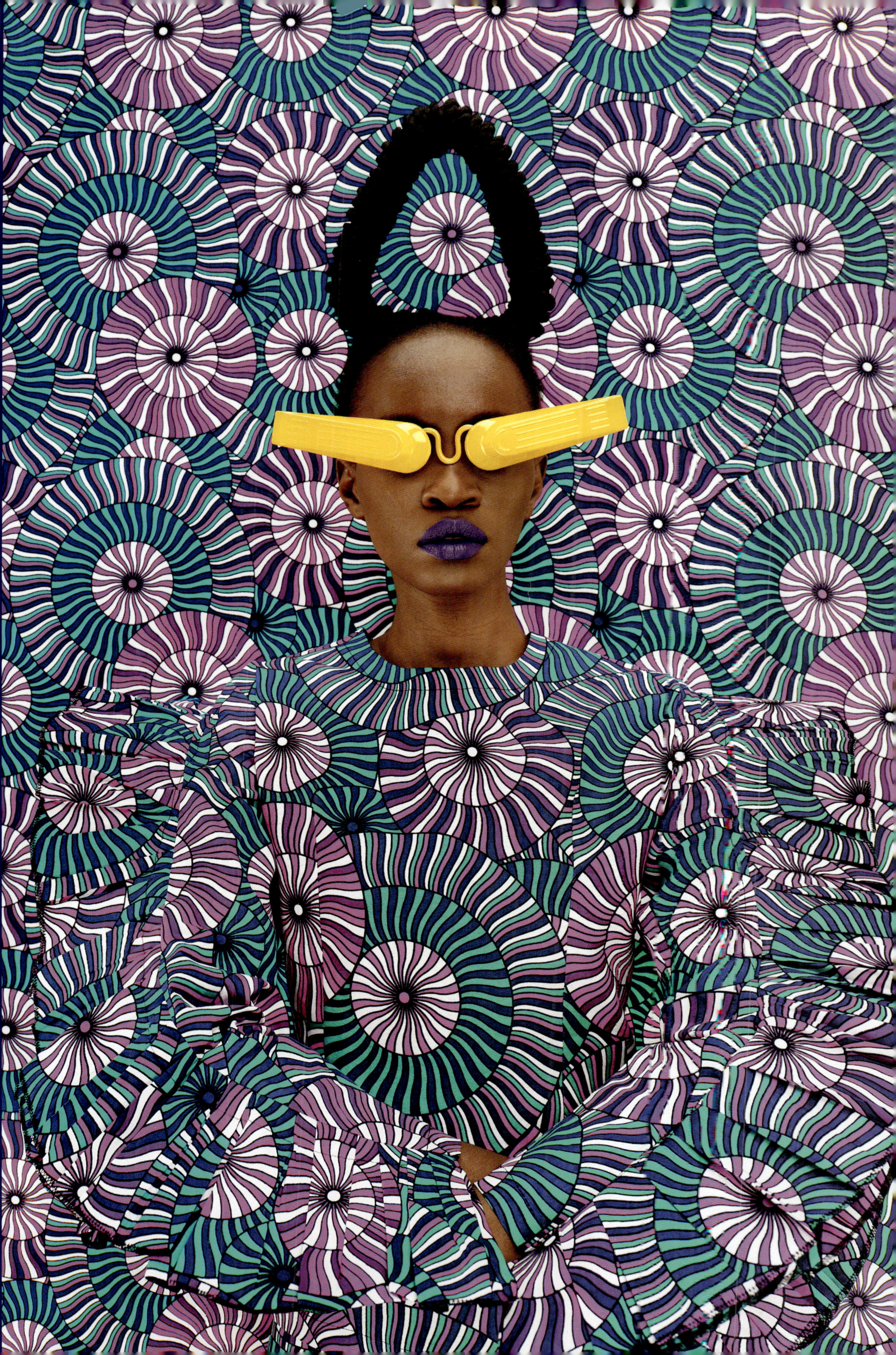

"It is not only giants that do great things."

"Sio majitu pekee wanaoweza fanya mambo makuu."

The coming together of women can produce great things. Their invisible labour—the small, simple, and seemingly meaningless things they do daily—produce sizeable results.

Whether it's a family gathering, a church fundraiser or a wedding in Kenya, to gather is to eat. Throughout festivities, there is often an invisible symphony of womens hands working in harmonious rhythm to sculpt sustenance out of maize flour and boiling water. From their teamwork, a mountain of the highly relished pillowy dough, called ugali, emerges. Served on large communal platters, the monumental steaming delicacy is mined by hands both big and small. As the towering wall comes down, previously unseen friends are noticed and warm satisfied greetings are exchanged.

With every stirring of the pot and sprinkling of flour, as aromas fill the air and laughter echoes, these women perform the miracle of satiating hungry masses. .

Eyewear constructed from kettle coils.

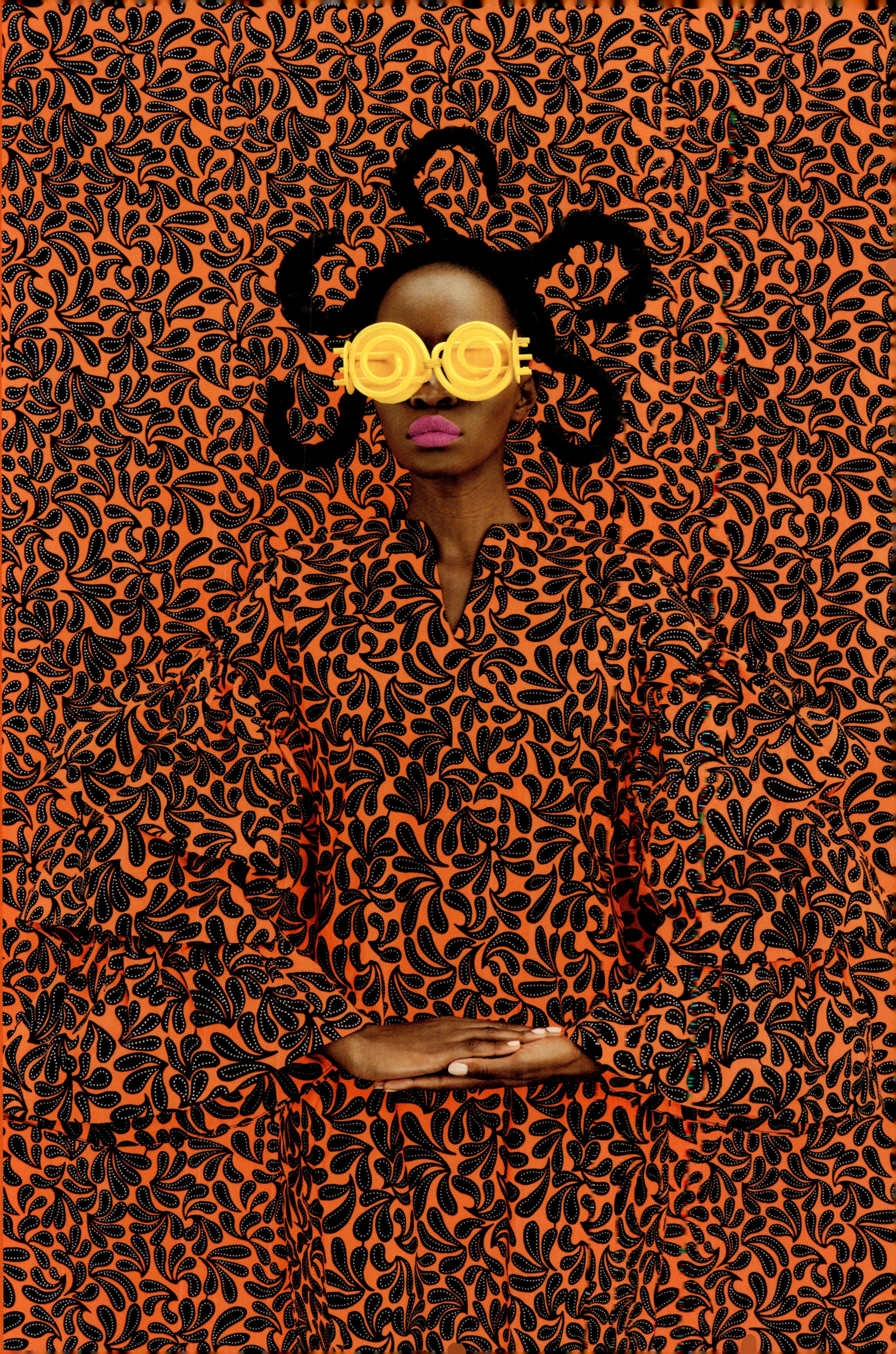

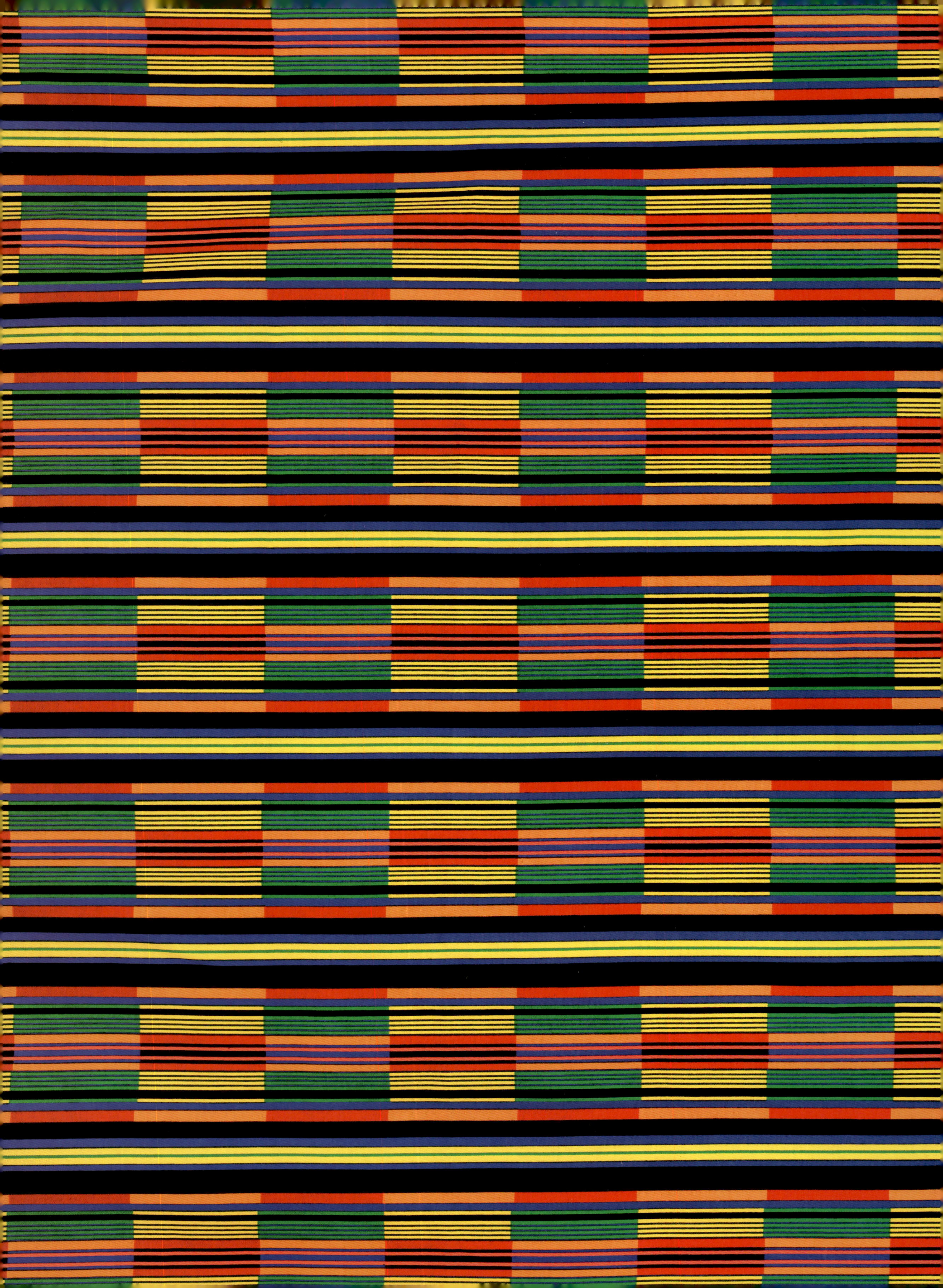

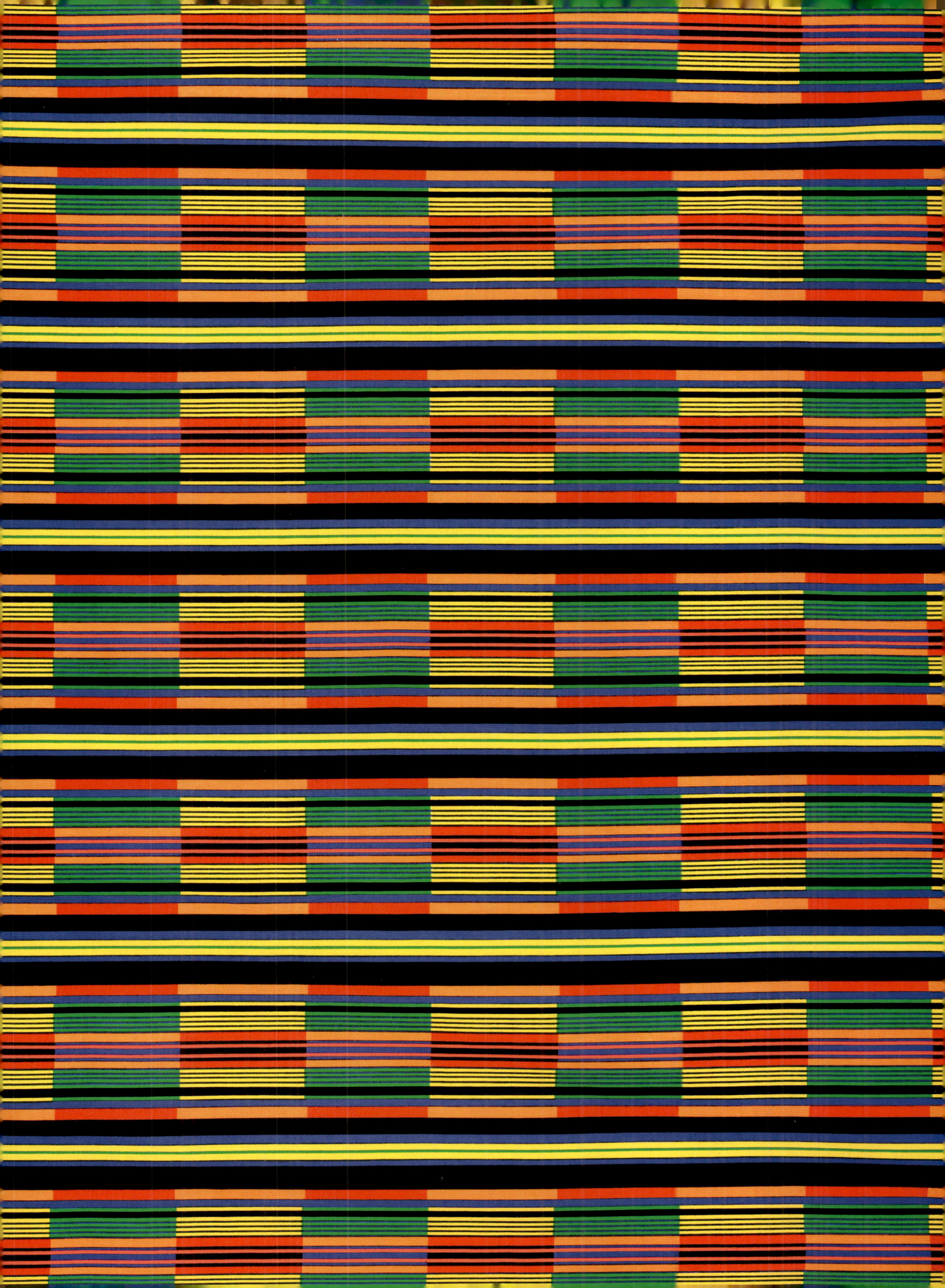

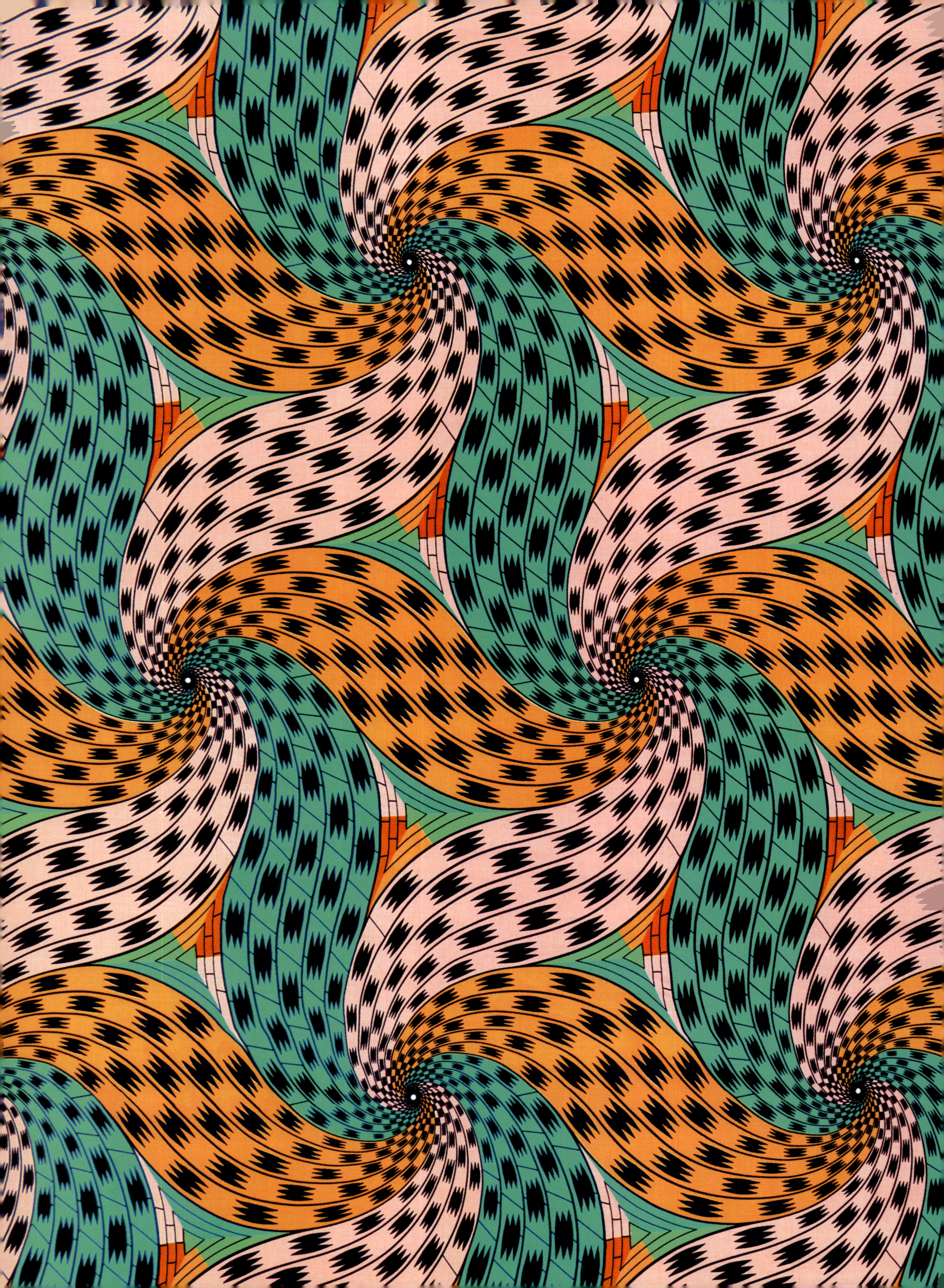

MATERIAL CULTURE

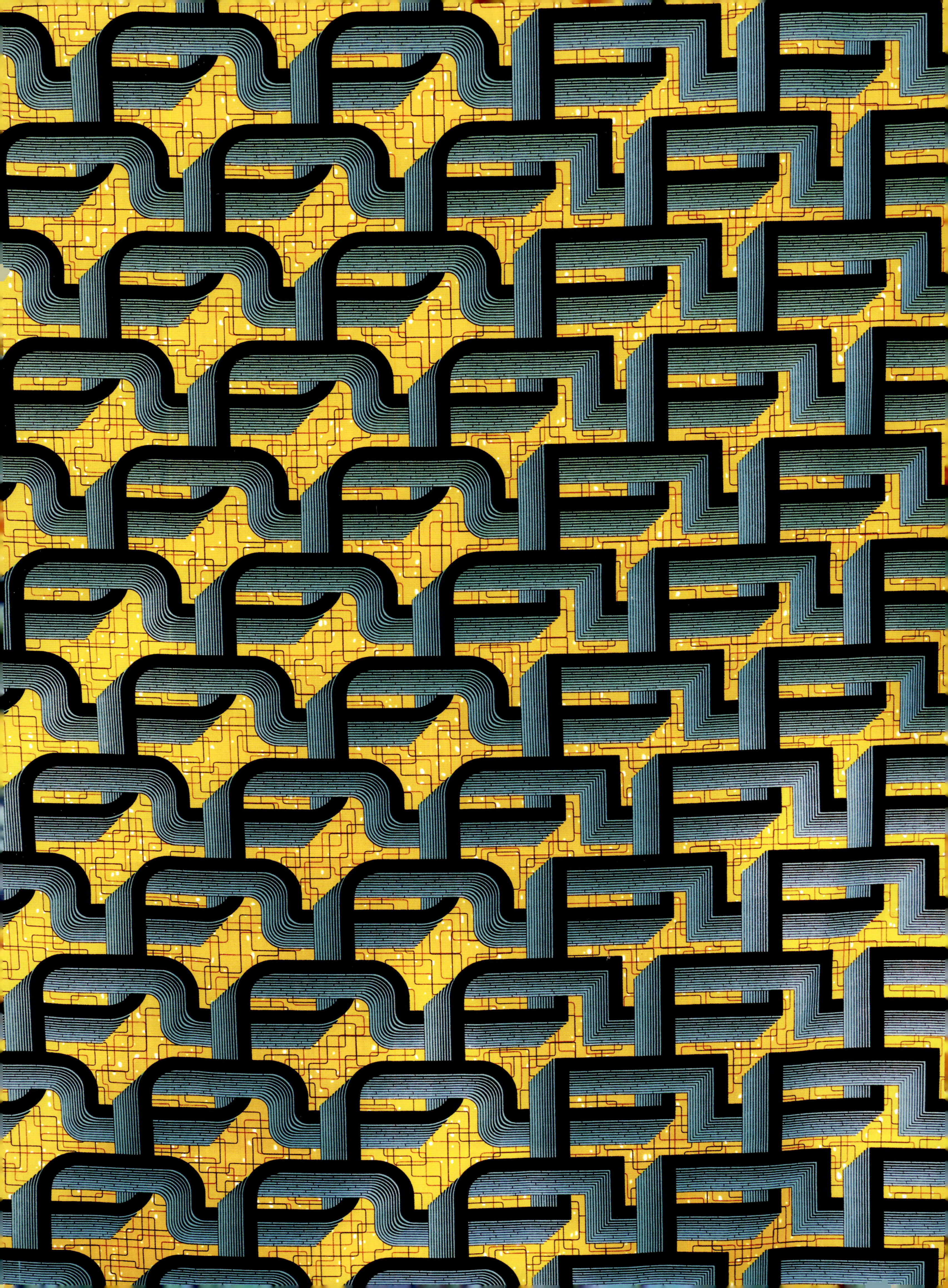

MATERIAL CULTURE

Headwraps are a key part of African culture. These colourful crowns hold immense significance during various social occasions like weddings, church gatherings, and other important social outings. The more prestigious the event, the larger and more elaborate the headwrap.

This body of work is inspired by this rich cultural heritage, one Thandiwe observed daily as her mother skillfully manipulated rolls of fabric into towering masterpieces in preparation for her weekly church attendance. No two headwraps are ever the same—they are draped for a transient moment and then gone as soon as they are taken off at the end of the day; and even if the same fabric, pins and method are repeated there will always be something new in the final drape.

Material Culture serves as a profound homage to the artistry of this beauty practise while inviting contemplation on the self-empowering nature of this ritual. Every time a woman puts on a headwrap, she adorns herself with the African equivalent of a regal coronet, the humble fabric transcends its material form, becoming an exquisite work of art that graces her head like the crown of a queen.

Sunday Best

English colloquialism, Kenya.

Eyewear constructed from baking whisks.

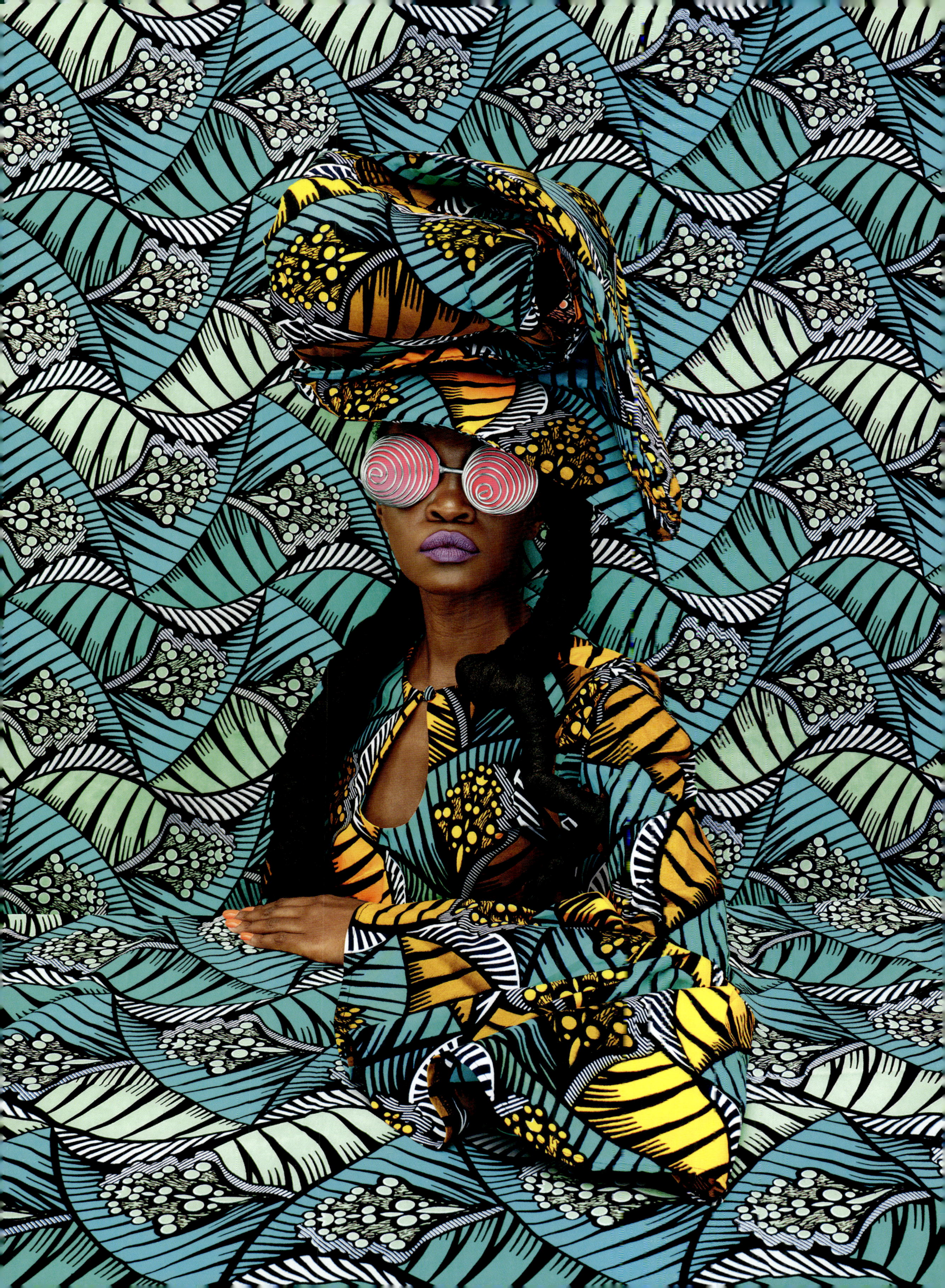

Rembeka

Meaning: to be beautified.
Swahili language, Kenya.

Earrings pay homage to the popular 'Pata pata' slipper in Kenya, used as an indoor slipper and spanking tool.

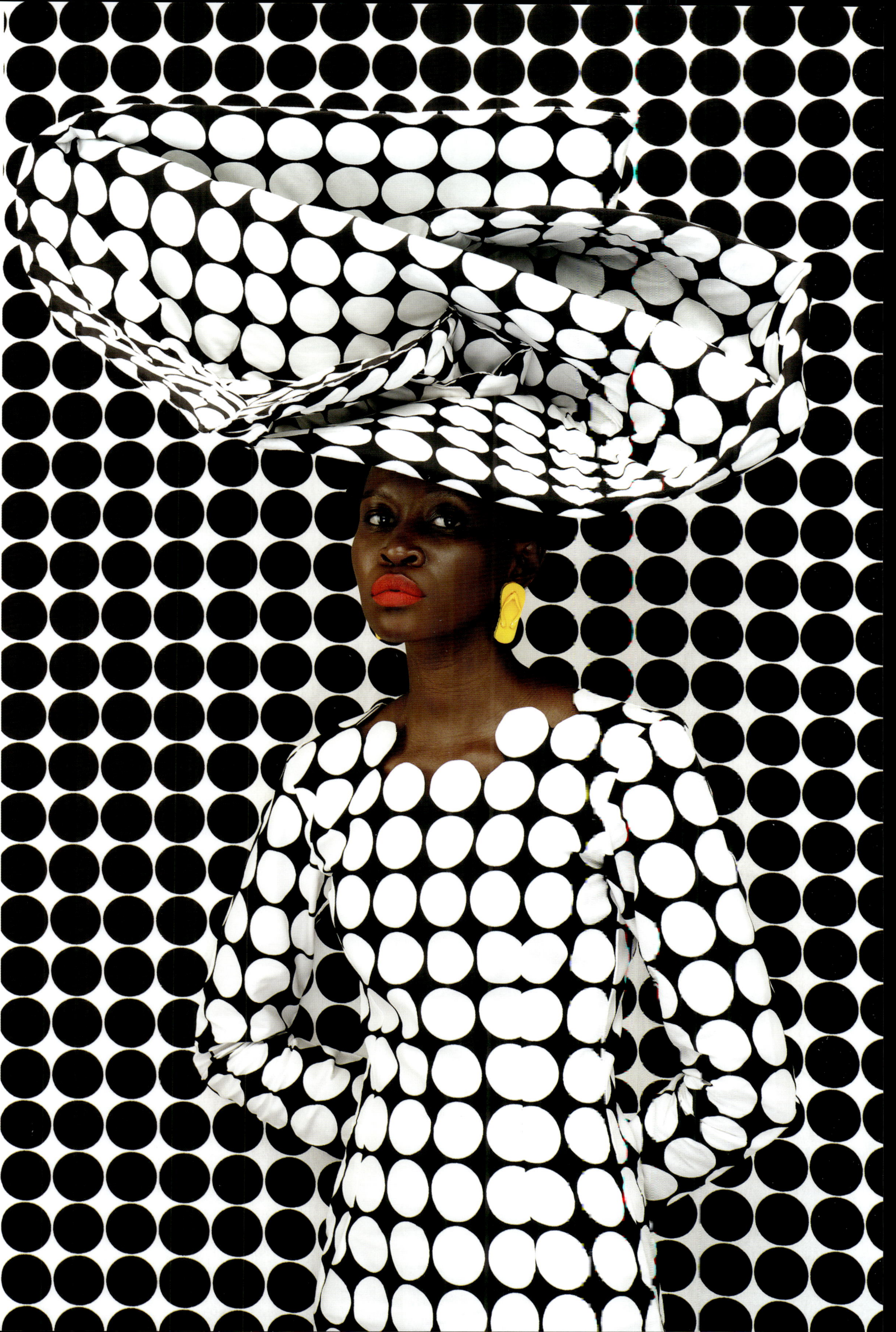

Maridadi

Meaning: beautiful with style or stylish beauty.
Swahili language, Kenya.

Eyewear constructed from bolts, nuts and washers.

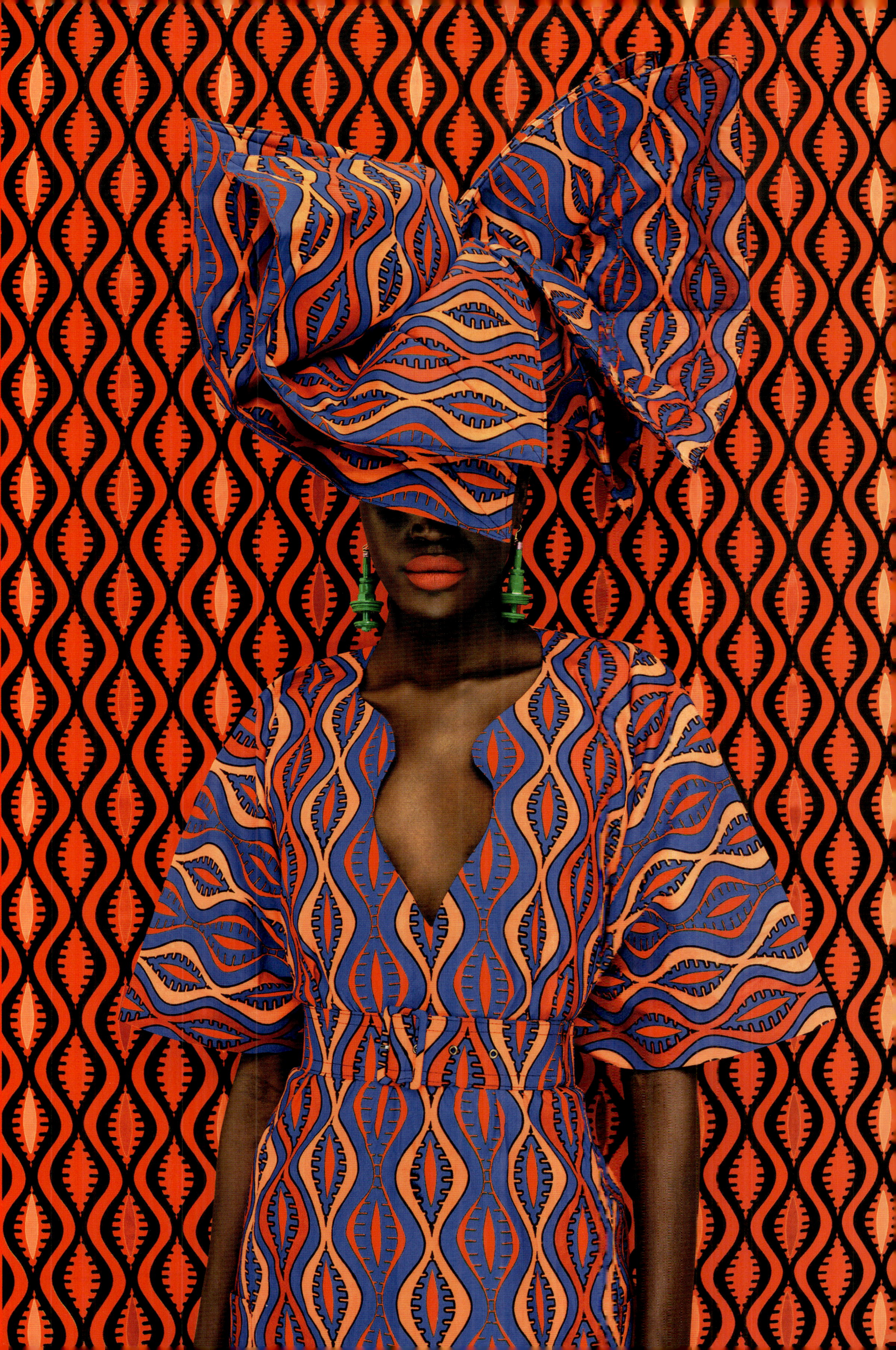

Madam President

Meaning: Liberian or Malawi female president
Chichewa colloquialism, Malawi.

Eyewear constructed from zips and beads.

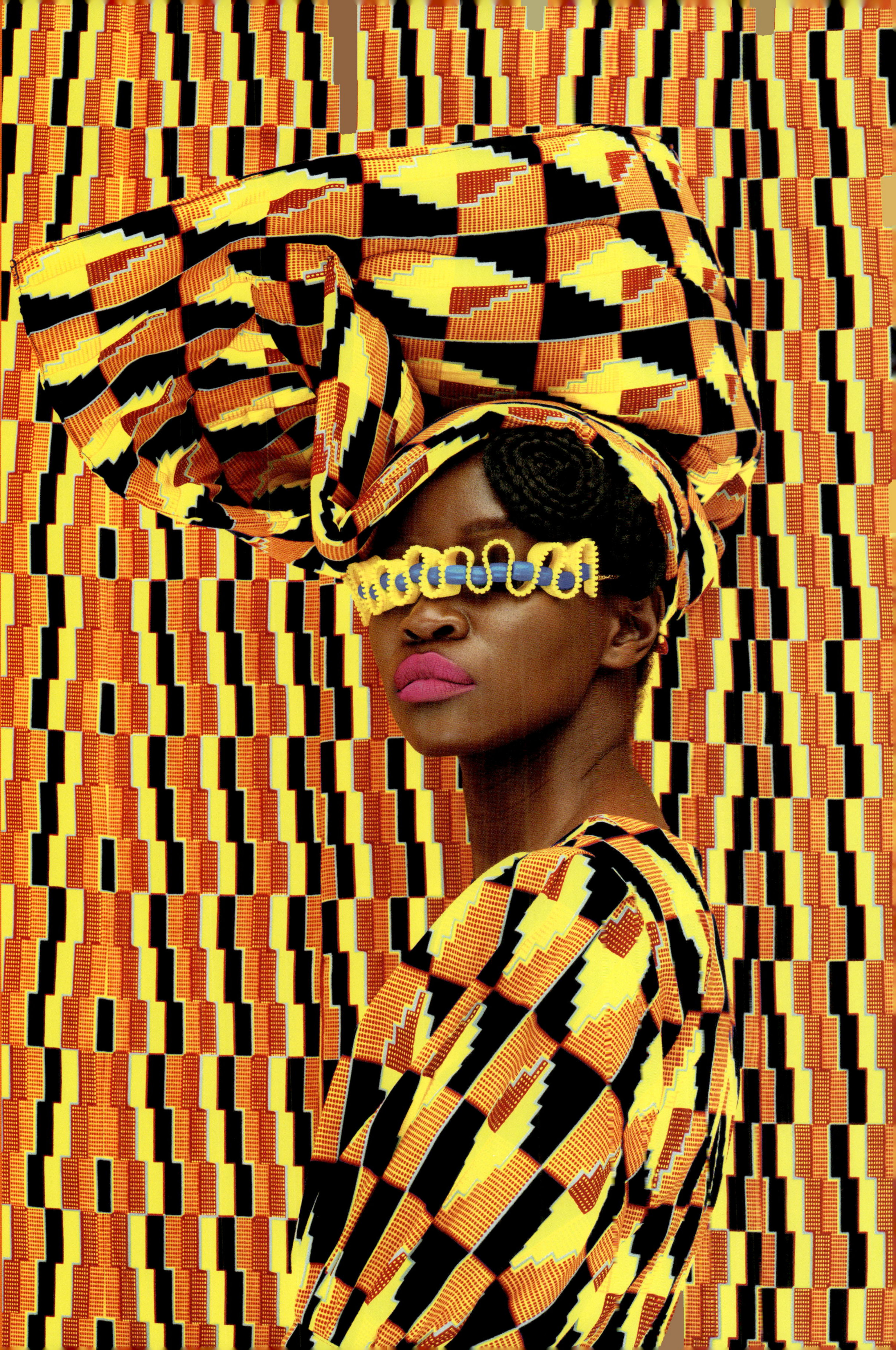

Eyewear constructed from pastry wheels.

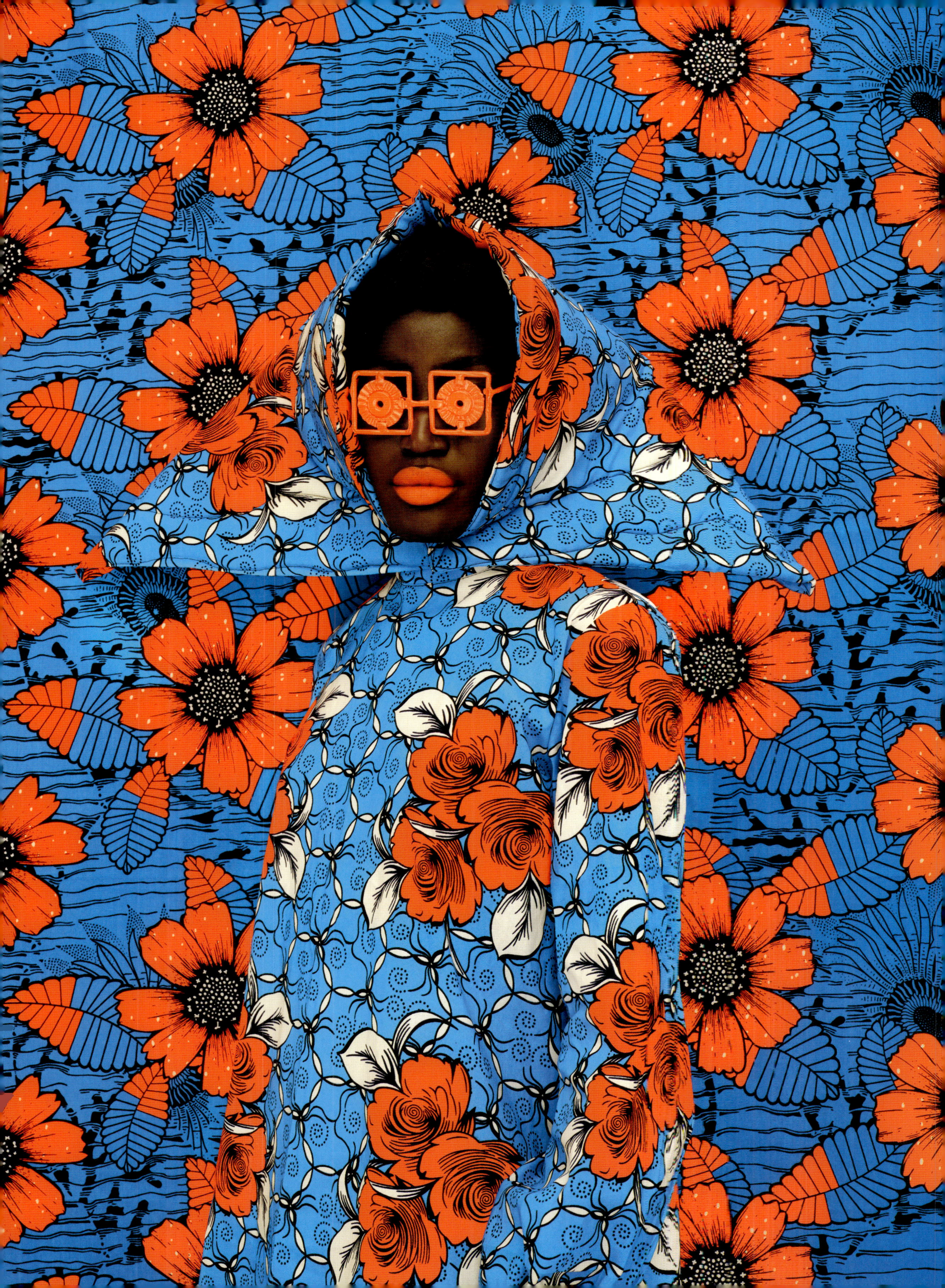

Eyewear constructed from pastry wheels.

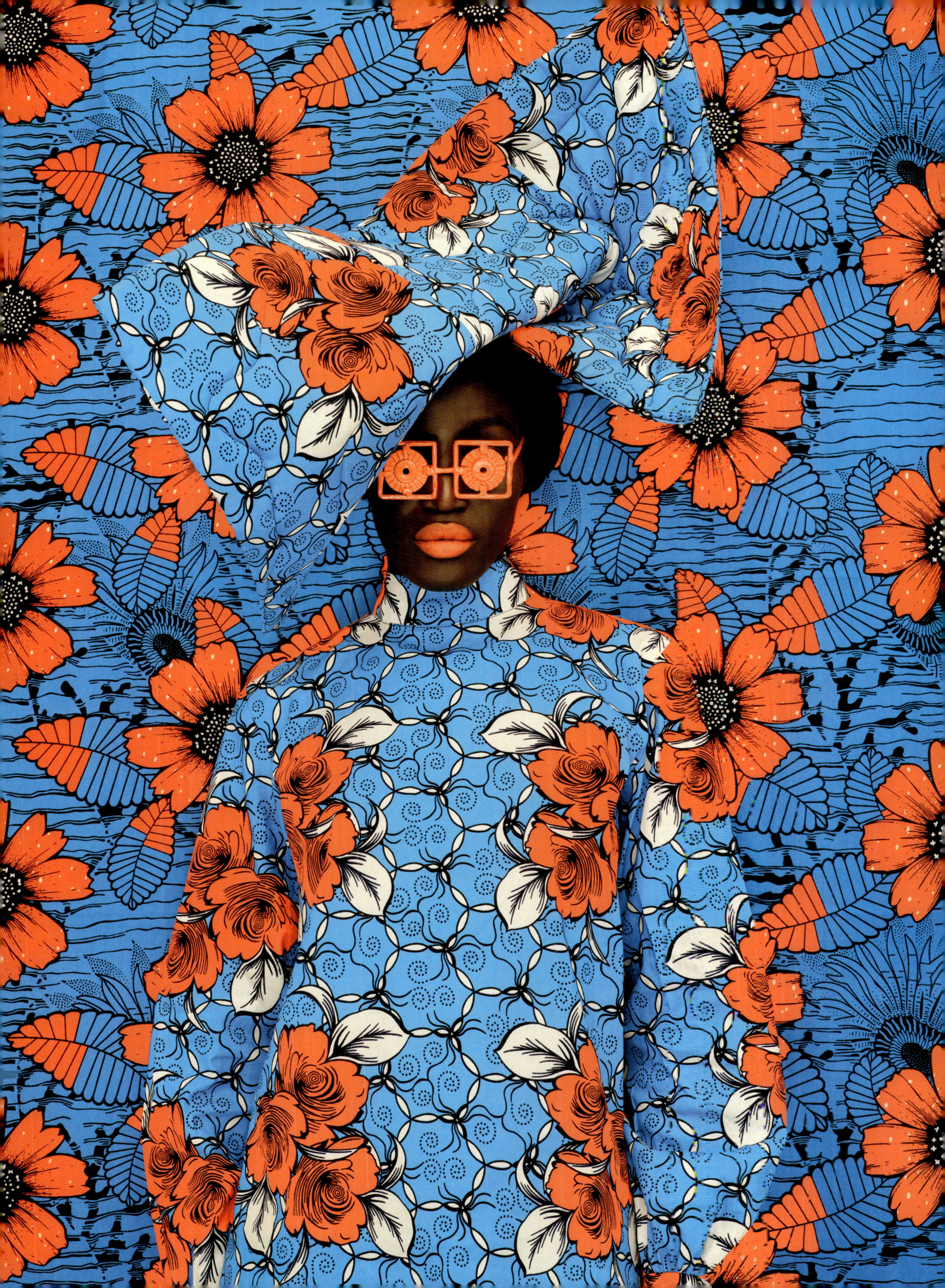

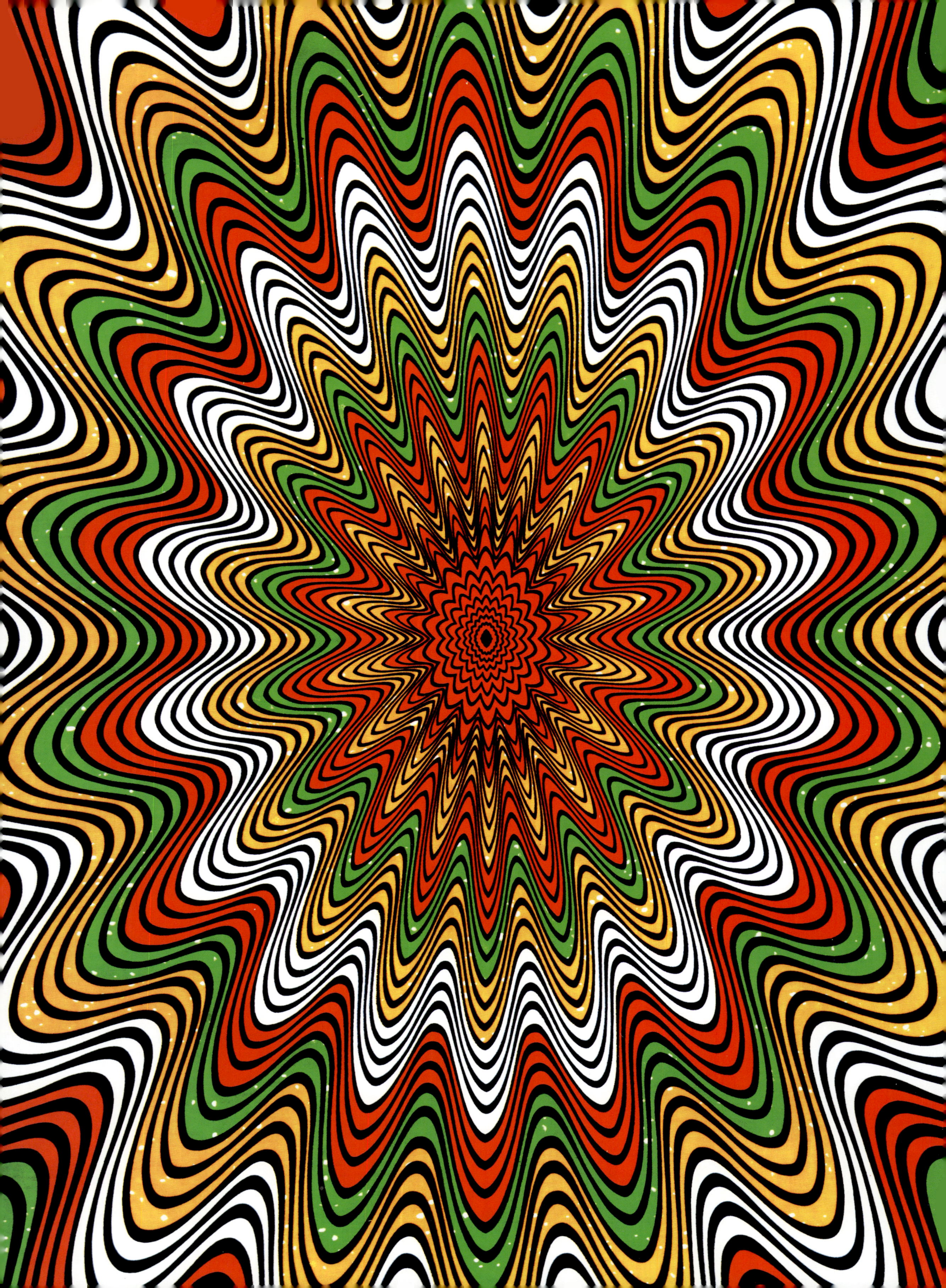

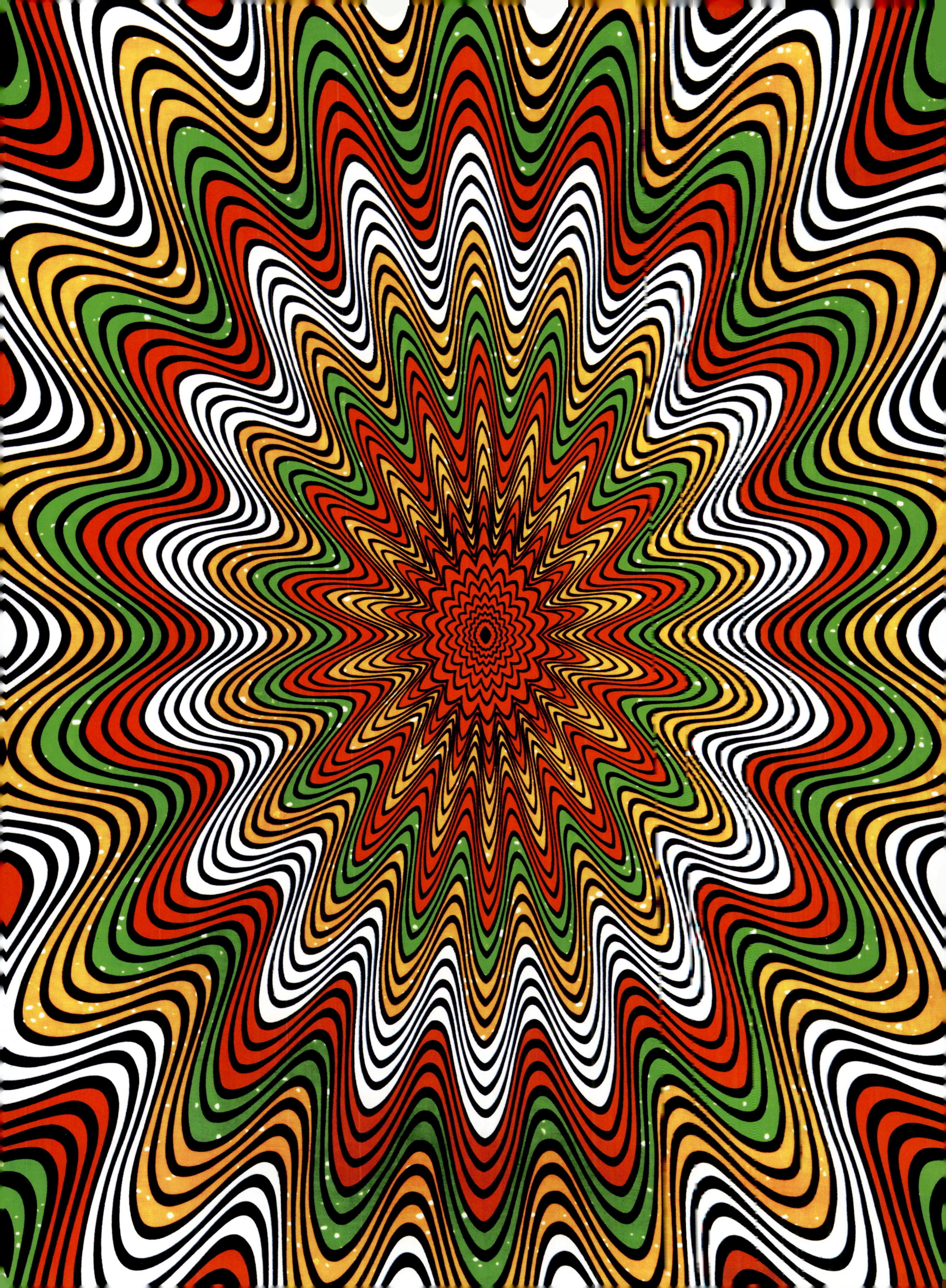

UNIVERSAL TRUTHS

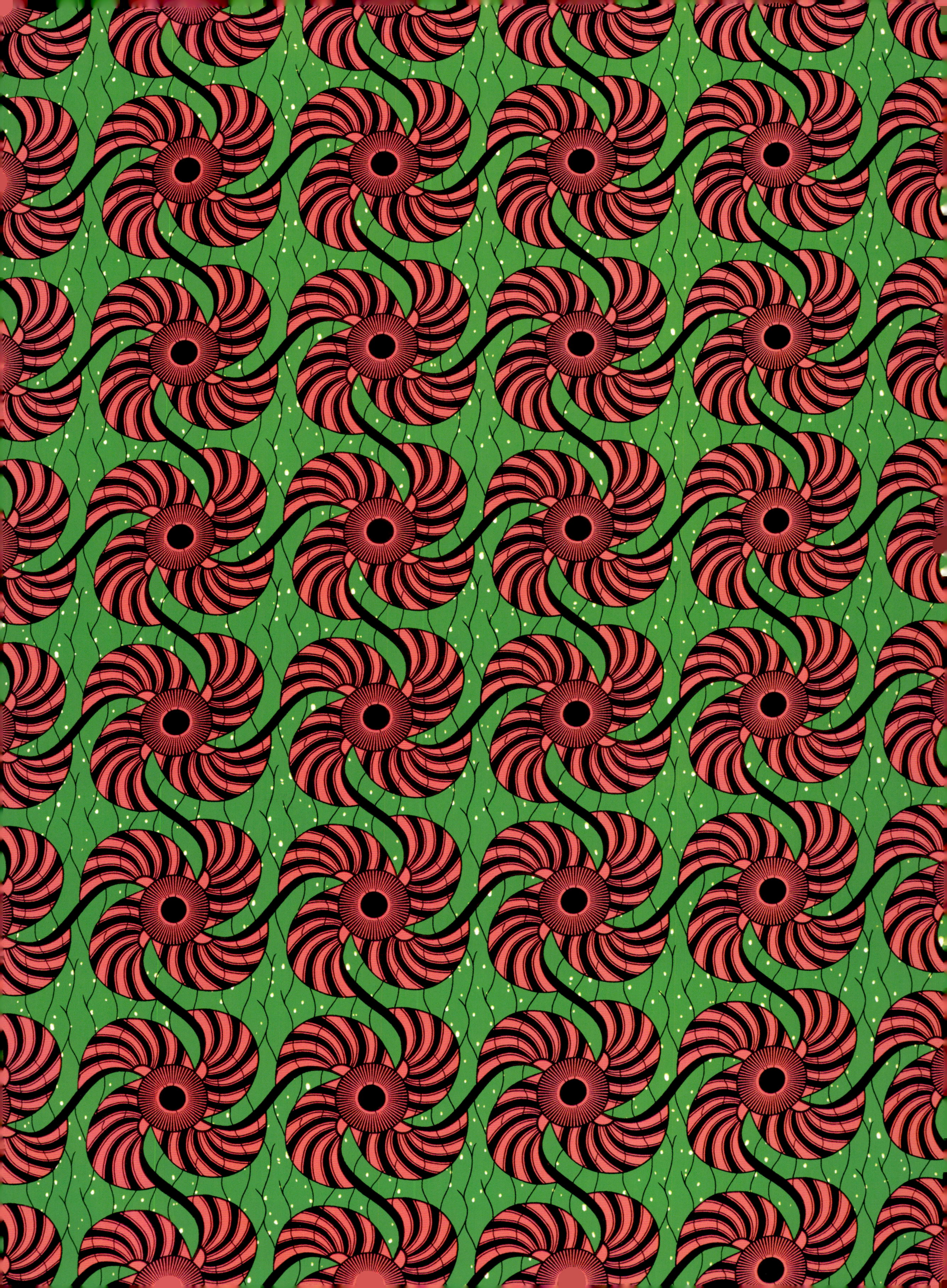

UNIVERSAL TRUTHS

"Universal Truths" explores the complexities of intimacy and the experiences transcending culture, country, and age, that connect all of us as human beings. At the core of humanity is the desire for connection, a longing for belonging.

Each culture responds to this call in distinct ways, delicately balancing the individual's need for communion while retaining independence. Within this vital equilibrium of connection lie some inescapable truths—conflict can exist where there is love, there is an inherent human pursuit of advancement, every soul is seeking a kindred spirit, support lifts a heavy heart.

This body of work is a visual discourse on the social intricacies of being and belonging, crafting a fable of the beauty of struggle underlying this eternal human yearning. Thandiwe's visual discourse forgos the superficial in favour of more meaningful, existential truths, inviting us to explore the presence of these perspectives in our lives.

"Unity is strength, division is weakness."

"Umoja ni nguvu, utengano ni udhaifu."

noun: unity
The state of forming a complete and harmonious whole.

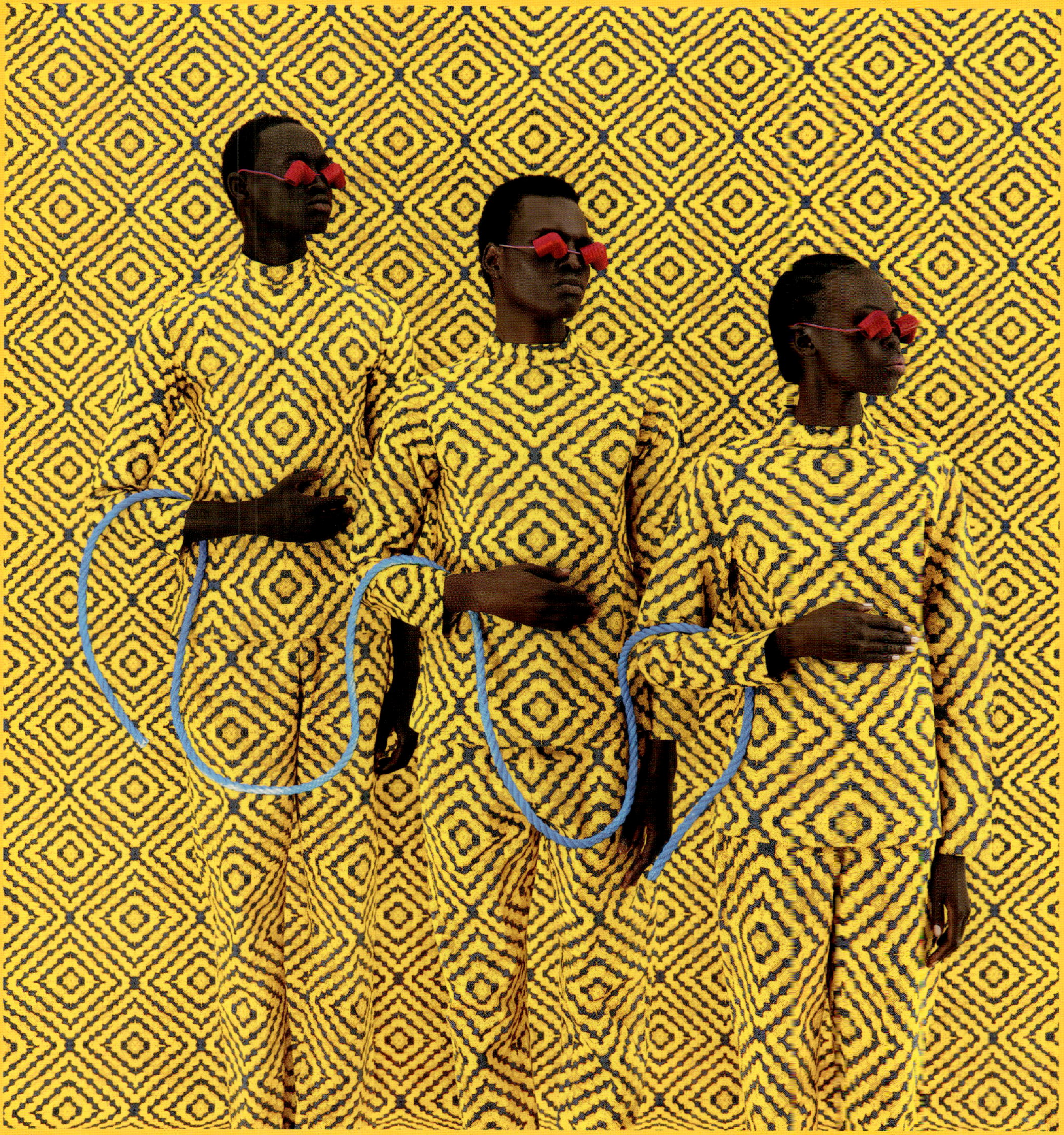

"A friend is someone who knows the song in your heart and can sing it back to you when you have forgotten the words."

"Rafiki ni mtu anayejua wimbo uliopo moyoni mwako na anaweza kukuimbia ukisahau mistari."

noun: brotherhood
A feeling of shared interests and support.

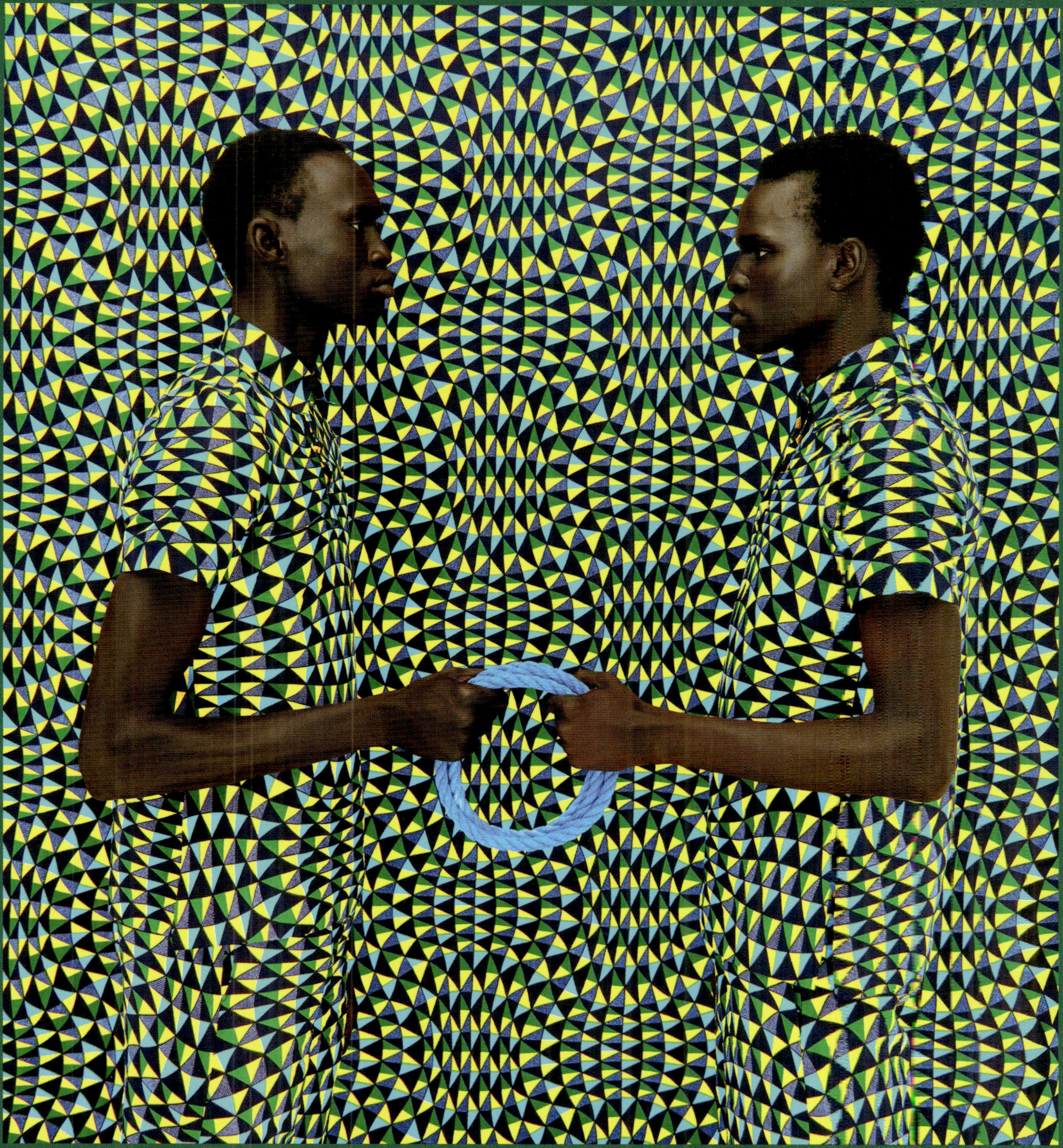

"Hope is a good thing and good things never die."

"Tumaini ni jambo zuri na mambo mazuri hayafi."

noun: discord
Lack of harmony between notes sounding together.

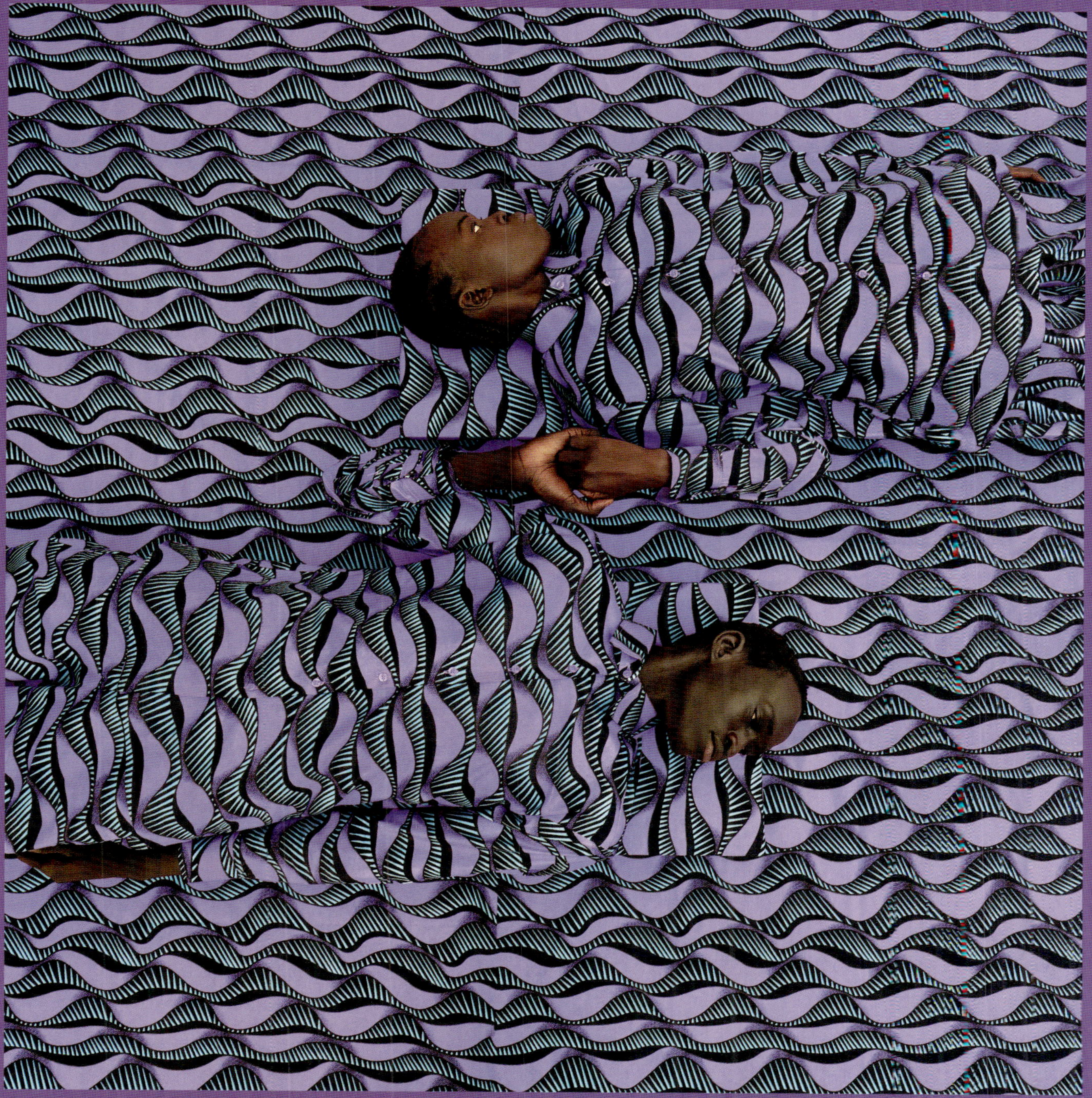

"If you want to go quickly,
go alone. If you want to go far,
go together."

*"Ukitaka kuenda haraka, enda
pekee yako. Ukitaka kuenda
mbali, enda na wenzako."*

noun: ascension
The act or process of ascending, rising or increasing to higher levels, values, or degrees.

The action of moving upwards.

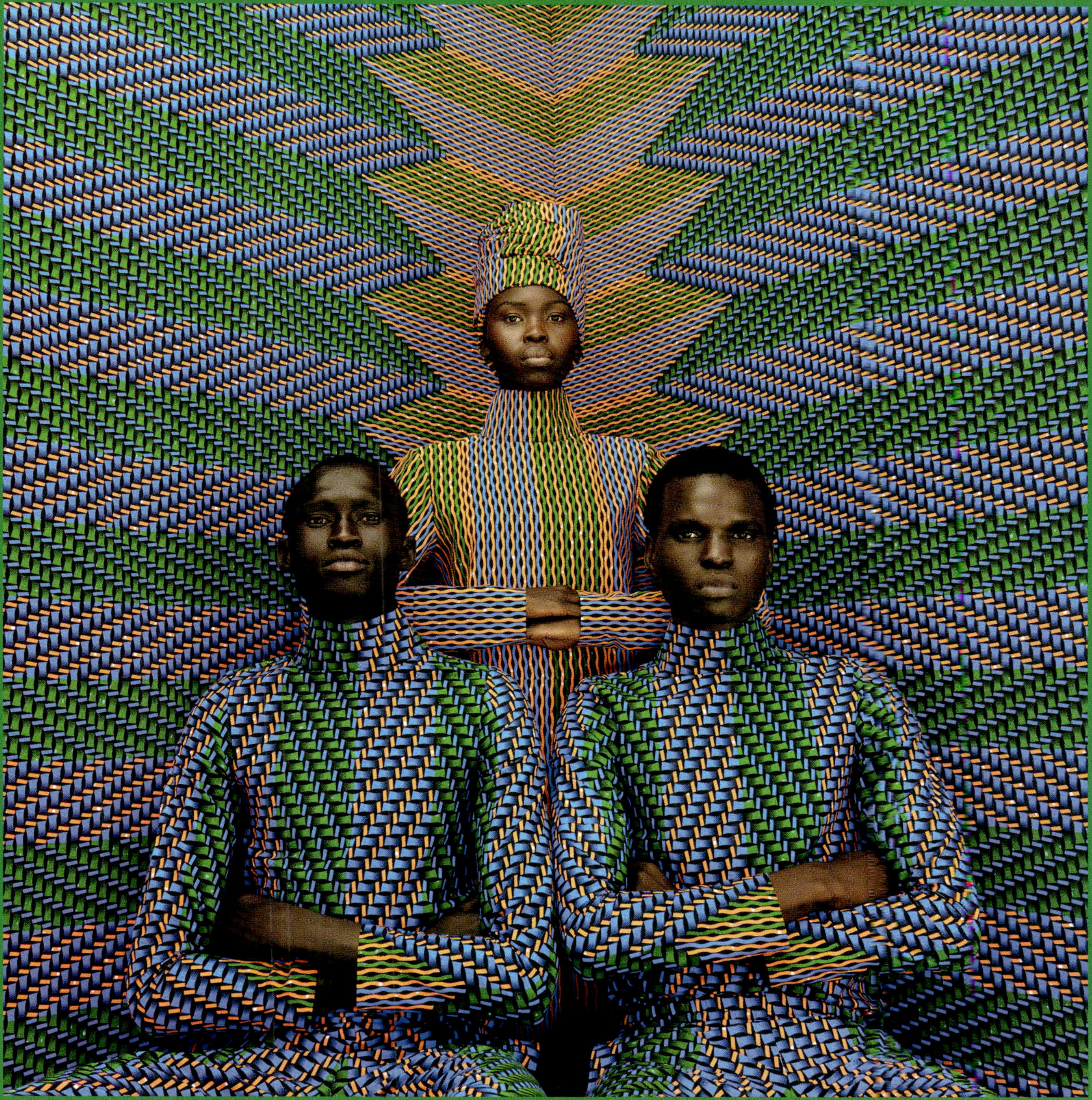

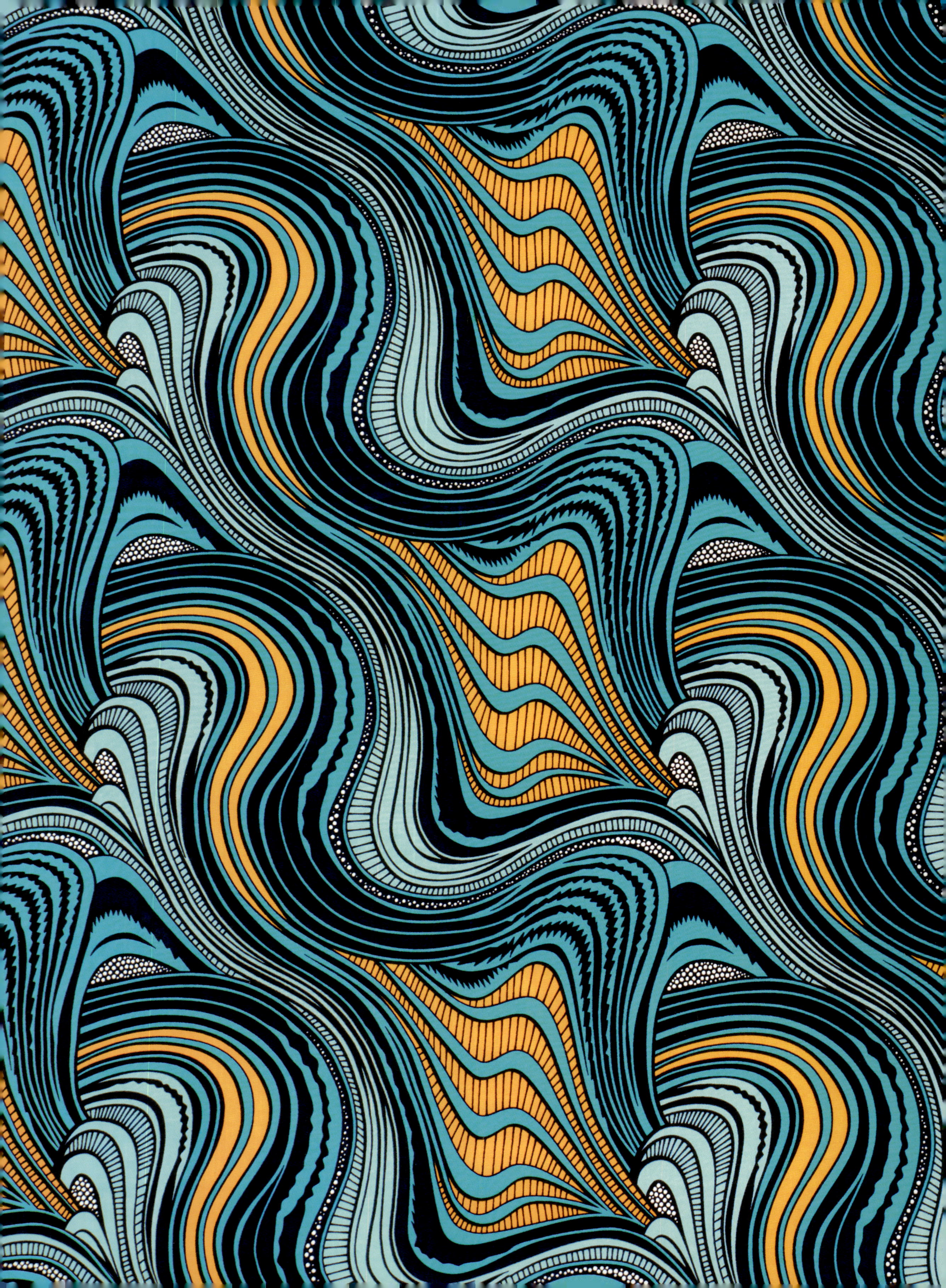

A GLOBAL LENS

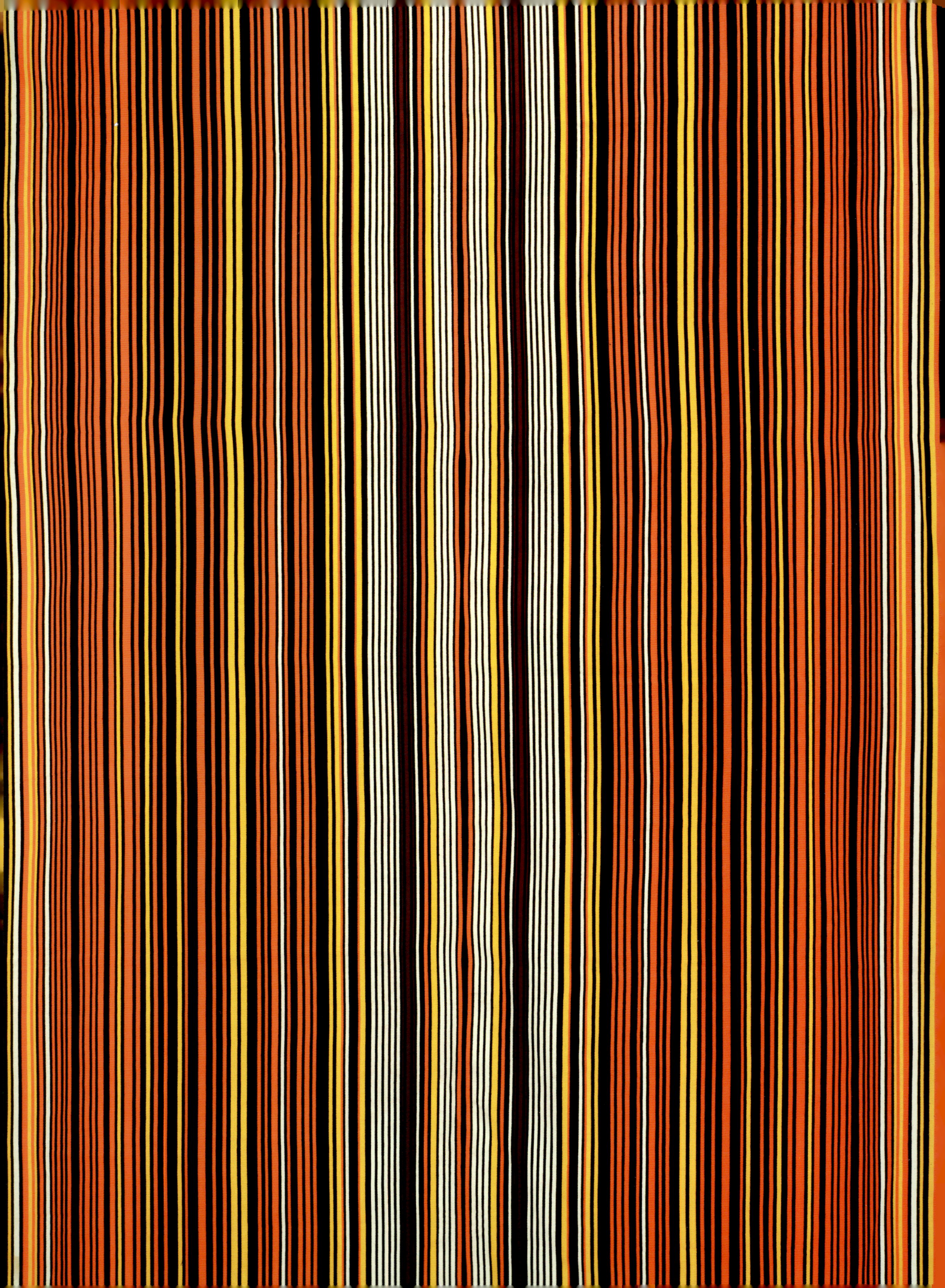

A GLOBAL LENS

Camo's uniqueness and ethos have opened new, unexpected doors. It has been a fulfilling adventure to have others connect with the body of work and assimilate my viewpoint and style to shape their projects.

There is a unique challenge to being an African-based creative. We face numerous issues in our attempts to travel across the globe. Access to visas is difficult. The application process is expensive, laborious, and without guarantee of success. There are often significant delays in processing times and extraneous stipulations that ultimately hinder our growth. Thankfully, Camo hangs on the walls of homes, galleries, and collections around the world. It transcends borders on my behalf.

Signing on with Institute, an agency that represents auteur-driven storytellers, further amplified the journey of my work. Institute afforded an opportunity to fuse my message with the well-recognized stories of high-value entities like Apple, the United Nations, and National Geographic, to name a few. I became the first African female photographer to shoot the prestigious Lavazza Calendar. Eager to show them my *New Africa*, I invited some of these brands to collaborate with me and my creative community in Nairobi. This was the first time many of these partners had travelled to Africa. I'm glad Camo became their gateway to a fresh perspective on the continent. And now this on-site Nairobi interaction has become part of the creative process I offer.

The symbols in the images may change, but the heart of the work remains. The mastery and grace of the Kenyan woman was at the core of the Dior commissioned work, *A Tapestry of Dreams*. An iconic Lady Dior bag resting daintily on my subject's head draws an elegant parallel to the stacks of firewood balanced on that of a countryside woman. Working with the Swiss Red Cross involved creating an image where hand-wound stethoscopes became eyewear, symbolic of the impactful medical care the organisation provides. No matter the partner, no matter the project, Camo's core values reverberate throughout the resulting image.

It is incredible the power a photograph holds. It provokes necessary dialogue and forges new connections. Building relationships in this way becomes transformative. Working with these collaborators in my city, with elements from my world melded to their creative ideas for a global audience, encourages a vibrant cultural exchange. The result? Camo's message of a self-assured woman continues to travel throughout the world and is stronger in its resonance. "If you want to go quickly, go alone. If you want to go far, go together" (African Proverb).

"With a little seed of imagination you can grow a field of hope."

"Ukiwa na mbegu ndogo ya dhana unaweza kukuza shamba la tumaini."

Across the undulating Kenyan coffee fields, rows upon rows of women gracefully move, their presence a symphony as their baskets fill with the berries of their labor, their laughter and stories mingling under the warm Kenyan sun.

These coffee berries adorn the subject's glasses in this work commissioned by Lavazza. The renowned coffee brand made the complete genome sequencing of Coffea Arabica fully available to the public for the first time. This groundbreaking effort will help the scientific community, symbolized by the subject's stylish lab coat, study solutions to combat the impact of climate change and improve the quality of coffee in your cup.

Woven into the fabric of Kenya's economy, coffee stands tall as one of its major exports, ranking as the third largest contributor to the country's GDP. This thriving industry owes its success to the diligent hands of the locals, particularly a group of industrious women who play a crucial role in the bountiful harvest. Baskets brimming with freshly picked coffee, they gather in loose circles, their experienced hands expertly sorting and grading the precious fruit. Their gentle touch and practiced techniques ensure that only the finest beans find their way into the cups of coffee enthusiasts around the world. The Crown of Curiosity encapsulates the essence of the women working diligently in the coffee fields, collectively shaping an economy. As the day draws to a close, songs of joy and hard work fill the air, an anthem of the Kenyan spirit that resounds through time. It is a spirit defined by strength, unity, and a commitment to agricultural excellence.

Eyewear constructed from coffee berries and filters.

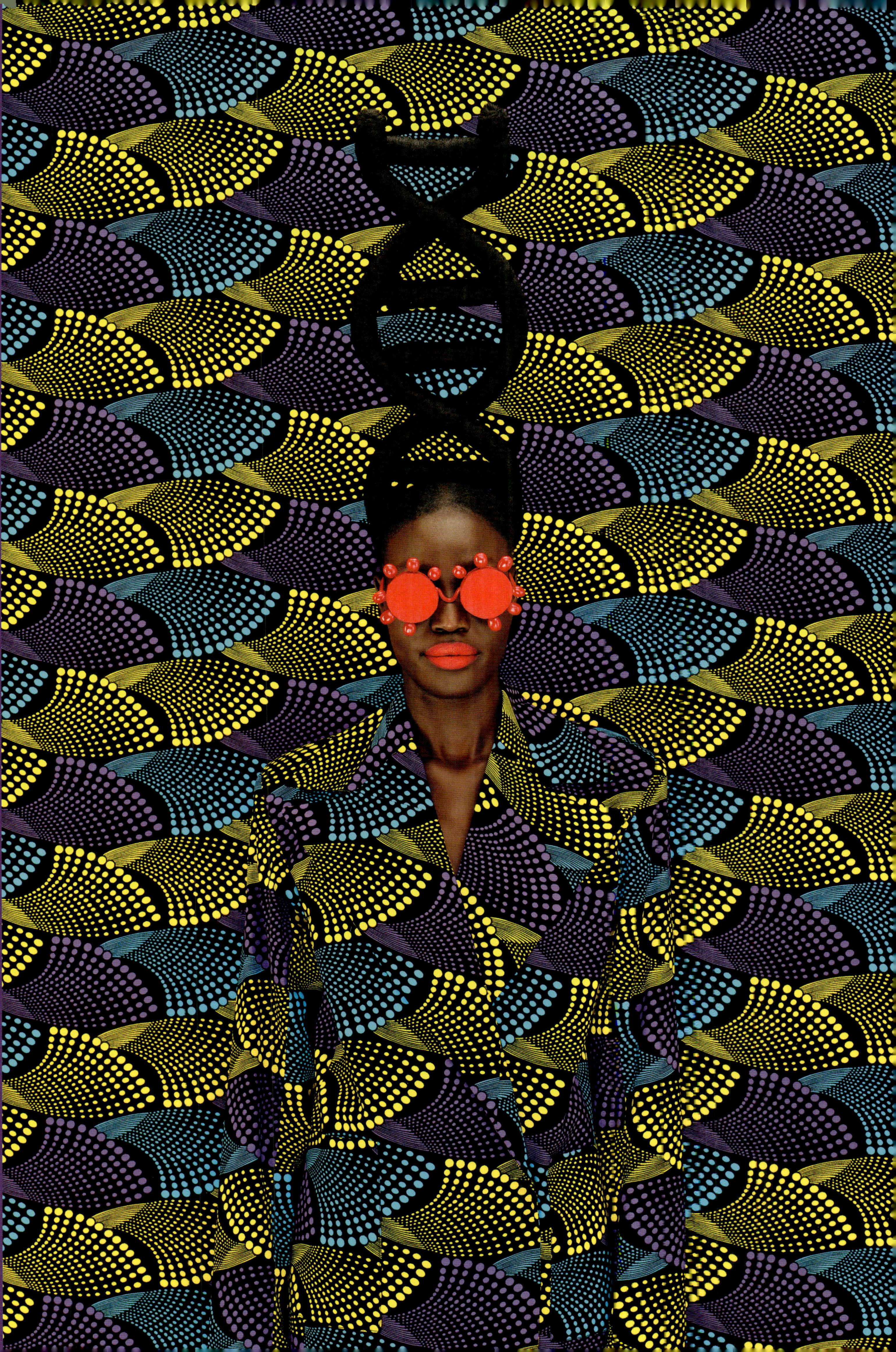

"There is no beauty but the beauty of action."

"Hakuna urembo, bali ule wa vitendo."

Commissioned by the Swiss Red Cross in relation to their activities with mothers and children in Togo, "Pillar of Courage" addresses universal challenges faced by many African countries, particularly the lack of access to adequate medical care for those living in impoverished conditions. This medical obstacle experienced by some Togolese women is many times reflected in Kenya.

It is this awareness that directed Thandiwe's reimagination of stethoscopes into mesmerising eyewear; symbolic of the medical care provided by the Swiss Red Cross. Within Togo, their medical partnerships and their rapid response during times of crisis highlight the beauty of taking immediate action to safeguard the well-being of mothers and children.

Tradition, innovation, and compassion are at the core of this piece. Pillar of Courage beautifully combines the elegance of Togo with the historical significance of its lavish kente cloth, a fabric traditionally worn by the Ewe people. Textiles are often overlooked as an art form, yet they possess the power to capture the history and cultural identity of a people; they are as dynamic as those who wear them. The cultural reference in this image extends beyond the textile to the subject's dress, which takes inspiration from the pagne, a distinctive traditional attire from Togo. Traditionally, the pagne is a long rectangular cloth wrapped tightly around the torso, with loose ends flowing freely. In this image, the subject's dress reimagines the pagne, transforming it into an elegant and asymmetric statement piece. Working with an ankara textile that features the kente's distinct patterns , it is this depth of tradition that grounds Thandiwe's message.

Eyewear constructed from stethoscope.

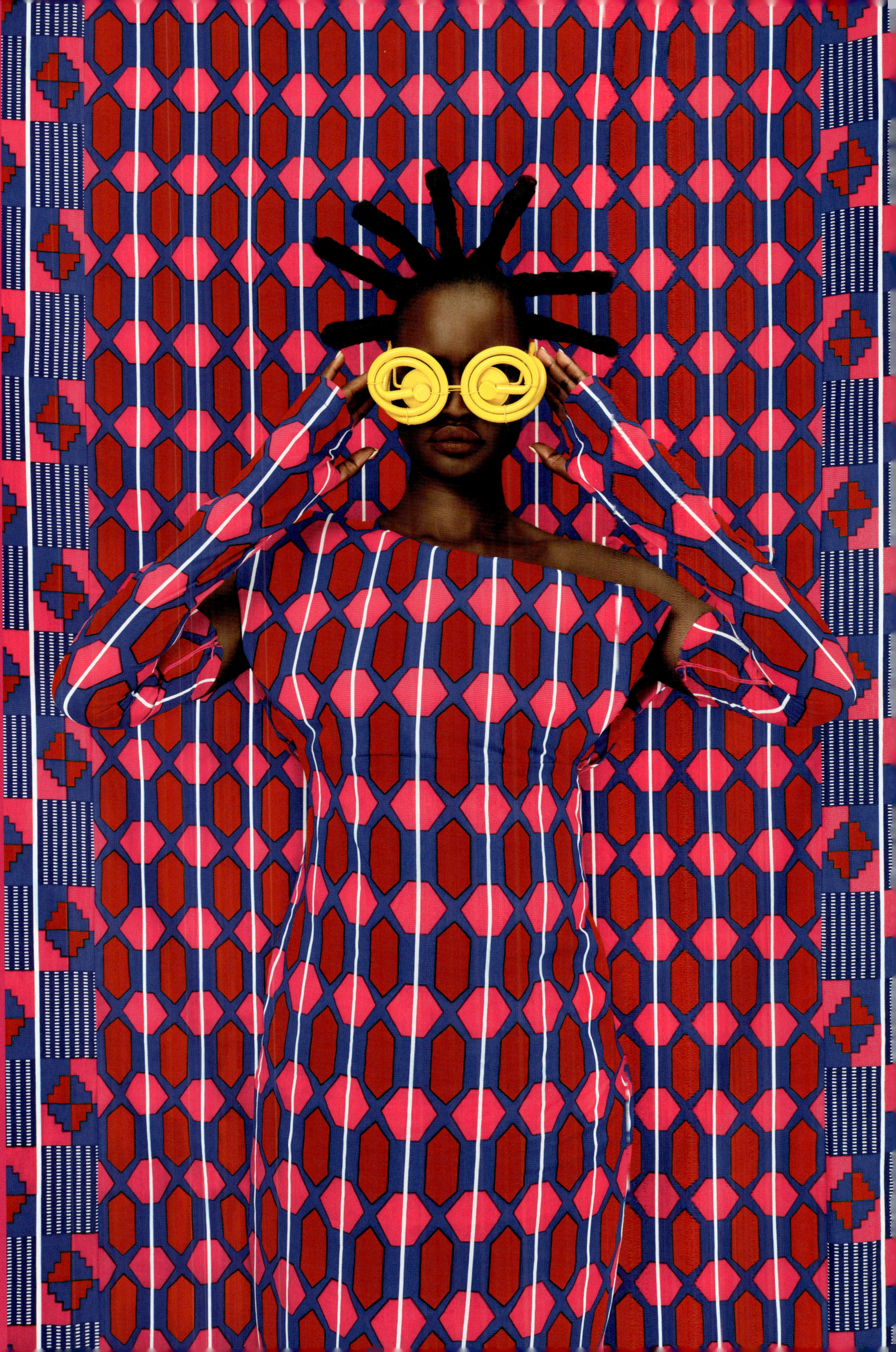

As the sun bathes the African cityscapes in a warm golden glow, a mosaic of women emerges, their silhouettes adorned with gracefully balanced baskets on their head. Bountiful harvests, jugs of water, and bundles of firewood masterfully perched, utilizing this ancestral skill passed down through generations. It is this timeless dance between tradition and modernity, an iconic image that's been photographed throughout the decades, that inspired this work. The legendary Lady Dior bag echoes the serene and sophisticated allure of this imagery.

In her homeland of Kenya accessibility to such luxuries often feels like a distant fantasy for the average woman. Thandiwe witnessed the power of community coming together to weave a tapestry of dreams—it took the effort of multiple hands to get the bag to Nairobi. So valued are these symbols, it is complicated to bring them into the country. In the journey to Kenya, it became more than a bag; a symbol of realised impossibilities for a Kenyan who never imagined she could hold her hopes in her hand. Fueled by a deep desire to stay true to her roots, where some women aspire to own high fashion yet cannot, Thandiwe embraced the challenge of accurately portraying this reality. In the African tapestry of dreams, women own Dolce Gabbbana, Pumba and Gucgi.

This piece acknowledges the power of fashion to transcend national boundaries and inspire the hearts of many.

Eyewear constructed from belts.

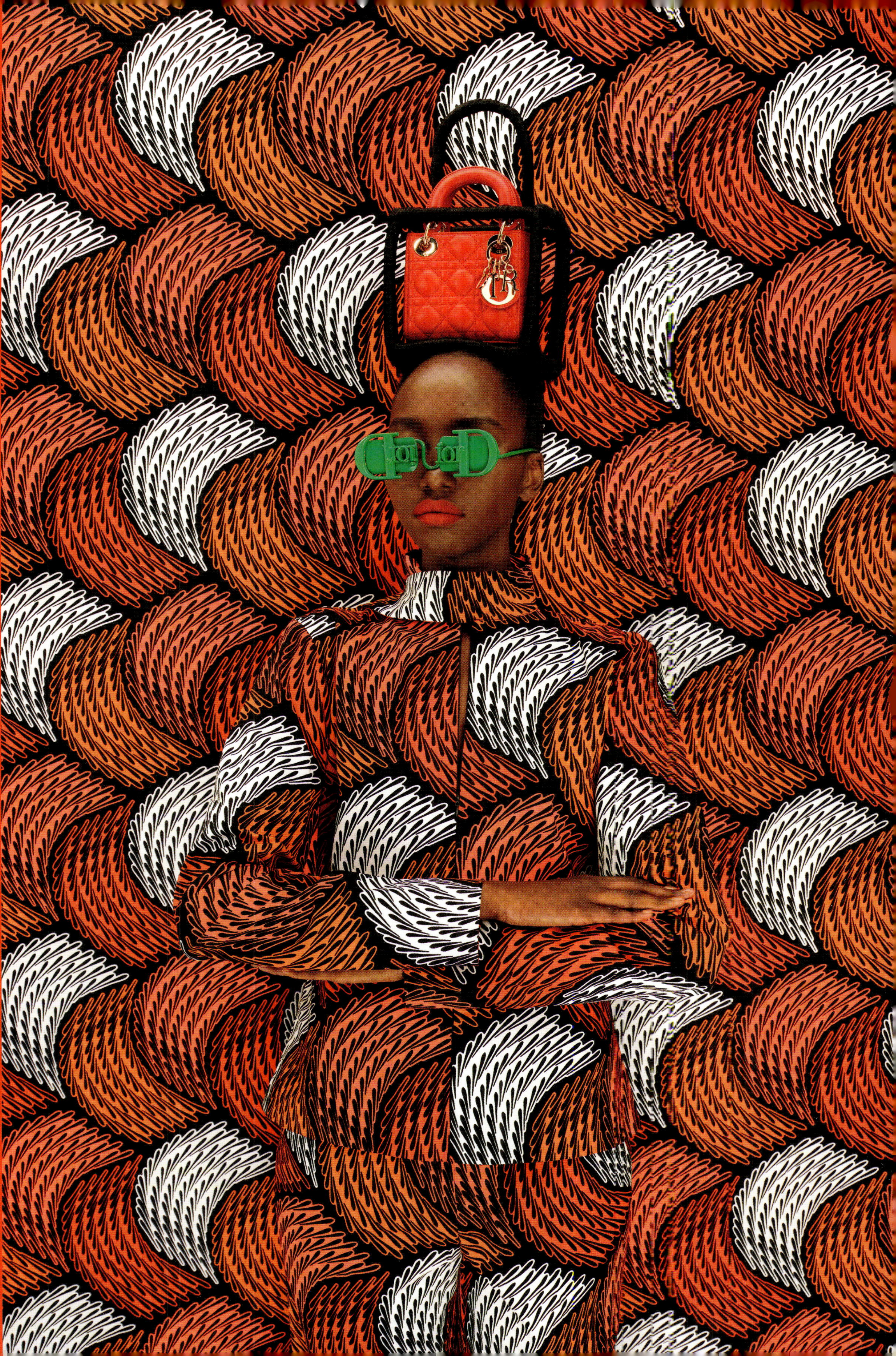

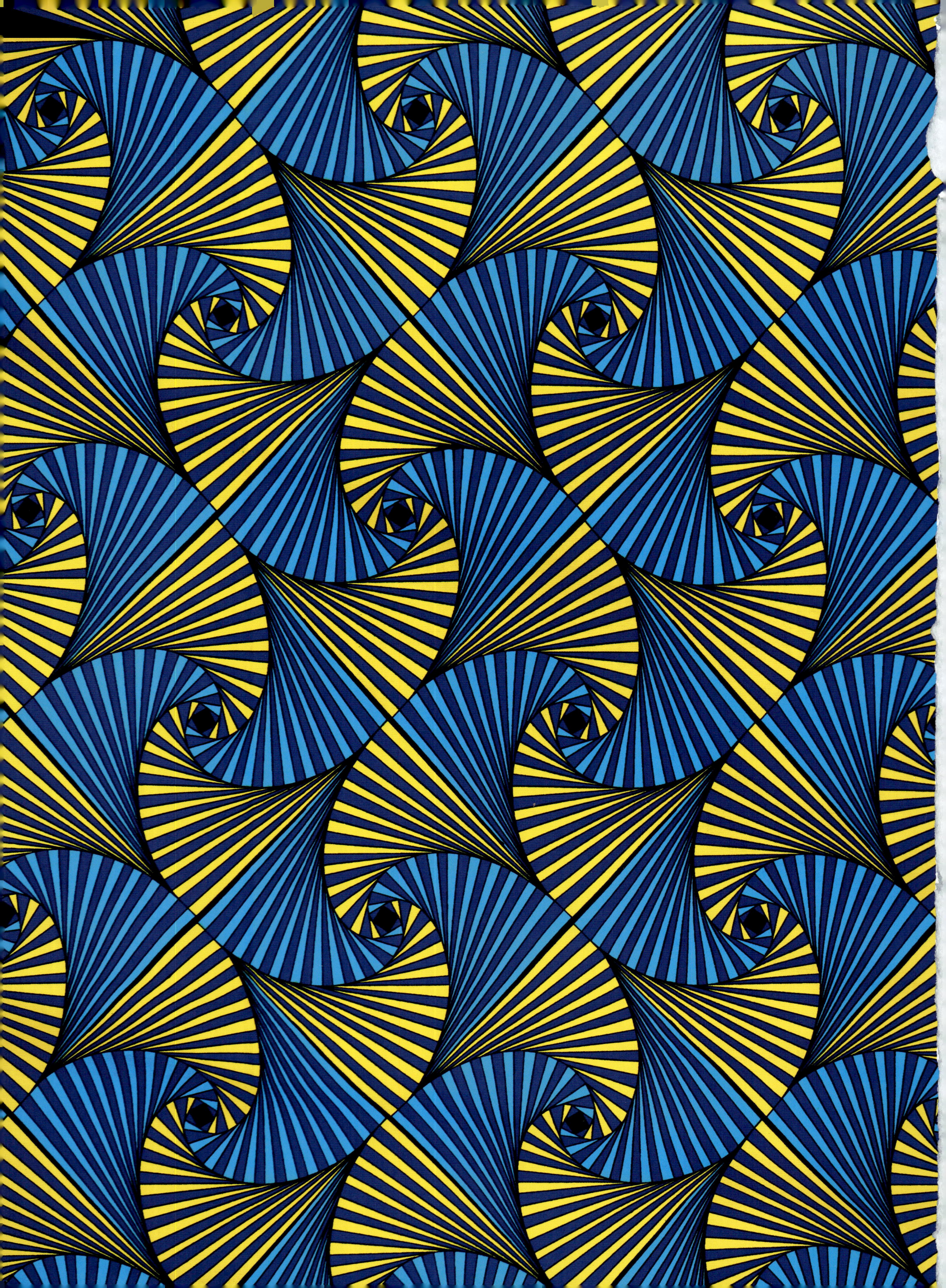

ACKNOWLEDGMENTS

To my sisters Wanjiru and Wanja, thank you for believing in me through the years. We have journeyed through life with each other, and together, I cannot wait to discover what the next seasons of womanhood hold for us.

Bruce, thank you for your support. My heart is forever full.

To César Levy, Linda Franco and Mary-Lou Ngwe-Secke—your confidence in my artistic vision has completely changed my life, thank you.

Writing a book is harder and more rewarding than I could have ever imagined. Thank you Matt Shonfeld and Frank Evers. This book would never have come to be without your vision. Matt, *safi kabisa*.

Thank you to my creative community who have grown with me through Camo: Quentin Ikiki, Osborne Macharia, Richard Kinywa, Jamie Kimani, Thomas 'TJ' Gachago, Kibe Nduni and Elizabeth Orario.

Thank you Wanjiru Anami, Wanjeri Gakuru and Awuor Onyango for writing this book with me.

Finally, thank you to all the incredible women who have agreed to feature in Camo images throughout the years.

CAMO by Thandiwe Muriu

Foreword: Oyindamola Fakeye
Introduction: Thandiwe Muriu
Captions: Thandiwe Muriu, Wanjiru Anami and Awuor Onyango

Publisher: Steve Crist, Gloria Fowler
Art Director and Editor: Gloria Fowler
Copy Editor: Sara DeGonia
Designer and Production: Alexandra Martinez
Production: Freesia Blizard
Cover Font Design: Tré Seals for Vocal Type

ISBN: 978-1-7972-3001-6

Library of Congress Cataloging-in-Publication Data available.

Second Printing

Manufactured in China

MIX
Paper | Supporting responsible forestry
FSC™ C104723
FSC www.fsc.org

CHRONICLE CHROMA

Chronicle Chroma is an imprint of Chronicle Books.
Los Angeles, California

Follow us on Instagram @chroniclechroma

chroniclechroma.com

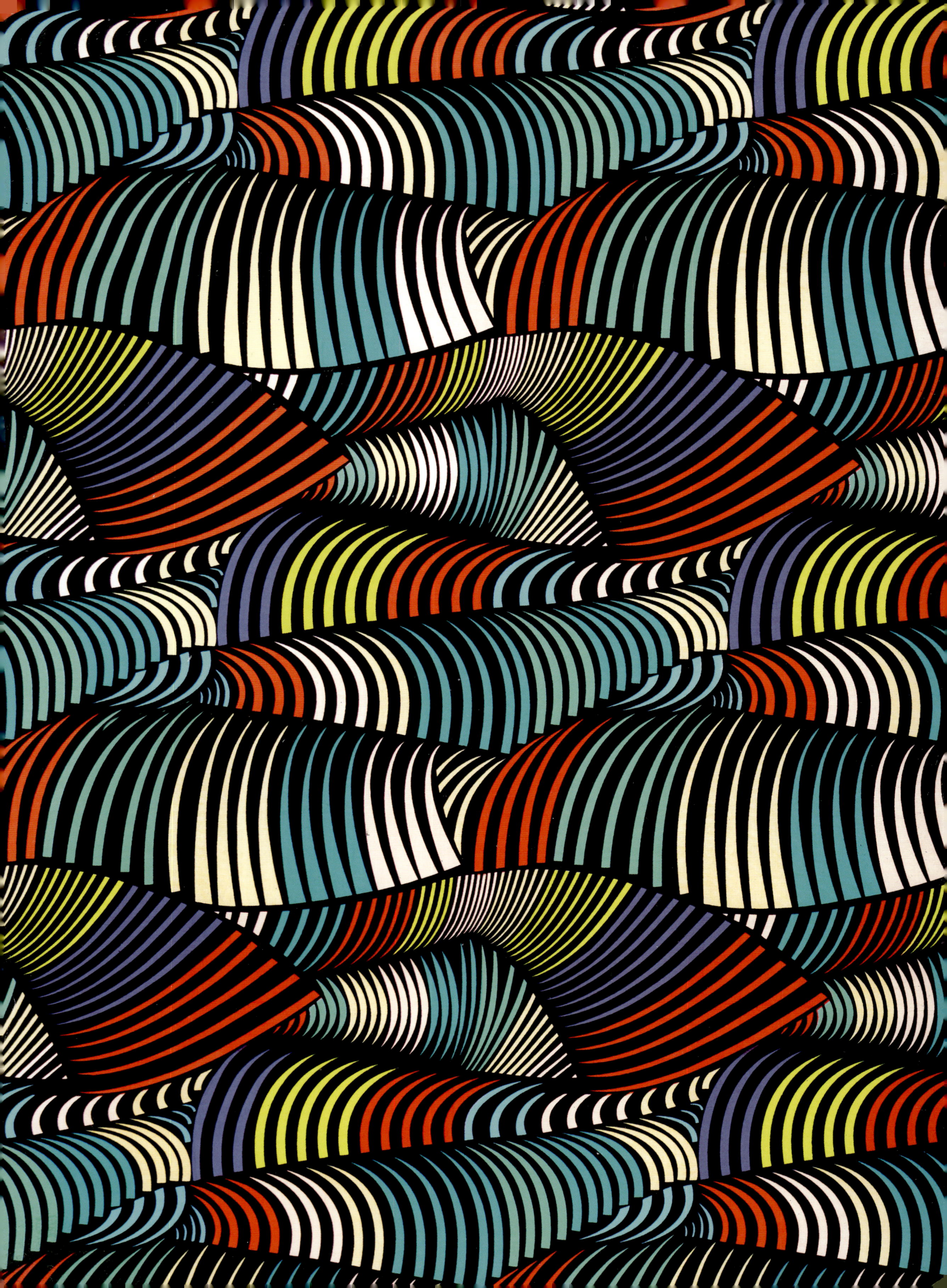